NATURAL BORN GUILT

My Tragicomedy: Happy to Hippie to Hooked

Jacqueline Mendelson

Me at Marin Town & Country Club

ISBN: 978-1-80128-031-0

Dedication

This book is dedicated to my ancestors, whose courage was beyond measure, to my mother and father for modeling their strong moral compass, generosity of spirit, and the meaning of unconditional love, and to my best friend Marilyn, my sister and teacher. I love you, Mare!

Marilyn and Me in Greece

Acknowledgment

I would like to thank Robin Kellogg, Sharone Rosen and Kenneth Kellogg for the hours of meetings, readings, and valuable feedback during this book's writing.

Thanks to Tory Abel and Nichole Helget for setting the bar higher for the sake of the writing and my readers (whether I liked it or not). For that, I am grateful and better.

I would also like to acknowledge the readers that hopped on and off this wild ride, providing encouragement and great ideas…. sorry if you do not see some of them here in print. No readers were hurt in the writing of this manuscript.

My gratitude goes out to the infinite number of fellow travelers on my life's journey so far with whom I have walked, learned from, loved and trusted. And to those others…you know who you are…thank you for helping me to gain strength, understanding, tolerance, and independence.

About the Author

Jacqueline Mendelson is a native San Franciscan. Her family migrated to the suburbs of the San Mateo Peninsula (Bay Area "bedroom community"), where she lived until she turned 18 years old.

She attended the San Francisco Art Institute after graduating high school. She embraced the Cultural Revolution by living in the Haight Ashbury, hanging out in Golden Gate Park, attending every Fillmore and Avalon Ballroom concert imaginable, and demonstrating against the war in Viet Nam.

Jacqueline "grew up" and established a career that covered a span of more than 30 years as a Senior Executive of several charitable organizations and foundations.

Natural Born Guilt: A Tragicomedy: Happy to Hippie to Hooked is the first book in a trilogy. Look for the next book in the trilogy titled Natural Born Guilt: The Truth Will Set You Free in 2021.

Preface

Growing up in the 1950s to 1960s, Northern California brought with it a lot of contradictions. Children were supposed to be seen but not heard. Girls were encouraged to be good students but not to outdo a boy they might like. Families were supposed to be perfect, at least in the view of the outside world. Television shows, like *Ozzie and Harriet,* said it was so. The world was considered safer than it is today, yet nuclear war was looming, and there were still pedophiles, drug dealers, and others lurking in dark doorways or sometimes on your very own block.

I assumed my older sister, who was adopted, felt the same closeness to certain relatives and family lore as I did. But then I wonder, how could she? We were her family, but at the same time, we weren't her biological family. We both have always felt like sisters, but I wonder what kind of sisters. Somewhere in there, we had to choose to be sisters... Didn't we? Growing up, I noticed that whenever adoption was discussed, the topic was usually with and about the adopted person, i.e.:

What were the circumstances for the adoption?

How old were you when you were adopted?

Did you feel you were treated differently by your family because you were adopted?

Have you ever tried to find your biological parents?

Seldom was the discussion about what it was like for the "natural born" child to have an adopted sibling. And, in my case, where there was just my older sister (the chosen baby) and myself (the unchosen baby).

I rarely had a conscious awareness that my sister was adopted, but my subconscious self was in a constant state of adaption and reaction. It went something like this:

Am I getting more attention because I am the natural-born kid?

Did that person look at her funny?

She must hate me because our mom "had" me.

She was chosen, and I was the booby prize.

Is it my fault that she is angry all the time?

I grew up with many of these contradictions and, most of the time was not sure what to do with them. I knew my family wasn't perfect. I had learned to appreciate those relatives who impacted my life in both wonderful and frightening ways. From my family, I learned the importance of a person's character, altruism, empathy, and why sometimes it's imperative to take care of yourself, despite the frenzy that may be going on around you.

But learning the conventions of a good person, and living by those principles, can be two different things when you are young and experimenting with drugs in the Haight Ashbury in 1967. I traded all the norms I grew up with in exchange for a backpack, my guitar, and a tribe of long-haired hippie freaks that became my "sisters and brothers." The times were historic, and we knew it. We were creating a revolution of thought and behavior, and we found our voice in defiance of the establishment.

And then the storm clouds came over our hippie haven, and the dream turned into a drug-induced nightmare. At least it did for me. So, this book is about peeling the onion to see how the layers of circumstances and random sets of events influenced my choices. What I would do, and what I wouldn't do, how I felt, and what I refused to feel, how I coped with change every day in a world that was changing minute by minute.

What turns a normal self-sufficient girl into a dope fiend? I try to address these pieces of my life in such a way as to show you through my experiences rather than telling you how I think it was.

I credit my determination, moxie, and a great sense of humor for getting me through many of life's ups and downs, to be able to recover in a heartbeat and go on my way... Or sit in the mess and become friends with my demons.

It's been a wild ride. At times, I never wanted the newness and excitement to end, and at other times, I wanted to jump off while careening down the slippery slope. What did I learn? Life is what we make of it, and there is no sleepwalking allowed!

Contents

Page Left Blank Intentionally

Chapter 1
How I See It

Almost every upper-middle-class Jewish mother wonders what she did wrong when confronted with the brutal truth that her child is addicted to drugs. My mom was exactly that Jewish mother.

What terrible thing could she ever have done to have me, her precious child, turn to drugs? How on earth could this have happened when she did everything in her power to raise me as a good person? Hadn't she taught me common sense and the need to respect myself and others?

Almost every upper-middle-class Jewish kid, when faced with their mother's tearful pleas to tell her what she did wrong, will almost certainly say, "You didn't do anything wrong, Mom! This isn't about you; it is about me!" And I was just that kid.

Growing up in the 1950s was idyllic. It was the post-war American dream where suburbs were spreading outside the big cities, and families strived to be just like those in *Father Knows Best, Donna Reed,* and *Leave it to Beaver* happy, agreeable, successful, willingly selfless, and adored.

Every time my parents begged me to tell them what was wrong, I would shrug and say "nothing." But the "something" that was "nothing" was that I did not look or feel like the kids who modeled perfection on the television shows and did not want to grow up to just be someone's wife.

My parent's values, which I was expected to internalize, were to get good grades, live as a faithful traditional Jewish woman, marry a Jewish man with a bright future, have children, volunteer at organizations established to help people less fortunate than myself, support my husband, children, and grandchildren to achieve all their dreams, and die peacefully in my sleep.

Coming of age in the '60s, the transition from the perfect families of the 50s to the demonstrations in the streets against the war in Viet Nam affected me more than my Jewish family's expectations. As a latch-key kid, I was left to my own devices while my mom worked, which made me independent and more prone to experimentation, seeking adventure and risky business like a heat-seeking missile.

Like many of my generation, I wanted to be a part of the historic cultural revolution all around me. My generation became enamored with shiny objects and creature comforts while claiming to be mellow with no interest in being encumbered with worldly possessions, even as we practiced "duck and cover" in fear of the USSR during the "Cold War."

Despite my parents' deep faith and integrity and their modeling of both, addiction was part of our story, too. Our family secrets had a great influence on how and why I came to find drugs and my longing to escape. Some addictive and compulsive behaviors were apparent in my family as I grew up. My grandmother and aunts were alcoholics, one aunt was seriously drug dependent, and my grandfather was a gambler and a polygamist. The hidden secrets were incredibly damaging and caused a distance and loneliness that could not be identified, only felt.

Even when I was in the worst of my addiction, I knew I was self-medicating, haunted by feelings of remorse. I had such guilt for being the natural-born child of my parents, felt anguish that my sister, Marilyn, was adopted, and felt even worse when I thought about how badly my sister and I treated each other.

I surrendered to the painless drift where nothing and no one mattered while stoned. In that state, it did not matter that I wanted to be invisible, was confused about love, couldn't process the physical, mental, and sexual abuse I suffered, felt guilt for being my parents' only biological child, or that they had hoped I'd be a boy.

What mattered was getting from one fix to the next in time to continue the float, getting the money, or being with the right friends who had the money to keep the drugs coming. This was my life among a tribe of hippies in the Haight Ashbury and the other hip and groovy neighborhoods of San Francisco in the late 1960s and early 1970s. I had indescribable fun living in the middle of history and then I became a dope fiend, unrecognizable even to myself.

Our Family with Cousin Cindy

Chapter 2
The Girls

The Mendelson family dynamics were so simple and yet so complicated. Everything seemed good on the outside, and anything unpleasant was scolded away. Strife between our folks was handled behind closed doors. I was hypersensitive and felt everything that was going on, but I had to keep it to myself because, in our family, no one would talk about feelings in an honest and authentic way.

Being the second daughter, I never knew when I became one of The Girls because it probably happened before I had the ability to reason. Sometimes I thought it was because they couldn't remember my and my sister's names, so people lumped us together and would say, "Did you girls do your homework?" "Will you girls please set the table?" "Which one of you girls spilled the ink on the carpet?!?"

Marilyn and I were one entity.

When I was three, and Marilyn was four, our family lived in a wonderful house on 42nd Avenue across from a park in San Francisco. Around the corner was the neighborhood grocery store. The two of us would walk to the store with tree leaves. The cashier would sell packs of gum to us for three or four leaves, and then when our mother would go in to do her shopping, the cashier would say, "I added three gums to your bill. The Girls were in today and did some shopping."

Marilyn was always taller than me. This was not only because she was older but because she clearly had been created from a different gene pool. Marilyn had a gorgeous olive complexion, almond-shaped brown eyes glistening dark long straight hair, and a sweet little pug nose. I was short, with huge bright hazel eyes and blonde curly hair. I was a package of energy and courage, while Marilyn was a big scaredy-cat. So, the true protector in our relationship, in our younger years, was me.

One early Sunday morning, Marilyn and I went out to play. A neighbor called my mother. "Do you know where your daughters are?"

My mom said, "Well, I suppose they are lying in bed. You know it is 7 o'clock in the morning."

The neighbor said, "Guess again. They are at the neighborhood playground playing on the swing set alone."

My mom and dad ran out of the house and around the corner where the fenced-in playground was attached to the grammar school. There we were – Marilyn and me swinging on the swings without a care in the world. Marilyn was in her favorite pink flannel nightgown and bare feet, but I had taken the time to put on my Raggedy Ann bathrobe and matching slippers. The two independent little Mendelson girls were having a morning to themselves.

I don't remember whether we got a potch en tuchus (a spanking in the Jewish culture), but I suspect that we did not– I suspect we got a grin.

Another time, when Marilyn had just turned four years old, she ran into the rumpus room, overcome with excitement. "Hey, the kitty next door just had kitties of her own. Do you want to go and look at them?"

"Yes!" I said. I was always up for an adventure. "Where are they?"

"In the neighbor's yard. We have to crawl under the fence to go get them."

What Marilyn really meant was that I had to crawl under the fence to get them. She would never do something that scary. So, I conquered the fence and found the baby kittens and handed them to her. We snuck them into the basement and put them in a little cardboard box filled with line-dried laundry.

We had these kitties down in the basement for all of about 20 minutes, feeding them milk with an eyedropper from some medicine bottle we found underneath the bathroom sink.

My mom heard a knock on the door, and it was the next-door neighbor telling her that The Girls had borrowed the baby kittens, and they could have another 10 minutes of playtime, and then they had to give them back. I can't remember getting a potch for that one, either.

Our adventures and escapades strengthened our sibling relationship. Marilyn and I were best friends. I was always looking out for Marilyn to make sure she wasn't too scared and certainly to make sure that she got her fair share of attention. Marilyn and I always knew that she was adopted. One of the pacts that our parents, Pat and Mel, made when they decided to adopt was that they would be honest with their adopted child and never pretend that the child was naturally born. They would always say that out of all the babies in the world, they chose that baby to be their very own.

When they first got married, Pat got pregnant and, hearing that the rabbit died, declared that day the happiest day of their lives. The story goes that one day when she was in her third trimester, Pat tried to open a window that was stuck. Somehow that pressure and force affected the baby, and the child they named Michael was stillborn. There was no gravesite for the baby, nor was there talking about any of it.

This was another pact that Pat and Mel made. Pat and Mel tried for an awfully long time to have another child. They even visited a fertility doctor – a step that was rarely heard of in the 1940s. The doctor told Mel to stop wearing jockey shorts and to start wearing boxers. But another child was not in the stars for them, or so it seemed, and so they decided to adopt.

Pat called the fertility doctor that they had seen for a referral to an attorney who could handle the adoption. After speaking to him, she hired him on the spot. Her next call was to her rabbi to ask if he knew if there was an agency that was dealing solely in the adoption of Jewish babies. Then it was on to the Jewish Community Center, which was the hub of Jewish life in San Francisco, to ask them the same question. Within no time, Mr. Cohen, their new attorney, called them back. "I just got a call from an agency, and they have a baby that was just born and can be adopted immediately. Please come over to my office so I can give you all the details," he said.

Upon their arrival, Mr. Cohen began, "The baby's mother is unmarried with no means to support herself. She had made this heart-wrenching decision to give her up so that her little girl would have a fighting chance for a good life. You should know that all records about this adoption will be sealed, including the agency that contacted me, which is The Adoption Bureau of the Catholic Archdiocese."

Mr. Cohen resumed speaking. "I know you wanted a Jewish baby, but this is the only agency that has contacted me so far. You can wait until a Jewish baby comes along, or you can start your family now, thanks to the 'Mount Zion Family Services' agency. It is up to you." He winked and shrugged his shoulders, hoping that they would pick up his cue.

They named the baby Marilyn Rochelle Mendelson and told everyone that the matter had been handled by the Mount Zion Family Services' agency. They would keep that secret to their dying days.

Nine months later, the rabbit passed away, and Pat became pregnant with me. When I arrived on October 9, 1949, the "Mendelson Girls" were born, and our parents and relatives showered us with attention.

Sometimes attention was the last thing that Marilyn and I wanted. As a function of being the Mendelson Girls, we were expected to attend certain social gatherings and, at times, to entertain the adults. You see, our mom was very involved with our synagogue, Hadassah, and all the women's groups promoting Jewish family values at that time. Every year we were expected to attend the Mother-Daughter Fashion Show put on by the Temple Sisterhood. It wasn't attending the event that bothered Marilyn and me as much as it was being forced to dress like one another and, even more humiliating, to dress like our mother.

Other times we would be summoned to perform "Sisters" for guests when our parents had cocktail parties, singing, "Sisters, sisters…there were never such devoted sisters". Marilyn and I entertained like poodles turning in circles before we could get a dog biscuit. Once we were done, we ran out of the room. While we ran down the hall, the guests clapped and laughed hysterically.

Sometimes it seemed like I was born for Marilyn, to be her playmate and support. We shared the same bedroom, played with and fought over the same toys, and, for the most part, were each other's best friends. I always knew that Marilyn needed me to protect her, that I had to take care of her emotional well-being.

When Marilyn was five, and I was four, I felt Marilyn separate from me for the first time. She went to kindergarten. I felt abandoned by her. I didn't know what was going on and did not know why all of a sudden, Marilyn was not there with me. I would cry when she would leave but never felt comforted by my parents. I was only told, "Stop crying. Marilyn will be back later. Go find something to do."

When Marilyn came home from her adventures, waving pieces of paper with little pictures, they immediately went up onto the refrigerator. Well, I wanted something on the refrigerator too, so I went and got my crayons and drew all over the empty spaces on the fridge. I had to have gotten a spanking for that, but I really don't think that happened. When Marilyn lost a tooth, you would have thought that the heavens opened up, and all the angels came downplaying harps and sprinkling glitter all around.

Apparently, this was another rite of passage that I could look forward to someday. That night, Mom and Dad put money under Marilyn's pillow and, in the morning, told her that she was visited by the tooth fairy. I ran and got my baby doll and pulled a little tooth out of its mouth that looked like a small piece of Chicklet gum. I ran in and told everyone that I had lost a tooth too.

When I was asked where that little tooth came from, I just pointed way back in my mouth and grunted, *"Ehrrrr!"* I put that little Chicklet under my pillow that night, and in the morning, I found that the tooth fairy had visited me too.

One afternoon, Marilyn and I were playing in our bedroom. We each had our own big girl bed, and we had taken blankets and strung them from the chest of drawers to the ends of the bed, making a tent. We were playing campout when our parents came in and said, "We are going on a short vacation. It will only be for the weekend, but we're going to have you stay with Mrs. Becker down the block. She is a babysitter and keeps children during the day, so you will really enjoy being there, and she's a genuinely nice lady."

We had no idea what our parents just said to us. Where are we going, and who is Mrs. Becker? We were literally dragged through the front door of Mrs. Becker's house crying and yelling, "No, we don't want you to go. Take us with you."

The door slammed shut, leaving Marilyn and me standing in the middle of Mrs. Becker's living room staring as we heard the fading sound of our mother and father's footsteps.

Mrs. Becker led Marilyn into a small bedroom that she would be sharing with another little girl. It was pink and pretty and had two big girl beds and a lot of dolls and really fun toys. She led me to the garage that had been converted into a playroom, and she told me that I had to sleep in the crib. I almost lost my mind. "I am not sleeping in a baby crib. You cannot make me sleep in that baby crib."

When Mom and Dad finally came home two weeks later to pick us up, Marilyn raved about what a wonderful time we had. I just wanted to scream, but I did not speak. Marilyn got the big girl bed, and I got a crib! Didn't they care at all about this terrible miscarriage of justice? If that was not bad enough, mean Mrs. Becker made me drink buttermilk.

I packed up all of my socks into the case where I kept my tap shoes and ran away. When no one came to the park to find me after two hours, I went home and ate dinner. No one had even known I was gone. Not even Marilyn.

A vacation with Nana and Auntie Harriet

Chapter 3
The Elephant in the House

Nana Hazel, Dad's mom, was living with us because she needed someone to care for her after my grandfather died. Someone who would understand her situation and tolerate her behavior.

Decades later, Uncle Stan, our Dad's brother, explained to me, "Your grandmother had a tough life, Jackie. After your grandpa Mannie died, I wanted all of your grandmother's attention, and any time she would have gentleman callers near the house, I would chase them away. When I look back on it now, it was quite sad, but I didn't understand what I was doing at the time.

"She started seeing this nice guy named Dick. He owned one of the most popular neighborhood bars down on the Embarcadero, and his flat was on top of the bar. She would go around to see him on some weeknights, and he would come over to our house to visit on weekends, but I would not give him an inch, and it must've been excruciating for your grandmother," he admitted.

"When your dad and I enlisted in the Navy and shipped out overseas, your grandmother married Dick, and the two of them were over the moon happy. I gave up the grudge and wrote her a letter telling her that I was incredibly happy for her and that I hope with all my heart that they would live to have a wonderful life together."

"One month after your dad got home from the service, he got a telephone call. It was your grandmother in a panic pleading with your dad to come and get her because a bar customer just shot Dick in the head and killed him. The coroner came and took Dick away; your dad came and took your grandmother away to live with him and your mom, and your Nana went into a pretty severe depression that no amount of gin could drown out. That is when your mom and dad adopted your sister Marilyn, and everyone thought that this would make everything better. They believed that, since Nana was adopted, she would bond well with her."

The detachment I experience and the feelings of being unprotected and unsafe have roots and seem to be a part of the entire Mendelson family's emotional make-up. As a kid, I didn't know where that feeling was coming from, but as I was developing and becoming more mature, I gained a better understanding of my own feelings and learned that holding secrets and pretending doesn't mean that others aren't affected! Withholding validation of your child's reality can be cruel.

As a toddler, I never knew where my mother was. I always knew where our caretaker, Audrey Ford, was, and I loved Audrey. And I always knew where my Nana was, and, because of that, I found the most fantastic hiding place in the closet.

Nana Hazel was not treated well as an adopted child, which is why she was going to make sure the same thing did not happen to Marilyn. She made it her business to make sure that Marilyn would never feel unloved or unwanted any second of her life.

The downside to that was that she made me a target, and in retrospect, I realize she abused me both emotionally and physically. When no one was around, Nana would pinch me hard and say something in my ear that made me feel afraid, so I would have to run to the closet and hide before Nana got to me. There were a lot of great hiding closets in that house on 42nd Avenue, but most of the doorknobs were too high for me to reach.

My very favorite closet was the walk-in in my parent's bedroom because the door was never closed all the way. I could slip into that big dark closet and nestle back in the corner, and nobody would know that I was there. My favorite spot was under my daddy's gray flannel slacks because they hung just low enough to cover my face, and they smelled like him.

I was too young for serious thoughts about why I was hiding the closet but certainly not too young to feel why I was in the closet. I developed intuition and learned how to trust it when it came to my safety. I was a vigilant little girl, always watching to see how people were reacting, what the looks on their faces meant, and how their movements affected me, eliciting feelings of love or the sensing of danger.

Nana Hazel very likely loved me, but because of her alcoholism, the hand that she was dealt in her life, and her overzealous protection of Marilyn, her actions seemed quite the opposite. Audrey Ford would always do everything she could to protect me because she was very aware of the dynamic, and she realized that my parents were oblivious. She would scratch her head, baffled at how Nana Hazel's drinking and abuse of me could be going on right under everybody's noses, but nobody was saying a word. I never ran to my parents after one of my abusive interactions with my Nana. Marilyn never said a word when she would see these cruel events occur. And Audrey supposed that because Mr. and Mrs. Mendelson had a duty and responsibility to care for Nana Hazel, they were not seeing anything that would rock the boat or make them have to confront her behaviors.

Audrey used to play with Marilyn and me, which irritated Nana. One day we were playing hide and seek. Audrey was hiding her eyes in the kitchen. Marilyn said, "Let's throw the ball down the back stairs to the basement and make Audrey think that you pushed me down the stairs." I looked at her like she was crazy and then saw she had this twinkle of light in her eyes that it would be funny. "Do you think we will get in trouble?" I asked.

"No, I will hide behind the door, and you throw the ball down the stairs and yell my name," Marilyn said.

Well, Audrey was so busy counting that she never heard me yell Marilyn's name. But Nana did. She came tearing around the corner, did not see Marilyn hiding behind the door, saw me looking down the stairs with a shy smile on my face. Nana grabbed me and slapped the back of my legs until they were hot with welts.

Audrey heard the commotion and stopped her from hitting me. And with sheer rage and girth, she forced Hazel back into her room and closed the door on her. When Audrey went to comfort me, I had already made a beeline for my hiding place. No one said a word.

Potty training was a big deal at the Mendelson house. Most people do not remember being potty trained, but I do because I came to understand the concept of *dirty*. That word came up a lot, and with it, disgusting sounds and squishy faces and all kinds of other negative reactions that I was trying to figure out.

I remember being taken out of my bed while I was sleeping and propped on top of a toilet seat with a big swan's head on the front. And there I was, riding this swan on the toilet seat, half-asleep with my head bobbing up and down, peeking out of one eye to see either my mother's face or my father's face smiling and making sounds of encouragement.

All I wanted to do was sleep, but I finally realized that if I went in the swan toilet instead of my diapers, I would receive appreciation, hugs and kisses, and no more squishy faces, dirty words, and discouraging grunts. I finally got the hang of this activity and almost always made the right choice. I was on the cusp of moving from my bulky cloth diapers to a thin little pair of undies just like Marilyn was wearing.

One day I was playing like a crazy girl in the rumpus room. I had dolls lined up and was directing my first play when I got the sensation that I should be visiting the swan, and I should get someone to help but chose to keep playing. Well, that was a big mistake. I went into a panic. My mommy wasn't around. Audrey must have been busy. So, the only one that could help me change was Nana. My blood ran cold.

I ran into the bathroom and closed the door. I pulled down my rompers, took off my diaper, and looked at what I had done, making squishy faces and grunting. I remembered seeing my mommy dunk the diaper in the toilet, so that's what I did. But I didn't remember what to do next, so I just left it there and closed the lid.

I grabbed my rompers and peeked out the door to see if anybody was there and when I saw the coast was clear, I ran butt naked into my bedroom. I tried to reach up on the changing table for another diaper. No matter how high I stood on my tippy toes and how far I stretched my two little fingers to grab the edge of that diaper, I could see right on top of the table, and I could not get it.

Without putting on a diaper, I put my pants back on, ran to the closet, and hid. I felt ashamed of myself and didn't want anyone to know what I had done, and I did not want Nana to see because I would get punished. Of course, tipsy Nana found her way into that bathroom, pulled up the lid, looked down at the diaper, and went on a mission to find the guilty party. She assumed no involvement on Marilyn's part, so it was either Audrey who did not finish changing me properly or it was me.

Hazel screamed Audrey's name, but there was no reply. At that point, Hazel decided to make another gin and tonic, and I fell asleep in the closet.

Marilyn and I loved laundry day with Audrey. The Mendelson home was two stories. However, there was a basement. The laundry chute was on the top floor and went all the way down to the basement ending right where the washer was. The most exciting part was that it did not drop straight down. It fell at a diagonal, which made it the perfect slide for us to play on. Audrey would throw clothes down from the top floor to make sure that nothing clogged up the chute. After the first load of laundry went into the laundry basket, we knew it was playtime.

If Nana Hazel had not been drinking liquids and could escape Audrey's discerning eye, she too would participate in the fun. This one day, Audrey was on the third floor, helping us get into the laundry chute, and Nana was at the bottom, making sure that the laundry basket full of fluffy clothes was placed directly under where the chute ended. Marilyn was first because she was the oldest. She slid down and shrieked with glee and then came flying out of the bottom into the basket and in Nana's arms.

My turn. Audrey lifted me by my armpits and dangled me into the chute, which I thought was fun in itself. Audrey yelled down, "Nana Hazel, here comes Jackie, ready or not." I went sliding down into the dark shoot full of anticipation and slammed into the closed laundry chute door. Audrey heard the sound and yelled down, "Jackie, are you okay?" But she received no response.

Audrey ran down two flights of stairs as if her bloomers were on fire. She unlatched the chute door to find me folded up in a bunch, with literally no expression on my face. Then I started to giggle and said that it was all fun, except the part where I slammed into the door.

Audrey stormed into Nana Hazel's room to find her sitting in the rocking chair with Marilyn in her lap, reading her a story. Audrey yelled at Hazel for closing the door and leaving the basement while I was taking my turn. Hazel looked up at Audrey, cut her eyes and said, "I did not realize that Jackie was going to play too, or I would not have closed the door and come upstairs for you to yell at me."

Audrey could not hold her tongue any longer, so she went to our mom and told her that she was worried about Hazel and her drinking habit. She also told Mom that she felt Nana Hazel was not treating me in a kind and loving manner and that she felt she had to protect me far too much. Our mom looked at her with disbelief, thanked her for her concern, and said she would talk to her husband about it. Audrey felt defeated and quietly walked out of the room. Every day at precisely 5:45 PM, Marilyn, Mommy, and I would run to the couch, kneel on the cushions, hang over the back of the pillows and look out the picture window waiting for Daddy to drive his Pontiac into the driveway. We made up a sing-song game that we would play every night, "Daddy, where are you? Daddy, where are you?" And the three of us would sing it in all different ways until he finally drove up and walked in the front door. We would all run to greet him with big hugs and kisses.

Dad would be out all day calling on clients that were ranchers, rawhide brokers, furniture manufacturers, and anyone else who used leather and hides in their industry. He wore beautiful suits and ties and spit-shined shoes, but he always smelled like a combination of cow manure and formaldehyde. But when he walked in that door, we wrapped ourselves around him as if he smelled like lilacs and cinnamon toast. Now that was one of the ways that Marilyn and I learned about unconditional love. No one knows where those suits ended up after he would take them off, but I knew one thing for sure, and that was that they were not in that closet that I loved so much to hide in. The cuffs of those gray flannel slacks had the faint smell of Old

Spice and comfort. On that particular night, our mom told us to play until dinner was ready, and we ran into the playroom and started to set up for a tea party. Our mom told our dad what Audrey had said, and he asked her if Audrey had quit. Mom said, "No, it seemed like she did not want to leave Jackie alone with your mom. The last thing Audrey would do is quit at this point. She is trying to tell us that she is afraid for Jackie."

Mom was looking in Dad's eyes for any sign that he may believe this to be true. And, true to form, his eyes filled up with tears, and he said, "I would love to say that this is not true, but I know my mother and if she thinks that Jackie is getting any more attention than Marilyn, she really could be doing something hurtful to her. I have not seen it myself with my own two eyes, but I do sense that there is a problem, and I don't know what to do about it. I have to think about this, and maybe I'll talk to Stan, but please, do not say one word to anyone until you and I think of a way to fix this."

Mom seemed to have more of a presence in the house during the day, and Dad made it a point to spend more time playing with us when he came home from work. Hazel seemed to back up a little bit from the gin and tonic bar, and Audrey's fear and stress level seemed to somewhat subside. It was not clear why all of these things were occurring because it did not seem as though anyone was talking.

Marilyn and I were in our parent's room, watching our mommy get dressed to go downtown to the sisterhood luncheon. She took such care to make sure that everything was perfectly pressed, perfectly matched, and appropriate for whatever the occasion. We especially liked to watch her put on her lipstick. When she was about to leave, she would put on her hat and her white gloves, and we would run to the front door to say goodbye. She bent down, first to kiss Marilyn, and then to kiss me on the cheek as she walked out the door. We both looked at each other and laughed because we each had a bright red lip mark. We were not going to take the lip marks off until mommy got home.

We saw Nana walking downstairs into the basement and decided to follow her. Maybe we would go out in the backyard and look at the birds and pick some flowers.

When we all reached the bottom of the wooden stairs, Nana turned to me and said, "Do you think your head could fit through these posts of the banister?"

Marilyn said, "Why do you think she would want to do that, Nana?"

Nana said, "I think it would be fun to see, don't you?"

Marilyn said, "No, Nana, I don't think so. That's not fun. Let's go outside and pick flowers."

I said, "I will if you want me to, Nana."

So, Nana smiled down at me and said, "Let's just see."

I sat down on one of the wooden steps and proceeded to stick my head in between the posts on the railing. To everyone's amazement, I was able to turn my head in such a way that it worked. I giggled and felt proud of myself. Marilyn giggled at the sight of my head sticking out from the posts.

"Okay," Nana said. "That's enough. Let's go outside and pick flowers."

Nana led Marilyn out the back door while I sat on the stairs struggling to release my head. No matter how hard I tried, I could not figure out how to get back out. My ears hurt, and I became afraid that I was never going to get out.

And nobody was around to help me.

Eventually, Audrey came down the stairs and saw me sitting there with my head through the posts and said, "Child, what did you do?"

I said, "My head is stuck, and I can't get out. Nana wanted to see if I could get my head through the posts and I did, but now I can't get out, and they're in the backyard picking flowers, and I don't know what to do."

Audrey tried everything, even put Crisco on the sides of my head to see if that would help, but nothing worked. Finally, Audrey called the fire department, and four big firemen in big black coats and boots walked through the basement door with a big buzz saw. One fireman asked Audrey for a towel, which he put over my head, and proceeded to cut the posts on the top and the bottom to free me.

Nana Hazel and Marilyn stood on the other side of the stairs watching in horror as they heard the saw chewing at the posts right over my head. And if looks could kill, Audrey would have cut Hazel's head off with that saw … that's how angry she was.

The fireman picked me up and held me in his arms. He told me what a brave little girl I was for letting him saw right by my head. I didn't move an inch. I didn't shed a single tear, and that astonished Audrey. She looked me right in the eyes and asked, "You alright, child?" I didn't respond to Audrey's question. The fireman bounced me up and down in his arms to check and then affirmed that I was fine.

Our mom had come home from her luncheon to see fire trucks in front of our house. In a panic, she followed the sound of voices down into the basement. The first thing she saw was me in the arms of the fireman staring straight ahead, and then she noticed woodcuts and sawdust and Audrey standing with her hands on her hips and shaking her head.

"What is going on here?" Mom asked.

Audrey told her the entire story right in front of Hazel as if she wasn't even there. And at the end of her story, Audrey said, "Mrs. Mendelson, I can't abide by this kind of behavior any longer, and this baby girl doesn't deserve to be treated this way. I appreciate you and Mr. Mendelson and everything you have done for me during these four years that I have been with you. And I love Marilyn and Jackie with all my heart, but I discussed this subject with my husband, and I said the next time something awful happens would be the last time I see anything happen here. I regret that I am going to take my leave."

I wasn't sure what Audrey had just said, but I felt that it was not good, and big tears started rolling down my cheeks, but I didn't make one sound.

The fireman handed me over to my mother and said, "Our work here is done. You look after this little girl now." The firemen left, Audrey left, and Mom, Nana Hazel, Marilyn, and I all went upstairs to sit in the window and wait for daddy to come home. No one was singing, *Daddy, where are you?*

Chapter 4
The First Closet

The first closet held all of my tears, whether they were expressed or not. Never wanting to be discovered, I learned to wail with grief without making a single sound. I learned that feeling vulnerable went hand-in-hand with feeling unworthy and neglected. Even if I was showered with love and kisses, the cold pit of worthlessness and abandonment overpowered me.

I spent hours in the closet, not always to hide or because I was afraid. Sometimes, I found sanctuary and peace in the closet and, at times, just wanted to think without interruption. I liked the solitude. Once in a while, Marilyn would find me. She would crawl in along the floor and find a spot that felt comfortable to her, and we would talk.

"This morning, I was on the front grass with a stick, and every time somebody walked by me, I would tell them to stay off our property," I rustled some pants for emphasis. "That little Billy, in your kindergarten class, told me that Audrey was dirty. I said she is not. Why would you say that? He said she never washed, so her skin looks dirty and dark. I got mad and poked him in the head with the stick and then ran back upstairs. Audrey isn't dirty."

"No, she isn't," Marilyn said. "That's how her skin looks. I hope you hurt him. Nobody likes him anyway."

"Today, while you were in school, Mommy and I went with Mrs. Stein to pick branches for the decorations for the Sisterhood luncheon. We drove up to where there was nothing but trees and then parked the car. Mommy opened the door and got out, and then I started to get out of the backseat, and Mommy closed the door on my hand. I started to scream, and she opened the door, and she was as white as a ghost. She kissed my fingers and told me I was supposed to stay in the car. How was I supposed to know? I thought I was going to get to pick branches with them."

Marilyn said, "Mommy didn't do it on purpose, so let me see your boo-boo." I held my finger up, but it was too dark in the closet to see.

Suddenly, there was a knock on the closet door. Marilyn and I jumped out of our skin. "Girls, you can stay in there. It's okay. Daddy and I are out here and just want you to know that we have bought a sweet little house in a wonderful new neighborhood in San Mateo. It's full of kids your age, and they just built a brand new school. Nana wants to stay in San Francisco, so she will be moving in with Uncle Stan and Auntie Harriet. Isn't that exciting, girls?" Mom and Dad waited for an answer, but we were silent. It was pitch dark in the closet, so I couldn't see Marilyn's face for a reaction, but I was sure I heard her crying.

The last time that I sat in the closet on 42nd Avenue, I was thinking about what it would feel like not to have this closet to sit in anymore. Maybe I wouldn't need the closet when we move. Maybe there will be a better closet in the new house. Audrey leaving was a heartbreaker for me. Leaving Nana was a relief. But leaving that closet left a temporary profound emptiness that I quickly remedied when I discovered an even better closet in the new house.

Mom, Dad, Nana and Auntie Betty

Chapter 5
And the Winner Is…Baba!

I enjoyed visiting my Baba's house because it smelled like fresh-baked bread and dill pickles. My Baba, Mom's mom, was always in the kitchen, cooking and making humming noises as she went from the counter to the stove to the sink. I knew that my Baba kept kosher, but to me, that only meant that she boiled her silverware and dishes in a huge pot with a big rock in it. I loved her cooking, but I never knew what I was eating. I guessed that my Baba was pretty old because she moved slowly; her hair was gray and worn in a long braid that wrapped around her head. She was a big woman but moved gracefully around the kitchen with her apron flying.

Baba would call Marilyn and me over to the kitchen table and set us up with dough so that we could make our own cookies while she was baking desserts for dinner. We loved baking with Baba because she would let us eat our cookies after we were done even though they were molded into shapeless mounds and filthy dirty from being touched. She never cared; she just sprinkled them with powdered sugar and said, "Enjoy bubbellahs (babies)."

Baba was so incredibly grateful that her oldest daughter, Betty, lived with her because she needed somebody there to care for her. Auntie Betty had never married. The family lore was a tale of woe. She once met a fella and got engaged; soon, the engagement broke off, and then it was all over. The guy was never spoken of again. She was the spinster who cared for her mother, made sure all the nieces and nephews got a card every year for our birthdays, drank cocktails and smoked cigarettes.

Every Saturday, Marilyn and I would each take one of Baba's hands, and we would walk with her to Shul for services. The synagogue was a storefront on Noriega Street just a few blocks away. We knew Baba was an important woman at her Shul because she would be greeted by everyone the minute she came towards the door.

Baba always looked stunning on Saturday mornings with her stockings rolled up above her knees, her thick heeled sensible shoes, beautiful blue silk dress, three-quarter length gabardine coat with the Peacock brooch, the blue hat with the black feather, and the thin black veil sitting on the brim. Marilyn and I were proud of our Baba.

Then I would think about Nana, and I would try to feel the same feelings that I had for my Baba. I thought, "I think Nana loves me because she is supposed to love me, and I think I love Nana because I'm supposed to love her. I don't like her, and I don't think she likes me."

I would remember Nana's hands pinching me with those bony fingers and that clear loose skin with blue veins and spots, and it would make the hair stand up on the back of my neck. Then I would compare them to Baba's hands, so smooth and loving with the ring on her wedding finger that always looks like it was cutting off her circulation.

I cannot remember a time when I ever tasted Nana's cooking, ever seeing her in the kitchen at all. We loved our Baba's cooking. We love our mommy's cooking. We laughed at our daddy's cooking because he tried so hard, and it always tasted so awful. Audrey could make a wonderful peanut butter and jelly sandwich, but there were no memories or gestures of love through food from Nana.

Baba's bedroom had curtains with beautiful flowers that looked like the fuchsias that we used to pop in her backyard. Baba had a heavy white bedspread with all of these bumpy dots on it that I liked to pick and twist. She had a big dresser with a huge white doily on it and an etched glass tray with glass perfume bottles I used to sniff. Different sized picture frames of the entire family filled her bedroom. But my favorite thing in my Baba's bedroom hung on the back of her door. It was a fox stole with all these little fox heads with mouths that could bite. I would make them bite her on the hand and giggle.

My Nana's door was always closed. I never saw anything in her bedroom at all.

Baba loved to hear us sing, and she always requested the song Volare. The lyrics were in Italian, but we would sing them anyway, and as long as we kept the right tune, nobody cared what we were saying. Auntie Betty decided to pay to have Marilyn and me go to a singing school.

Marilyn and I took several lessons and then went to Baba's house to perform. They always mused, "Marilyn sounds like a songbird," and then they would laugh and say, "And Jackie croaks like a frog."

It was true that I had a very deep voice. I learned to sing "Blueberry Hill" in the same key as Fats Domino, and that was very funny, but I did know all the words, and I had perfect pitch. It hurt my feelings whenever people laughed at me. I later realized that they were laughing because they loved me and because I was cute. That didn't fix the hurt.

When Marilyn was six, and I was five, we moved away from San Francisco to the suburbs and bought a house with a wonderful backyard. Our grandmothers, aunts, and uncles, all the friends, cousins, and children came down to the peninsula for a barbecue on Sundays. Everyone would bring something to add to the feast, and Auntie Betty made sure that Baba had kosher food so that she could eat with everybody.

I giggled when Baba played in the sprinklers with us. She didn't run, she waddled, and when she picked her skirt up, you could see her long salmon-colored bloomers hanging down around her knees. I always loved seeing them on the clothesline flapping in the breeze. I felt a little embarrassed seeing them on Baba. One morning, before a family barbecue, Marilyn and I were on our beds preparing games to play with all our cousins when they arrived. Our parents walked into the bedroom, and each one sat at the foot of a bed.

"Girls," Mom said. "We have something very sad to tell you. Your Nana passed away this morning, and she has gone to heaven."

Marilyn ran, crying into our mother's arms. Mom rocked her back and forth while rubbing circles on her back and gently patting her. I went into a panic because I knew I had to run to my father, but I didn't feel sad. I ran into my father's arms and buried my face into his chest and shook my shoulders up and down, pretending to cry. My dad held me in his arms and wept in my ear and said, "It's okay, sweetheart. Everything is going to be okay." I believed him.

Many years later, I learned that my uncle Stan had removed all of the empty pill bottles and gin from Nana Hazel's bedside table before he called the coroner. I thought about all of the new things that I had learned about my grandmother and things I had already known, and I felt a profound and honest sadness for her. I felt sadness for my grandmother and the severe ups and downs of her life. But most surprisingly, sadness that I was so affected by my grandmother's behaviors that I had never really considered her as a person or knew her at all for all those years.

Bertha Siegel...my Baba

Chapter 6
We Are Moving

The move to the Peninsula meant buying a home in San Mateo County, selling the house on 42nd Avenue, and saying goodbye to family and friends. We followed the Bekins moving van down the Bayshore Freeway to a whole other world.

The house that Mom and Dad bought on 31st Avenue in San Mateo was a single-story home with a big front lawn and an even bigger lawn in the backyard with trees and flowers all around. The street was lined with beautiful magnolia trees, and right across the street was a big neighborhood park with swing sets, slides, and a rocking boat swing.

Although I was only five years old at the time, I could see the differences in my surroundings, and I was interested in trying to understand those differences. In San Francisco, there had been very well-defined neighborhoods and specific places to play, like parks and school play yards. On the Peninsula, little towns defined the areas; neighborhoods were all clustered around schools, and kids could play anywhere. There were parks, schools, recreation centers, beaches, and bays, but the most fun was that all the kids could play in the streets and not have to worry about getting hit by a car. The only worry was getting home when the street lights went on and to be back in time for dinner.

The tract homes that were being built in the 1950s were developed off main thoroughfares, and the residential streets were shorter than city avenues. This was the age of the cul-de-sac, and every young couple with children tried to buy their homes on one of those streets within 2 to 5 blocks of the schools, but not directly across the street from a school. The parameters were very clear.

The move took place in the middle of the school year, so Marilyn had to leave her new best friends from kindergarten behind and walk into a strange classroom in the middle of the year where nobody knew her.

Our mom and dad looked around for a Jewish Temple so that we could start Sunday school, and that was not easy. Mom started calling everyone she knew who was Jewish, who had also migrated to the Peninsula. She found a few families who met on Friday nights in the back of a carpet store. They all decided to start a Temple together and began the hard task of creating Peninsula Temple Shalom. They started a Sunday school, got an ark with two Torahs, and hired a Rabbi and a Cantor

The day finally came when I was allowed to go to kindergarten. I was so excited. Marilyn was told to take my hand and walked me to school that morning, so I wouldn't be afraid and would learn how to get there. Marilyn took my hand and walked me out the front door, but when we were five houses away from our home, she dropped my hand, ran away, and left me in the dust.

I had no idea how to get to school. I didn't even know the name of the school. So, I just started walking in the direction that Marilyn ran.

After walking several blocks, a man came up to me and asked me where I was going. I told him it was my first day of kindergarten, and I had no idea where I was going. The nice man took my hand and walked me right to the school and directly into the kindergarten room. I was late, but I was safe. I got to finger paint that day, so I had beautiful pictures for the refrigerator.

Marilyn had run away from me so fast that she got lost, too, and could not find her way to school. She ended up at the Saint Gregory's Catholic School. Marilyn had never seen a nun in her life, so when a nun came up to her in full habit, it scared the living daylights out of her, and she could not stop crying. Finally, she was able to tell them who she was and who her parents were. The nuns called our Mom and told her to come over and pick up her daughter.

Mom swung by the public school to pick me up from kindergarten after rescuing Marilyn from what was only described as "these tall penguins that helped me find Mom."

There were definitely no spankings handed out that day to the Mendelson girls. But The Girls were no longer one unit. A line of demarcation was established.

It was the defining moment when I started to see myself as an individual and separated myself from my bond with Marilyn. When Marilyn ran away, I knew I was on my own. Moreover, I didn't know if I should have those feelings at all, but I did have them, and they were mine.

I thought things were getting comfortable in our new home until I would look at Marilyn.

"Marilyn, why are you so mopey and upset all the time?" I asked. "When you get home from school, you sit on your bed, and it takes me forever to get you to play with me. Then when you do start to play, you are happy again."

"I miss all my friends at my other school, and I don't know anybody in my new class. Nobody talks to me or plays with me. I hate it here. And I miss Baba and going to Shul with her on Saturday morning," Marilyn confessed.

I loved the social part of going to grammar school. I felt fortunate to know some of the kids in the neighborhood that were also in my class. I liked my teachers so far, but it soon became apparent that for me to understand some of the things I was learning, I had to contend against them.

My teacher demonstrated the proper way to fold a piece of paper. She doubled over a sheet of paper, laying it corner to corner on the desk and pressed her finger down the middle, making a perfect crease. "Class, always keep the paper flat on the desk when you fold so that it will not tear." I doubled over my sheet of paper and decided to pick it up and make my crease with both hands starting at the middle of the fold. All you could hear in the classroom was the ripping of my paper and then the scolding from the teacher. Then I learned why you always fold your paper when it's lying flat on the desk. I learned just about everything this way. When I was in second grade, my reading and writing skills were excellent.

My teachers liked me enough and found my curiosity intriguing, but their feedback was always the same; 'Jackie is a particularly good student but spends too much time visiting with her neighbors. Jackie plays well with others but needs to spend more time paying attention in class'. I loved school; it was just that sometimes I forgot that I was there to learn and not to discover.

During the three years that we lived on 31st Avenue, more and more families moved down to the Peninsula and joined our temple. Most of the families socialized with each other, and Marilyn and I made wonderful friends with the kids that were in our Sunday school classes. Our folks started going out on Saturday nights and leaving us with babysitters. The babysitters were the older girls from the families in the Temple that were all a part of our growing community. The minute our parents closed the front door and we were left alone with the babysitters, all hell would break loose. Marilyn and I tortured those babysitters, putting gum in their hair and forcing them to eat tablespoons of mayonnaise. After a night with us, most would never sit for us again. We learned to watch out for each other, and our relationship equalized. We were equal parts companions and equal parts brats.

One day, Marilyn and I were walking home from playing, and it was getting late. All of a sudden, a man stepped out of the bushes and went up to Marilyn and said, "Do you know where Bay Street is?"

She said, "No, I don't know where Bay Street is, but I know it's not anywhere around here."

I didn't notice the man because I was walking ahead and thinking about what I was going to have for dinner when I heard Marilyn scream. I looked around to see the man grab her arm and try to pull her down the street.

I ran back to where they were and started screaming at the top of my lungs, "You leave my sister alone! You take your hands off her right now!" I kicked and punched the man until he let go of her arm and ran away. I took Marilyn's hand, and we ran home, and we told our parents what had happened. Within minutes, the police were at the door asking us for a description of the man. We told the policemen everything.

After eating a delicious dinner of meatloaf, mashed potatoes, and string beans, we went to play in our room. Our mom and dad walked into the room, sat me on the foot of my bed, and sat Marilyn on the foot of her bed, and our father said, "We are moving."

Marilyn and I looked at each other in disbelief. Dad went on to say, "This has nothing to do with that man trying to grab Marilyn. I have been offered a transfer to Los Angeles, and we have decided to take it. Your cousins live down there, so you're going to love it."

Marilyn started to cry. "I don't want to move again. I like all my friends, and the fourth-grade teacher I am going to have is nice. Please don't make us move again," she screamed. Our parents laughed and said she should be glad it is the summer, so we are not moving in the middle of the school year. I just sat there and stared.

Marilyn ran out the backdoor heading for the swing set. That was her go-to place for comfort when she was bereft. She would swing and cry until she was exhausted and too rung out to care about anything. I found my way to my secret closet floor and rocked back and forth, wondering how I was going to cope with the coming upheaval. It was clear that my first order of business when we found a new house in Los Angeles was to find my next closet to soothe my soul.

"The Girls"

Chapter 7
Hooray for Hollywood –
NOT

The Mendelsons moved into a small two-bedroom apartment in what was affectionately called the Jewish Ghetto of Los Angeles. We lived in one of the bottom apartments of a two-story stucco building, and everything around us was cement. There was one tree on the property, but it was in the back where the garbage was burned. None of the kids were allowed to play back there because the incinerator was white-hot and hazardous.

I decided not to think about my personal taste in terms of apartment living and Los Angeles until I started school and met some of the kids in my class. My first observation of our neighbors was that all the women had bright red hair, bright red lips, and wore gold shiny stretch pants. Everyone talked loudly, and the neighbor ladies called each other "Doll" and were in everyone else's business, always telling what they knew. Selma Bernstein lived next door with her husband and daughter, Leslie.

Leslie and I were the same age and grade, so we started to play together. Every day at 4:00, Leslie had to go home and change out of her play clothes and into one of her many party dresses with matching tights.

"Why do you dress up every afternoon in a party dress? You must have a lot of friends with an awful lot of birthdays!" I said.

Leslie laughed, "I am not going to a party. I get dressed up because my father is coming home, and I need to look perfect when he sees me, and we sit down for dinner."

"What happens if you wear your play clothes to dinner, but you washed your hands?" I pondered aloud.

"It is not about being dirty; it is about respect. He is the man of our house, and we can never look or act unpleasant in his presence. If I make a mistake, he teaches me how to be better. I stand on a stool in the closet with the door shut until I know what I did wrong, why I did it, and how never to do it again. Then I knock, and he tells me if I can come out. I tell him what I thought about and apologize, and I tell him I will never do it again. He teaches my mother too."

I discovered that I had very little in common with Leslie except for the closet.

We spent the remainder of the summer swimming in our cousin's pool in Beverly Hills; we caught a crab off the pier in Santa Monica; we saw Audrey Hepburn at the Big Top Market; we found a really good cheeseburger at Nick's Coffee Shop on Olympic Boulevard, and we went on the pony rides on La Cienega Boulevard right in the middle of the city.

School started, and we could not believe how lucky we were to be served hot chocolate and cinnamon toast at recess. Marilyn and I liked our teachers, my classmates were nice, and most of them were Jewish.

Nevertheless, within the first three months of the new school term, Mom and Dad told Marilyn and me to pack up again. We were moving back to San Mateo.

Marilyn did not cry.

We moved into another apartment, and it did mean going to a different grammar school yet again. By this time, even I was starting to get a little irritated with all this moving around.

I knew one thing; I did not like apartments. I felt it was way too close to other people, and you can hear and see everything everyone was doing.

I was also agitated with my mother and father for not talking to us about anything they were doing as though our feelings didn't matter at all. The more decisions they made without talking to us, the more control they exerted over our behavior; they would try to control who we could play with, how we dressed, and how we acted.

It felt like our reward for getting hauled around from house to school was punishment. The luckiest thing for Marilyn and me was that there were dozens of children to play within this new apartment complex. The Hillsdale Garden Apartments had a lot of places to play, a big community swimming pool, and the grounds were not all covered in concrete.

My mom decided that it was time to give me a haircut. She said it was because it was still hot out and that I would feel much cooler with shorter hair. I didn't want to get a haircut. I liked my curls the way they were. I was not going to win that battle, so I just went along with it and got in the car.

When I saw where my mother was driving me, I got sick to my stomach. My mother took me into a barbershop with all these men standing around and getting haircuts. She asked if they would cut a little girl's hair. I was mortified, and all I wanted to do was run out of that shop and keep running.

The man laughed and said, "Sure, we will cut any hair on any head." He picked me up by my armpits and sat me in the barber chair on a booster seat. He threw a drape around my neck and proceeded to cut off all of my curly blonde hair. The only thing that I heard through my rage and powerlessness were the words "pixie cut." When it was all over, and he handed me the mirror, I wanted to die. Tinker Bell is a pixie and looks like a little girl...this was Peter Pan!

I climbed in the back seat of the car and would not say one word to my mother. Mom kept looking in the rear-view mirror at me while she was driving, saying, "Oh honey, it looks so cute, and it'll grow out. Don't worry about it. All the kids are getting short hair for the summer. It looks adorable, sweetheart."

I was thinking, *All the kids are not getting all of their hair cut off, and Marilyn's ponytail has grown so long that it touches her waist. And my mother is just stupid.... I don't even look like myself!* I went out to play, and all the kids laughed at my hair and said things like, 'what happened to you?' 'Did your mother put a bowl over your head and just chop?' 'Are you a boy or a girl?' That was the one that I hated the most. How could somebody ever think that I was a boy? And they all knew I was a girl, so they just wanted to hurt my feelings, and it worked!

I didn't understand why my mother felt that she had the right to change the way I looked so dramatically without even considering how I would feel about it. I had a mind of my own, but my mom always wanted me to think and feel the way she thought and felt.

I was confident in my instincts and decided to let my mom say whatever she wanted. I would nod my head and say I understood, and I would keep my feelings and thoughts to myself. I began to discern what a teaching moment from my parents was and what an imposition of my will was. I decided to become willful! One day on one of my escapades, there was a huge trout barrel in the center of the mall, and you could catch a fish for twenty-five cents. I gave the man my quarter, grabbed the pole with the baited hook, and put it in the barrel. Within a few seconds, I felt a sharp tug, and there was a trout on my line. The fight it put up was exciting to me, but I was even more fascinated that I caught a fish myself! Catching that fish felt so invigorating that I had to do it again.

By the time I had to get home, I had five trout in a plastic bag and was running fast, so I would not be late for dinner. I was singing and skipping. The bag of fish was flying around, and all of a sudden, I stopped dead in my tracks.

My mom is going to kill me. I spent my whole allowance on fish that she is going to have to clean and cook. She is not going to want to do that, and she is going to tell me I don't have a brain in my head. I panicked. Instantly all the joy and exuberance were replaced with fear, and I tossed the fish under the bushes and ran home.

I flew in the door. "Go upstairs and wash your hands and get ready for dinner, sweetheart. And ask your sister to come down and set the table. Daddy will be home any minute."

"Okay, mom, what's for dinner? I'm starving." I said, panting for breath.

"Frozen fish sticks with that tartar sauce you love!"

Chapter 8
A Short Time Out

It was the first day of summer, and we were over the moon excited to be able to go swimming every day. I was 8 ½, and Marilyn had just turned 10, and we had passed all our swimming lessons with flying colors. Our mom and dad agreed that we could go to the pool one hour after we ate lunch. Mom was a sun worshiper, so she went with us most days, but when she didn't, we were instructed to announce to the lifeguard that we had arrived, so he knew we were in the pool, to be safe.

All the kids swam every day and Marilyn and I were having so much fun. After swimming, we would walk to the mall and get a soda or visit friends at their houses. We realized that it was our first taste of independence, and we felt trusted by our parents. We had good playmates, we were obeying our parent's wishes, we didn't get into trouble, and we came home when we were supposed to for dinner. I asked my parents to buy me a bicycle because all the kids were learning to ride, and I wanted to ride around the walkways of our huge apartment complex with them.

Dad said, "We'll see, Jackie. Bikes can be dangerous, and I am studying to be an insurance agent right now, so I may not have time to teach you. Your mother and I will talk about it and maybe… for Chanukah." I was disappointed.

I went outside and saw my little friend Hans from Germany, learning to ride his bike. I sat on a bench and watched his father hold the seat steady and run behind him until he could catch his balance.

"What do you think, Jackie? Am I doing good?"

"Yes, Hans, you don't even wobble now. Is it fun?" I asked.

"It sure is. Do you want to try? My dad will teach you, too, if you want."

I looked over at his father, and he was smiling and nodding his head, so I decided to give it a go. The bicycle was a perfect size for me. I got up on the seat and tried to balance while pushing down on the pedal. I wobbled from side to side but soon realized that Hans' father had a firm grip on the bike. In no time, I found my center and pedaled down the street and made a wide turn to find Hans and his father standing down the road, clapping and hooting! I had been on my own and didn't even know it! I was consumed with the exuberance of accomplishment. I couldn't wait to get home to tell my parents that I learned how to ride a bike. I was proud of myself for learning without waiting until my father had time to teach me.

The family sat down to dinner, and Mom served the first course, a small salad.

"How was your day, girls?" Dad started. That was the time every day when everyone got to tell their story and hear what each other had to say.

Marilyn said, "I had fun. Sylvia and I played with her dog Tazzie and dressed her up in doll clothes. Then we watched American Bandstand, and I came home."

I went next. "I was outside watching Hans' father teach him how to ride a bike. They asked me if I wanted to learn, and I said yes. So, I got on the bike and the next thing you know, I was riding it all on my own. I learned without even training wheels. I think it was because the bike was so small. But I did it!" I looked for a reaction. My folks and Marilyn started clapping and laughing.

Then I began to confess, "After that, we were eating cookies, and my friend, Diana, came over to say hello. She asked me for a bite of my cookie. I said, close your eyes and open your mouth. She did, and I squirted Elmer's Glue in her mouth. She started to cry and ran home. I ran after her telling her that I was sorry, and I thought it would be funny, and I asked her not to tell her mother, but she did."

"What did her mother say," they all asked in unison.

"She asked me why I did it. I said it was an accident. Her mom just stared at me, and she said I could not play with Diana anymore, and she told me to go home."

"I don't know why I did that. I eat paste in school, so I did not think it would hurt her, but it was mean, and I made her cry. I am sorry!"

"Jacqueline Suzanne, I am surprised at you. That is not like you to be cruel to anyone! What got into you?" Mom may have been harsh, but I was overcome with guilt. There was no need for admonishment.

We all sat quietly.

My father broke the silence, "I finished studying to take my test to get my license to sell insurance today. I take the test tomorrow, and if I pass, that will be my new job. There aren't any insurance agents in our Temple, so I am hoping I will be the insurance agent for all our friends."

We were genuinely happy for our dad because he had a lightness and look of joy in his eyes, showing that he was pleased. Mom saved the best for last.

"I found a new house for us to buy, and your father and I are putting an offer in on it tonight. It is up on the hill on the street called Sunset Terrace, and it is a beautiful neighborhood. When we went up there, all you could see were kids playing everywhere, and the new grammar school is supposed to be fantastic. Also, once your father gets started selling insurance, I am going to study for my real estate license. Buying and selling houses seems to be in my blood."

Marilyn looked down.

Our offer was accepted, escrow closed, and we all went up to the house to decide what had to be done before we could move in. We walked in the front door and stood dumbfounded. The place was a disaster area, and it was hard to determine where to start.

Mom walked to the kitchen. "First things first; I will scrub down all the appliances. Daddy, will you please peel down all this hellacious wallpaper and prep it for paint? Girls, will you please take bags and go all around the house and put every scrap of garbage you can find in them and take them to the side of the house?"

It was like that for two weeks until the last finishing touches were put on the vacant house so we could move in. Mom looked around and said, "Oh boy, we forgot to paint under the sinks in the bathroom and kitchen. No one can fit under there but Jackie."

"Honey, can you crawl under the sinks and paint the walls while we vacuum and finish straightening up?"

I took a small paint can and a brush and slipped under the sink in the bathroom. I was proud that I got to do a job that nobody else in the family could do. After I was halfway through with the enclosure, I started to get very lightheaded.

It was a ridiculously small space, and I was inhaling strong paint fumes. My head was spinning, and I thought I was going to get sick, but then I realized that I liked that feeling. I pulled the door until it was almost closed and sat there with my eyes shut.

Dad walked in. "Oh, my God! These paint fumes have gone to her head. Look at her; she could pass out!"

He grabbed me and pulled me out from below the sink and ran me outside to get some fresh air. I opened my eyes and smiled. I was very aware that this was the first time that I was in an altered state, and I loved the feeling and knew it would not be the last time.

He looked down at me with a very puzzled look and his face and said, "Well, we won't have you doing that again anytime soon."

It was nearing the end of the summer of '58, we moved, settled in, and Sunset Terrace was everything Mom and Dad promised and more. The streets were filled with kids to play with, and it was as though all children had a sonar signal that drew them to the corner every day to gather to play.

At the end of the day, some of us kids went to visit Mr. Hanky, and the rest said they did not want to and went home. Mr. Hanky was a nice old man who lived with his sister in a house in the middle of the block.

He had a greenhouse in his backyard, and he would show all the kids how to grow plants from seeds. Mr. Hanky's sister served cookies and Kool-Aid at the beginning of the visit, and she would always come around to see if we were enjoying the refreshments.

We decided to end the summer with a block carnival to raise money for Polio, so playtime turned into planning time every day. I ran over to Mr. Hanky's house to tell him and his sister about the carnival in case they wanted to help. Mr. Hanky's sister wasn't home, and Mr. Hanky must have been in the greenhouse, so I went through the gate and around back to tell him the news.

"Hi, Mr. Hanky! We are having a carnival, and we thought you and your sister might want to help. It's for charity."

"Come over here and sit on my lap and tell me all about it," he said. He sat down on his stool and slapped both his knees and waved me over with his arms wide open.

I walked over and climbed up on his lap and started to tell him all the plans so far. As I was telling him what everyone agreed to do, I felt him pushing down on my legs and holding me tighter to his lap. I did not know what he was doing or why, but I got a bad feeling in the pit of my stomach and jumped off his lap and walked to the other side of the workbench.

I kept talking about the carnival, and Mr. Hanky said, "Where did you go? Come back over here and finish telling me everything". I kept talking as if I did not hear him, and just then, Mr. Hanky's sister walked into the greenhouse with cookies and a panicked look on her face. I said, "No, thanks! I just came by to tell you about the carnival, and now I have to get home. Bye!"

As I ran home, I thought, *I don't think I am going to go visit Mr. Hanky anymore.*

Two days later, Marilyn and I went out to play and saw all the neighbors standing in the street talking. We walked up to our whole group of friends and asked what was going on.

Billy Barth said, "Mr. Hanky and his sister are gone. Bonnie was getting ready for her bath, and my Mom asked her why she had dirt in her underpants. She told her that

Mr. Hanky's hands were dirty. My Mom told my Dad when he got home from work, and he ran, screaming out of the house. Boy, was he mad! So, this morning, a moving van pulled away with all their stuff, and they just disappeared."

Bad move, Mr. Hanky. Billy Barth's father was a member of the San Mateo Police Department.

Marilyn said, "He touched my boob once." None of the other kids made eye contact or said another word about it...... ever again.

Summer on Sunset Terrace

Chapter 9
Finally,... Solid Ground

Mom was faithful to her word and successfully passed her real estate license exam. Dad established a large client base of newly insured Temple members. That meant that Marilyn and I were home alone after school until both our parents returned from work.

We were old enough to look after ourselves during the day. Mom and Dad taught Marilyn and me how to take a perfect telephone message and what to do in an emergency if they were not home.

I went to the park every day after school. After about two weeks, I walked up and introduced myself to the Recreation Director, Dennis Nelson. "Hello, my name is Jackie Mendelson, and I would like to work at the park after school. I notice that you need someone to be in the equipment room to check balls and games in and out after school. Also, I can set up checkers tournaments that we can hold on the picnic tables. I have to be home by 6:00 p.m. for dinner."

Dennis looked down at me and chuckled. "Alright then, I guess you've thought this through, so let's get you acquainted with the routine. Here is a whistle to put around your neck in case you need to get my attention." He ran off, and that was that. I was an official unofficial volunteer at the San Mateo Parks and Recreation Department with my very own whistle.

I ran all the way home that night in utter disbelief; I knew it wasn't a real job, but it was real to me.

I also started to take doodling and drawing more seriously and was turning into quite a little artist. I divided my indoor time between doing art projects and studying the heart. I was fairly certain that I wanted to be a heart surgeon when I grew up, and my art was my way of expressing my emotions. One night at dinner, I announced my decision to the family. "I have done a lot of thinking, and I have decided that I want to be a doctor. Not just any doctor but a heart doctor. And I want to be just like the doctor in *Love is a Many Splendored Thing*".

My folks looked at each other and then at me with an expression that I could only interpret as sympathy. "Oh, honey," Mom said, "You can't be a doctor. No one will go to you. You have to be a nurse. Women are nurses, and men are doctors."

"That isn't true!" I protested. "The doctor in *Love is a Many Splendored Thing* is a woman, and everybody loved her."

"That was a movie," Dad said, "and this is real life. Besides, you better concentrate on getting better grades so that you can make it out of high school."

I felt deflated, and I knew I should never have told anyone what I wanted to do. I knew I wouldn't get any support. Why was I so stupid?

I decided to tell Dennis Nelson, the Park Director, what I wanted to do and see what he had to say. He wasn't my family, so maybe he had a different opinion. When I went to the park the next day, I told Dennis the conversation, and he said, "Jackie, I think you can do anything you want to do if you put your mind to it. You walked up to me and took over the equipment room. That's a big deal. You have to get good grades to make it happen. There are plenty of people that will go to a woman doctor if she is good!"

"Thanks, Dennis."

I ran to check out the equipment and felt relieved.

It was not lost on me that I intentionally sought guidance from Dennis, much in the same way that I looked to Audrey Ford for emotional cues that I was not getting from my family. I gravitated toward people other than my mom and dad for reassurance and different points of view.

In part because of my disappointment in the lack of encouragement I was receiving and also because I was learning to value "the others" entering my life, alternate thinking and other's influences as valid and worth considering.

Chapter 10
Childhood is Real Life (and Death)

I was working almost every day at the park after school, and Dennis Nelson started driving me home when he could. I liked that a lot. I would ask Dennis questions that I would not ask my parents.

"Dennis? The other day you were playing baseball, and the ball bounced up off the ground and hit you in the crotch. You looked like you were going to die, and you rolled around for a long time. What happened, and what should we do to help? I mean, it seems like the more we grow up, the more we do dangerous stuff. You can break your bones playing sports and just trying to run across the street before a car comes can be a big mistake."

Dennis was taken aback. "Jackie, do you know the difference between a boy's body and a girl's body?"

"Not really. I have never seen my parents without their clothes on."

"Okay, let me try and explain this." Dennis began. "Boys have extra parts between their legs that girls don't have. These parts can be very sensitive if they get hit, and there is nothing anyone can do to help."

I got out of the car in front of my home, thanked Dennis for the ride and the explanation, politely closed the car door, and ran into the house to find my parent's book on Greek art history. I found some photographs of statues and got an idea of what those extra parts were that boys had and how they stuck out from the body. I decided that if they can hurt that badly when they get knocked around, I was glad I didn't have them.

On the last day of school, I ran to the park to give Dennis a card that I made because I would not see him again until the fall. It was a pink card with a big heart, and I wrote. "Thank you for giving me a chance. You are like my big brother, except I have a crush on you."

I made him promise not to read it until I was gone. He gave me a little peck on the cheek, and I ran away. It took a few days for me to find my bearings after school got out, and I had to devise ways to entertain myself for the summer.

It was August 6, 1960, and Marilyn and I were excited because it was the first day of the County Fair, and all the kids on the block got permission to go as a group to the fair without parental supervision. I was only 10, and Marilyn was 11, but our parents trusted us.

Everyone had a great time, and no one fell down and got hurt or got lost. Marilyn ate too much cotton candy and hot dogs on a stick, and she threw up on the Tilt-a-Whirl all over the back of Dean Manders' head, but he forgave her.

As we were walking home, we had to cross the train tracks. The boys ran ahead, but we walked slowly to be safe so we could look on the ground for potential treasure. Marilyn and I looked to our right, and we saw three people looking at something at a distance on the side of the tracks, and the energy coming from those people was intense.

Marilyn and I went over to see what they were looking at. I looked down to see a young boy covered in blood and all twisted up. His legs were tucked back under his body, and his arms were out to the sides, and his fingers were twitching. His eyes were open, and his lips were moving, but I could not hear any words.

At that second, I knew I had to kneel down to be in the boy's field of vision so that he would know that I was there with him. I looked into his eyes and got as close as I could to see if I could hear what he was saying. I softly told him that everything would be alright and that I would stay with him until the ambulance came. He looked right into my eyes, and tears started to roll down the sides of his face. I took one of his hands and held it gently.

The ambulance came, and one man pulled me back as they lifted the boy onto the gurney and started to wheel him away. I yelled, "Stop! You forgot his shoe. Take his shoe!

The ambulance driver said, "Little girl, we have to go, and he doesn't need his shoe!"

"Yes, he does!" I screamed. "His foot is still in it!"

The driver looked right into my eyes as if he were looking at the oldest soul in the world, and he said, "You are right, Sweetheart. He does need his shoe. Thank you." He raced back to pick up the shoe, and then the ambulance took off with the siren blaring. Marilyn and I stood on the side of the railroad tracks shaking and trying to speak, but nothing would come out.

The rest of the kids were long gone and never even saw what had happened. We tried to walk, but our knees were weak, so we sat on the curb outside of the Thrift Store until we could find the strength to walk home.

"We have to know who that boy is, Marilyn. It just isn't right to have seen something like that and not know who he is."

Marilyn agreed, "I know. We can go home and call the hospital and see if they will tell us his name. Did you see his foot in his shoe? His shoe was soaked with blood, Jackie." Marilyn's speech was so shaky, as though her tongue was frozen from eating popsicles.

When we finally got home, Mom and Dad were still at work. We got on the phone and called Mills Hospital because that was the nearest one to the fairgrounds.

"Hello, my name is Jackie Mendelson, and my sister and I just saw a boy get hit by a train. We think the ambulance brought him to your hospital. Can you please tell us how he is?"

"One moment, please, and I will transfer you to the Emergency Room nurse."

When the nurse came on the line, I explained what I needed, and the nurse told me that the boy was there but that she could not tell me anything about his condition because I was not a family member.

"Please. We stayed with him and held his hand until the ambulance came. We just want to know his name." I begged. The nurse would not tell me anything and said she was sorry and hung up the phone.

When our parents came home from work, we told them what had happened, and Dad held me, and Mom held Marilyn, and all four of us wept from sorrow.

The next day, we all ran to get the San Mateo Times newspaper on the front porch. Each one took a section to see if there was anything in the paper about the accident, and there it was! On the front page of the Local News section was a picture of the train tracks, and the caption said. "MICHAEL HATHAWAY, A 14-YEAR-OLD BOY FROM BURLINGAME, DIED AFTER HE WAS HIT BY A TRAIN LEAVING THE COUNTY FAIR."

"Michael Hathaway!" we both whispered in unison. Now we knew who that boy was that stared into our eyes in his last moments on earth.

On Friday nights, when the Rabbi would say, "Who are you saying the Kaddish prayer for on this Sabbath evening?" all the Temple members would say aloud the names of those that had recently passed or those on the anniversary of their passing.

"Michael Hathaway." Marilyn and I whispered. We've never forgotten to whisper Michael Hathaway in our Kaddish prayers.

Chapter 11
Who Are You? And What Did You Do with My Sister?

Marilyn's body started to change. She was getting a waist, and she was ready for a training bra. She also seemed to be getting moodier and more short-tempered. She picked fights for no reason, bit her nails, and ate more.

I flew in the door after working at the park because I was "starvin' like Marvin" and hoped that dinner was ready. I found my mom and Marilyn huddled in the bathroom doorway. "What is going on?"

Marilyn looked like a deer in headlights as our mom waved a big fat gauze bandage and something that looked like a garter belt in her face and gave her instruction of some sort. Then, out of nowhere, our mom slapped Marilyn across the face and said, "This will keep your cheeks nice and rosy. You are now a woman."

I gasped. "Why did you hit Marilyn? What are you doing?"

"Your sister came home from school early because she started bleeding. She got her period, which means that she now has to wear a napkin. I slapped her because it is a tradition in our family that whenever a girl "falls off the roof," she gets a slap as a blessing that her cheeks will be rosy, and she will be a good woman."

I looked at my mother, said nothing, and thought, *Has my mother lost her mind? Let me get this straight. Marilyn fell off the roof and started bleeding. Did she fall off the roof at school? What was she doing on the school roof? I see no blood. What in the hell does that mean "she has to wear a napkin"? If she is bleeding, she should wear a Band-Aid. I know one thing, if I ever start bleeding, I will never tell a living soul.*

In the months to come, Marilyn and I fought about everything and nothing. Marilyn started pushing me, pounding my back, and giving me rope burns: she would grab my arm and twist each hand in a different direction to cause a burning sensation that hurt for hours. Mom and Dad would yell "knock it off" from the other room but did not intervene. I started steering clear of Marilyn by coming home just in time for dinner and avoiding her at night. If I started to feel threatened, I knew I could always duck into the closet for a little distance and peace.

Even so, when Marilyn would set the table for dinner, she would make me a glass of chocolate milk. This ritual lasted for years. No matter how terrible things got between the two of us, that was one loving gesture that I could count on. I wondered, on more than one occasion, whether Marilyn spat in my glass but, I would toss that out of my mind and give the milk an extra stir.

It seemed like every night, Dad would scold Marilyn. "Get those fingers out of your mouth! There is nothing left to bite, and your cuticles are bleeding! Your hands look horrible." They put Quit-It on her nails and even hot red chili powder, but nothing worked, and the yelling continued.

It seemed like every night, Mom would scold Marilyn. "You just had an ice cream sandwich, and now you are eating cupcakes! You are getting as big as a house, Sweetheart. Get out of the kitchen right now!"

It seemed like every night, Marilyn would run out of the kitchen sobbing and saying that she hated our mother, and she hated our father and that she wished they were dead. At first, no one but me could hear what she was saying, but after a while, she would scream it at the top of her lungs.

I kept doodling. My doodles started to look like cartoons. I added color, and my drawings were turning into art. In an attempt to control my anxiety when the yelling commenced, I retreated into my room, and colors, and forms, and images poured out of me. I escaped from the turmoil. I shut everything and everyone out and discovered an inner life where my creativity and expression lived. Drawing soothed me as much as the closet.

During the summer, when I would be going into fifth grade, and Marilyn would be going into sixth grade, our mom and dad signed us up for the day camp that was run by the San Mateo Recreation Department at Coyote Point.

Every weekday, for twelve weeks, we walked to the Hillsdale Mall to catch the camp bus then spent days fishing off the pier, swimming, making lanyards, singing camp songs, and learning about nature.

Marilyn ignored me, wouldn't even sit next to me on the bus. I did not know what I had done to make Marilyn treat me with such contempt.

The camp season ended with a weekend sleepover campout in the woods at a campground in La Honda. All the kids were singing "100 Bottle of Beer on the Wall" during the entire bus ride, and we were so excited to sleep outside in our sleeping bags, cook meals over a fire pit, swim in the lake, and tell ghost stories around a real campfire. I had a crush on Bobcat, my counselor. I followed him around like a puppy and tried to do everything right, so he would notice me and recognize how smart I was. I made the perfect S'mores at the campfire and sang all the camp songs in perfect pitch.

When it was time for all the kids to roll out our sleeping bags and get ready to sleep, I rolled my bag out right next to his. I checked my flashlight to make sure it worked just in case I had to run to the latrine. I went with the other girls to brush my teeth and saw Marilyn leaving the bathroom.

"Hey, Mare! Come put your sleeping bag next to mine, and we can share the hard candies I took from the candy bowl before we left the house."

Marilyn walked right past me as if she didn't hear a word I said and went down to the farthest end of the campsite away from me. That hurt me right down to my core, but I caught my breath and told myself that I was not going to let Marilyn ruin my good time. Bobcat walked around with his flashlight making sure that all the kids were in their pajamas zipped snuggly in their sleeping bags and that all the fires were out. I heard him slip into his bag, and he turned the flashlight on me. "You didn't change into your pajamas, Jackie. Why are you wearing your clothes to bed?" Bobcat asked.

"I was too cold to change, but it's okay because I have slept outside in my clothes before. Good night." What I was really thinking was that Bobcat had his clothes on, and I wanted to be just like him.

"Suit yourself, Kiddo, but I think you would be more comfortable in your pajamas. Goodnight."

At around 3 a.m. in the morning, I woke up, and my sleeping bag was sopping wet, and I was freezing. The first thing that came into my head was that it had rained on us, and the wet earth had soaked into my sleeping bag. I took out my flashlight and shown the light down into my bag, and I realized I had wet the bag. A wave of horror tore through me like a freight train. All I kept thinking was how to make this go away without anyone knowing. If I had only been wearing my pajamas, I could change into my clothes. Those were the only long pants I had, and my pajama bottoms had pink balloons on them, so there was no way they could be mistaken for pants.

Even if I did have another pair of pants, I had a wet sleeping bag that I could not crawl back into. I was mortified. The sad thing was that my very own sister was there, and I could have gotten some comfort and reassurance from her, but she wouldn't even look at me.

I inched over to Bobcat in my sleeping bag and gently shook his shoulder until I could feel him move. "Bobcat. Bobcat. Please wake up. I had an accident, and I don't know what to do."

Bobcat rolled over toward me and whispered, "Don't worry, Kiddo. It happens all the time. You probably had a dream that you were in the bathroom going and went in your sleeping bag in your sleep. Do you have another change of clean clothes?"

"No. Just my pink pajama bottoms with balloons on them. I have clean underpants and socks and my bathing suit," I whimpered.

"No worries, Kiddo. I have another sleeping bag and some jeans that are about your size in my trunk just for this type of emergency."

Bobcat came back from his car with a bundle tucked under his arm and kneeled down next to me. He told me to take the jeans and dry underpants to the latrine, go to the bathroom if I needed to, dry off, and change. He said he would fold up my sleeping bag and lay out the dry one for me while I was gone. He promised that this was our secret and that not a soul would know what happened.

The next morning, Bobcat winked at me and asked me to help him scramble all the eggs while he cooked the bacon. We quietly cooked breakfast for all the campers, and the only sounds that I could hear was that little voice inside scolding me for wetting my pants and embarrassing myself in front of Bobcat. Marilyn could see that something was wrong with me and, at one point, came over to me to engage in a somewhat sarcastic way, but I remained quiet and did not respond.

The bus pulled into the parking lot. Bobcat handed each child a certificate of achievement for completing the camping experience. He handed me mine, tussled my hair, and whispered that I was his favorite camper this summer. I smiled, took the certificate, and, when no one was looking, tossed it into a trash can and got into my mother's car.

"How was camp, girls? Your daddy and I missed you!" Mom smiled while looking in the rearview mirror.

"I had fun!" Marilyn said, smiling.

"It was good," I said while bending down, pretending to tie my tennis shoe.

Chapter 12
You Are Never Too Young to Hit the Slippery Slope

It was in sixth grade that I lost interest in school work and in being a doctor. My grades slipped, and I got kicked out of class at least once a week for talking, not doing my homework, or being disruptive.

My curiosity about alcohol increased, and I thought back on Nana Hazel sneaking gin cocktails at any hour of the day. Mom and Dad did not drink much unless they were having one of their rare cocktail parties. After the cocktail parties, Marilyn and I would help clean up; we would sniff all the half-full tumblers and try to guess the flavor of the adult beverages.

I did sneak a gulp once, and it burned down my throat, all the way into my stomach. I did not like the taste, but I didn't hate it either. And it gave me a sensation a little bit like the time I painted under the bathroom sink and almost passed out. I went to my father's liquor cabinet and pulled out a bottle of vodka and poured some in a glass. I grabbed three oranges from the fruit bowl on the kitchen table and ran into the garage. I found a syringe from an old dentist's kit that once belonged to my cousin Earl. I filled it with vodka and injected it into an orange. I did the same to the remaining oranges, hid the evidence, and took the spiked oranges into my room, and buried them in my sock drawer.

The next day at lunch, I sat on the benches that lined the schoolyard with all my friends and proceeded to peel my orange. I did not know how it was going to taste, but I did know that I could not react.

I peeled away my first slice and slipped it into my mouth and started to chew. The orange was deliciously sweet, so the alcohol did not burn too badly. By my third slice, I liked the orange a lot. When I was finished with the entire orange, I started to giggle.

"What are you laughing at?" asked Sarah Weiss.

"Oh, some kid playing kickball just fell on his butt."

That afternoon, I sat as still as could be in the classroom and didn't make a peep. I looked straight ahead because when I didn't or if I closed my eyes, I started to get the whirlies. I was happy, my teacher was delighted, and that was one way not to get kicked out of class anymore.

A few weeks later, I took a Parliament cigarette out of Mom's pack and went into the back yard behind the bamboo lanai and lit it up. I had seen my mother and father smoke; hence, I knew how to puff and blow the smoke out. I started to cough uncontrollably and couldn't catch my breath. As a result, I started feeling dizzy.

I tried it again, and, again, I started to cough... only this time, I coughed, passed gas, and almost wet my pants. I decided smoking wasn't for me and put the cigarette out. What I failed to do was brush my teeth, so when I went to kiss my mom goodbye for school, she took one whiff and grabbed my arm.

"Were you smoking cigarettes?" She gave me such a "hairy eyeball" that all I could do was lie.

"No, Mom! We all smell like smoke around here.... as much as you blow your smoke on us! See you when you get home from work. I love you. Bye!" I ran out of my parents' bedroom like a bat out of hell and briefly felt bad for lying, for blaming the smell on my mother. Then that was that. The next concoction I created was one I planned to share with Gary Seaput. He was the cutest boy I had ever seen, and he sat right in front of me in class. I thought he liked me too because he teased me a lot, and we traded stuff...like I traded Gary some of the best stamps from my collection for his confederate paper money from the Civil War that he swore was real.

I bought some malted milk balls on one of my trips to the mall, trips that occasionally ended up with me stealing stuff. I decided to inject the balls with rum. I slowly filled each one until it felt heavy. I decided to taste the first one to make sure it was worthy of sharing with Gary. It was really good but a little strong. I decided that it was because I just made them, and they would settle down by the next day.

That night after dinner, my father asked me to join him in the living room for a talk. A wave of fear came over me. My dad never took me into the living room for a private conversation before. Did he find out I was taking his alcohol?

Dad sat me on the couch, stood over me, and started, "Jackie, I am going to ask you a question, and I want you to tell me the truth. Have you ever stolen anything from any of the stores at the mall?"

My mind raced out of control. *Holy cow! What am I going to tell him? What does he know? At least my stealing his alcohol is not going to come up, so I have to give it my best guess.*

"Yes. I took some crystal mounts for my stamp collection from the stamp and coin store at the mall. I'm sorry, Daddy. I know that was wrong." I turned bright red from embarrassment, shame, and fear. I stared into my father's eyes. All I was hoping for is that he did not look at me with that disappointed look that made me want to curl up and die.

"I went into that store on an appointment with Sid Barth, the store owner, to take an application for a life insurance policy. When he saw my business card, he asked me if I had a daughter about ten years old. When I told him I had two daughters, he described you and told me that he saw you steal the cellophane stamp sleeves."

"They are called crystal mounts, Dad," I corrected.

"I don't care what they are called, Jackie! If you care more about my mistake than showing remorse for your mistake, then you and I have a problem! Do you understand me, young lady?" My father bellowed right in my face for maximum emphasis.

I nodded.

"Tomorrow, you will go into the store with your allowance, and you will give that man the money for the crystal mounts."

That next day, I went into the store to apologize to Sid Barth for stealing the crystal mounts. When he came out of the backroom, I gasped because I recognized him from Temple. He was Karen Barth's father. Karen had been in my Sunday school class since kindergarten, and we shared many a birthday party. I felt nauseous.

"Mr. Barth, please forgive me for taking from your store. I did not mean to disrespect you. I hope you will accept my apology because I am sorry."

I tried to look into his eyes the whole time I was talking. It was hard because I was ashamed and wanted to hide my face. Mr. Barth acknowledged me for doing the right thing.

Crying with guilt, I dashed out of the store, ran toward my home, and hid in the hall closet behind the vacuum cleaner. My dad must have kept my indiscretion from my mom because she never said a word to me about stealing.

I knew that breaking one of the Ten Commandments was a missed opportunity for my mother to correct my behavior, and so she must not have known because she would have lectured my ears off. I thanked God, and my dad, for small favors.

Chapter 13
Obligation Regardless of Consequences

After our Baba died in 1958, Auntie Betty had moved into a small studio apartment on Leavenworth Street in San Francisco. She did not want to stay in the house with decades of memories that she and her mother shared. She was left adrift and alone with no one to take care of and no one to watch over her. It had been four years since Bertha Siegel died, and we all missed her very much.

I missed baking cookies with her and the smell of dill in her house. I missed watching her light the Sabbath candles with her hands over her eyes, rocking back and forth, hearing her muffled prayers through her tears. I missed her soft hands and her warm hugs. I can only imagine how deeply the loss affected Auntie Betty.

Mom, Marilyn, and I would drive up to "The City" to visit Auntie Betty at least once a month. I marveled at the Murphy bed that was always so perfectly made up, despite being lowered from the wall. I looked at her figurines placed just so on the dresser and admired her armchair and ottoman positioned directly in front of a small television set with rabbit ears.

The older I got, the more interesting I found Auntie Betty. She had a very deep voice and short, finger-waved, bleached blonde hair, and she wore bright, red lipstick and matching nail polish on both finger and toenails. Her skin was very tan, and she had fine lines around her lips. She smoked non-filtered cigarettes and would spit bits of tobacco out into the air when no one was looking.

But, Auntie Betty's health was failing, and she was struggling with the decision of having to quit work and finding a safe place to live where she could be cared for.

After our last visit, we could barely get into the front door before Mom grabbed Dad's arm and pulled him down the hall into their room and closed the door. I pressed my ear up to the door.

"Honey," Mom said. "I am so sorry to ask this of you, but I cannot see any other solution. Betty has had several heart attacks and has to stop working. She took such good care of Momma, and she is now left with nobody but us, really. How can we not take her in? She would be here when The Girls get out of school, so they won't be coming home to an empty house."

He sucked air into the side of his mouth. It was loud enough that I could hear it through the door. Then he replied. "I guess it is only fair that we do for your family what we did for my family when we took my mom in. We'll take the TV into the living room, and she can have her own bedroom. Please make it clear to her that she is welcome into our family but that you and I are the heads of this household."

He sucked in more air. "She also has to cut back on her drinking because, honestly, her personality changes. And she has to be fully clothed unless she is sunbathing in the backyard. I mean it, Pat. I won't have her walking around here in her underwear and swearing in front of The Girls."

There. He said all he had to say for the moment.

Uncommonly meek, Mom said, "Thank you so much, Sweetheart. I know this may be difficult, but I feel like it is an obligation of love. I will call Betty tomorrow, and if she refuses with false pride, I will tell her it will help us because The Girls will not be alone after school. Let's tell The Girls."

I ran like the wind just in time to get around the corner and out of sight. Marilyn and I tuned out to whatever our parents said. We had no choice in the matter, so we had nothing to say. Mom and Dad kept prompting us to talk, but we just nodded and said, "Okay. Whatever needs to happen."

We went to our room, and Marilyn turned to me with an unusually civil tone and said, "We don't come home to an empty house every day after school. We are out playing and having fun. I will have a cow if we have to come home every day when she moves in because she needs our company. I am not going to babysit our grumpy old Aunt. I swear to God!"

The year that Auntie Betty moved into the house on Sunset Terrace, I was in the 6th grade, and Marilyn had started junior high school, the first time in six years we did not go to the same school.

Auntie Betty nestled right into the groove of the house and family. She carved out her role and level of authority with us. Mostly, we humored her because we were busy with school, Sunday school, choir practice, and after school activities.

During the day, Auntie Betty would lay out in the sun in her bathing suit and tan. She made a concoction of baby oil and mercurochrome, which she would rub all over her body, and it made her skin almost instantly bronze. She would read magazines and smoke cigarettes all day.

When Marilyn and I would come home from school with friends to play in the backyard, Auntie Betty would get irritated. One day the Sunset Terrace gang, our group of friends, was in the yard putting on a play that I wrote. Auntie Betty came out to the yard in her underwear and shouted that the noise was giving her a heart attack and put a nitroglycerine pill under her tongue, clutched her heart, and ran back into the house. That was the end of my play rehearsal, and the last time we brought kids home after school.

Auntie Betty took it upon herself to confront Marilyn about her eating habits and her weight when Mom and Dad were not around. That caused constant arguing, yelling, and crying from both of them. Then, Auntie Betty told Marilyn that she was not really part of the family because she was adopted. Marilyn's loathing of Auntie Betty grew stronger, and she seemed to use food to comfort herself even more.

Sunday was a ritual "call all the brothers, sisters and other living relatives and talk for hours" day. Every time a new call was made, we would be handed the phone to say hello to whoever was on the line.

We did not mind saying hi, but it was the long silence after that which was so uncomfortable. What do you say to a 70-year-old uncle that really just wants to speak to his sisters in Yiddish and tell jokes? We would try to be out playing when the calls started. Dad was always out playing golf on Sundays, so he found his escape from the cackling and loud carryings-on over the telephone wires that reverberated throughout the house.

During one call, Mom was in the bedroom on the phone, and Auntie Betty was on the kitchen phone. Uncle Joe was telling a long joke, and Auntie Betty had to go to the bathroom. Instead of putting the phone down and running to the bathroom and getting back for the punch line, Betty took a bowel movement in the kitchen garbage can.

Dad came back from golfing and went into the garbage can to throw away an empty carton.

"What in the hell is in this garbage can! Everyone get in the kitchen this minute! I want to know who put this poop in the trash, and I want to know now!" Dad shrieked.

Everyone came running.

"Not me! I didn't do that!" I said with my nose scrunched up.

"I wasn't even in the kitchen!" protested an indignant Marilyn.

Mom looked at Auntie Betty, who stood against the doorway, looking very defiant and smug.

"I did it," Auntie Betty admitted.

"We were on the phone with Joe. He was in the middle of a story, and I had to go, so I went in the trash can. Why are you so mad? You men go out golfing and pee all over the trees. Why is that different?" Auntie Betty curled her lip at our father.

My mind raged. *How could she say such a rude and spiteful thing to my Daddy?*

Marilyn and I turned on our heels and walked into our bedroom and closed the door. We did not hear what happened next, and we did not care what the grownups had to say. We had been getting along a little better lately.

"I can't believe she did that!" I said. "How do you think she got her butt over the trash can?" I laughed until I could not breathe, and tears streamed down my face.

Marilyn stuck her head under a pillow, and her body shook uncontrollably. All of a sudden, she stopped and looked out at me, wide-eyed and said, "I wet my pants!"

That made us laugh even harder. "Oh, good," I said. "She poops in a can. You pee in your pants. What is next? Am I going to barf in my shoe?"

Auntie Betty stomped into our room in a rage and yelled, "Oh, so you think that is funny, do you? Well, I'll show you funny! I am packing my things and leaving this house before I have another heart attack. I know when I am not wanted!" She put a nitroglycerine tablet under her tongue and stormed out.

That Sunday dinner started out very somber. The freshly baked rolls were crunchy on the outside and soft in the middle. The roasted chicken had a perfectly crispy skin, and I was happy to see the gizzard on my dish. The potatoes au gratin steamed on the plate, as did the green beans, so I started to calm down and let the "normal" of a lovingly prepared dinner soothe my soul.

Auntie Betty joined the family at the table. Her eyes were red from crying, and she had the sorrow of a lifetime on her face. "Please forgive me for my behavior. It was wrong to do what I did. Mel, I was unkind to you when you confronted me because I was ashamed of myself. I know that is hardly an excuse for how I spoke to you in front of The Girls. There is no excuse for being rude. Please forgive me, and if you want me to leave, I will understand."

Everyone looked at each other and then at Auntie Betty, but no one said a word. Out of nowhere, I reached across the table and stole my mom's last and best bite of her bread and screamed, "Last bites!" While everyone was still looking at me, Dad reached across the table and stole my gizzard and tossed it in his mouth and yelled, "Last bites!" I was stunned! I really wanted that gizzard. I just wanted to make everyone laugh. Well, it worked, and the five of us sat at the table for hours after dinner playing Yahtzee and laughing. Then Mom and Auntie Betty unpacked her bag, and we all felt better and went to sleep in peace.

Chapter 14
Go to Your Room This Minute!

By the end of 6th grade, I became very distracted. I strolled home from school one day, thinking about how hard it would be to say goodbye to my friends. After all, I was not going to be at the same junior high school with many of them in the fall. My favorite boys would be going to another school.

Suddenly, I gathered my thoughts. *Oh no! Marilyn is going to kill me! I rode her bicycle to school today because mine was stolen from the bike rack last week. I promised I would not leave it at school, and I did. I forgot all about it and walked home.* Panic set in.

I ran back to the school like a bat out of hell to try to retrieve the bike before someone could steal it, but when I got to the playground, the racks were empty. Marilyn's bike was gone. I was terrified.

Guilt set in again. I felt genuinely bad that I got Marilyn's bike stolen because I was careless and preoccupied. If that meant that I had to be Marilyn's personal punching bag tonight, I figured I deserved it. I would tell her after dinner.

I walked in to see an already prepared meal and set dinner table, and Marilyn had placed my iced cold chocolate milk on the table above my knife. Oh, the guilt.

The family had a delicious stuffed breast of veal with French cut green beans, shaved almonds, butter, and a hint of garlic. I loved the sticky, translucent little bones of the veal and marveled at how we could be eating such a perfect meal on a school night. But the weight of my crime and worrying about telling Marilyn wore on me.

The dinner was over, and Auntie Betty made her usual declaration of 'elegant sufficiency,' and she and Mom sat back, and each lit up a cigarette. Dad stopped smoking a few years ago, so he stared at them both and sucked air. They giggled and said, almost simultaneously, "I love a good cigarette after a great meal!"

Auntie Betty looked at me and said, "I have a wonderful surprise for you. I am going to Los Angeles to visit our relatives, and I am taking you with me, and we are going to

Disneyland. Isn't that fantastic?"

I looked at her, then at my mother, then at my father and then at Marilyn and said, "What about Marilyn?"

"Marilyn will have to stay home this trip, but I will plan something for her next time. This is going to be just you and me. Isn't that exciting?"

I was stunned and not even the least bit excited. Who in this family thinks it is okay to take one sister on a trip to Disneyland and not the other? Marilyn and I were fighting like cats and dogs over nothing, but this little bit of business could cause a murder.

Finally, I said, "Thank you, Auntie Betty, for asking me, but I do not want to go to Disneyland without Marilyn." I smiled sweetly and lowered my eyes.

"Well, that's too damn bad. You are going whether you like it or not. I have already planned the trip, and I have the tickets too!" Auntie Betty must have had vodka in her water glass.

Our parents didn't interfere. Marilyn ran out of the room, crying, and I seethed with rage until I was about to combust. "I won't go without Marilyn, and you can't make me!" I screamed at the top of my lungs.

"Go to your room right this minute, young lady, and don't you come out until you are ready to apologize to your Auntie Betty!" Mom yelled.

I ran into our bedroom to find Marilyn sitting on the edge of her bed, crying. I walked up to her and put my arms around her and said, "I don't want to go without you, Marilyn."

Marilyn said, "I know, Jackie. You would never have agreed to this if it were up to you. I just hate Auntie Betty and wish she were dead!"

I whispered in her ear, "I know Mare. Today is a crummy day. Someone stole your bike from school while I was in class."

Marilyn looked up at me with a stricken look of disbelief and then such a sad expression of hopeless defeat. "I don't care about anything anymore, Jackie. I hate my life, and I just want to die."

I gasped. I had never heard Marilyn turn in on herself before. She was always hating everyone else and lashing out at others around her but never had I heard Marilyn say she wanted to die.

Then Marilyn pulled up her sweater sleeve, and I saw a big gauze pad with bloodstains in the center. "What happened to you, Marilyn?"

"I like this guy named Jim. So, my girlfriends and I decided to carve the names of the guys we liked in our arms with a razor blade. I was scared, so I went last, and it stung. Lorraine and Marnie said we should show them to the guys to prove how much we like them. When I did, Jim glared at me like I was insane, and then he turned around and stomped away; now, he refuses to even talk to me. It is badly infected, and I don't know what to do."

I ran into the bathroom and snuck out with a bottle of hydrogen peroxide, cotton balls, squares of sterile gauze pads, and white tape. I cleaned out the wound and put a nice fresh dressing over the cuts.

Marilyn looked soothed for the moment and exhausted from the burden and pain of her life. She looked down at me and said, "Thank you, and please don't tell Mom and Dad."

"I won't say a thing, I promise. If they make me go to Disneyland with Auntie Betty, I will bring you back something that you will love, and I promise not to have a good time. And, I am sorry about your bike, Mare."

We gave each other a sideways hug and climbed into our beds without kissing the grownups goodnight.

Auntie Betty

Chapter 15
Little White Lies

I was sitting on the edge of my bed with an 'outburst hangover.' I knew I was going to be expected to apologize to Auntie Betty for what I had said, but I also knew in my heart that I was not sorry.

If I did say I was sorry, I was going to tell a lie. If I told a lie, I would be loved again by the two most important people in my life and would then have to go to Disneyland without my sister. My head was spinning.

The concept of 'little white lies' had never before been something that I had to ponder with such moral implications. I began making a list of little white lies that my parents had told me like they were charges on a criminal indictment. The more I thought about it, the longer the lists got. I remembered my father would snore loud on the couch when we would all be watching TV, and whenever he would wake up, he would say, 'I'm just resting my eyes. I'm not sleeping.' I recalled the time my dad took me golfing and said we would go again soon.

I remembered the time Mom and Dad sat us down and told us that money was tight, so they were going to borrow our college funds that Auntie Sarah set up, but that they would put it all back as soon as they could. I recalled all the times that my mom would answer the phone in her hairnet and bathrobe, and I would hear her say, 'no, I was just running out of the house, but I have a second.' And then the times that Mom would promise to quit smoking.

As the list grew, I expected myself to feel angry at the deception and betrayal, but I didn't. I started to smile, and then I started to laugh. I was too young to understand hypocrisy, deception, and betrayal fully; however, I could feel the emotions they evoke and was beginning to understand those feelings for the first time. I laughed so loud that I woke Marilyn up.

"What's so funny? You are sitting on the edge of your bed, staring into space and cackling like a moron." Marilyn snorted.

"Mom and Dad tell white lies all the time, and I know I shouldn't be laughing, but it is kind of funny. They are going to want me to say I am sorry for opening up my big mouth to Auntie Betty last night. I am going to do it, but it is going to be a white lie. I am not at all sorry for what I said, but to have peace in the house, I will apologize."

Marilyn was still half asleep and looked at me in a very puzzled manner. Then there was clarity in her eyes."

"A few months later, I asked Mom again how I came to be adopted. I could see I took her by surprise and a story just flew out of her mouth that my father died in the Korean War, and my mother died in childbirth. She said she thought she told me that once before and said that I must never feel as though I were unwanted. It was just something that happened, and it turned out to be the luckiest day of their lives." Marilyn looked truly distraught and hurt.

I was stunned when she told me and much later realized that Marilyn lived with those two stories crashing up against each other her entire childhood.

Our Mom lied to Marilyn. The car crash could not be true because the second story was completely different, so she concluded they were both lies. The second story caused deep pain because Marilyn was already born in 1948 and the Korean War began in 1952. Telling her that her mother died in childbirth could have been the cruelest lie of all. Feeling responsible for her own mother's death must have been agonizing.

Later that day, I made an apology to Auntie Betty, and the next thing you know, I was on my way to Los Angeles on my very first airplane ride. My aunt was pulling out all the stops to make me feel excited about the trip, and at some point, I set myself free and decided to have a good time. We jumped in a cab and headed for Beverly Hills to stay with our cousins.

Ruthie and her husband, Jack, were my mom and Auntie Betty's first cousins. They lived in what I believed to be a mansion with polished terrazzo floors and beautiful furniture with art on the walls by Picasso and Chagall.

In the Mendelson family, all cousins who were not young were addressed as Cousin so and so. So, I thanked Cousin Jack and Cousin Ruthie for inviting us to stay in their beautiful home and went into the backyard to swim in the pool. I did not want to sit inside with the old folks, and I missed Marilyn and wished she were there too.

That evening, Cousin Jack took me by the hand and led me to the back of the house and into his bedroom. He closed the door and locked it and said, "I am going to show you something, but you have to promise never to tell anyone you saw this. Do you promise?"

I could feel my heart pounding out of my chest, and I nodded my head in agreement.

Cousin Jack reached into his pocket and pulled out a ring of keys, and opened a very wide drawer in his built-in dresser. I looked inside the drawer to find stacks of $100-dollar bills, in bundles, covering every square inch of that drawer. I had never seen that much money in my young life.

He put his arm around my shoulder and whispered in my ear that he was very rich, and all I could smell was alcohol. I felt embarrassed.

I was let out of the room, and I ran to the other side of the house. Later, I heard screaming between Auntie Betty and Cousin Jack.

"You are just a small little man! Mr. Big Deal Grease Monkey that made it rich. You were a blowhard in Iowa, and you are an even bigger blowhard now," sneered Auntie Betty.

"Well, you are just a drunk old cow, and I wouldn't cross the street to go to your funeral," slurred Cousin Jack.

Doors slammed, and Auntie Betty came running into the room and told me to pack my things and that we were leaving in the morning.

"But what about Disneyland?" I questioned.

"There will be no Disneyland!" shouted Auntie Betty.

The next morning, a cab was honking, and Auntie Betty grabbed me by the arm and ran me to the waiting vehicle. She scurried me out of the cab at the airport and ran with me through the terminal, through the gate, and into the plane. She did not say anything to me until we were almost ready to land at San Francisco International Airport.

'We could not stay where we were not wanted' was her only explanation to me.

When Marilyn came home and found me there, she just shook her head and said, "Auntie Betty did something to ruin your trip, and you never made it to Disneyland, right? I am not surprised."

I nodded, "Cousin Jack and Auntie Betty got in a fight, and Auntie Betty had a cow and said we were leaving, and that was that."

Marilyn asked, "Do you want to know something else that isn't a surprise? Mom and Dad sold the house, and we are leaving Sunset Terrace. We bought the Altschul's house on Sylvan Avenue, and we are moving there just in time for you to start 7th grade at Abbott Junior High School. How about them apples?"

Chapter 16
A Day to Remember to Forget

The move down the hill to the flatlands was complete. The Mendelson family, plus one, could unpack and set up a house at breakneck speed.

Pat Mendelson assumed all roles, dispatcher, coordinator, interior designer, coach, and critic. By the end of that moving day to the house on Sylvan, the beds were made, the pictures were hung, and Mom had a chicken in the oven.

That night I was looking in my closet to pick out my outfit for my first day in junior high school. I turned to Marilyn and said, "Am I going to like going to Abbott? Is it a good school?"

"It is an okay school, but the part I like is that there are no little kids around and you change classes for different subjects. The cafeteria has better food, and I made some good friends to talk to. Just make sure you act cool because I don't want you to embarrass me."

I thought to myself, *When Marilyn started junior high, she started talking about boys, and she started smoking. She would leave the house like a normal girl, and when she got to school, she would go into the school bathroom and roll up her skirt at the waist, so her hem was way above her knees. She would rat her hair until you could see through it and spray it into a solid mass. She painted eyeliner above and below her eyelids and caked her lashes with mascara. Last on her routine was the swooping on of her white lipstick; a few lips smack, and she was ready for class.* I was sure if anyone were to be embarrassed, it would be me.

The next morning, the alarm sounded, and I popped out of bed. I got dressed and checked my pockets to make sure I had lunch money. I ran into the bathroom to be first because Marilyn took forever. I turned on the water, put toothpaste on my toothbrush, and looked up into the mirror.

The house rumbled from the sound of me, bellowing, "Noooo! This cannot be happening! Please, God, make it go away!"

My parents ran into the bathroom to see what had happened to me. There I stood, staring at them with one of my eyelids six times its size, bright pink and swollen shut. I had a sty on my eye. My dad ran for the ice to try to calm it down, and Mom went for the makeup because that pink was so bright, I could guide in the ships at the Coyote Point Marina. I slammed the door behind them because if Marilyn got one look at my eye, she would tease me for the rest of my natural life. I could hear Auntie Betty lurking in the hallway, trying to see what was going on. What a nosey body.

There was no amount of ice or makeup or camouflage in the world that could cover up that screaming defect, so Dad slapped a pair of sunglasses on me and told me not to take them off all day.

The homeroom teacher in the first period asked me to remove my sunglasses while I was indoors, so I responded, "I wish I could, but I scratched my eyeball, and I cannot let any light on it, or it hurts. My father told me to keep my sunglasses on all day because it is medically necessary."

I had to tell that story six times that first day of school, and every time I told a new teacher, I said it just loud enough so that the kids in the class could hear me. Each teacher made the same skeptical face when I told my white lie, but I made it through the day.

When I got home after school, I went into the bathroom and removed my sunglasses to see if my eye was any better. Auntie Betty saw the sty and came back with a warm teabag and told me to lay down and put it on my eye for at least ten minutes. She patted my head and went to her room.

That night Marilyn saw my eye for the first time, and she showed great compassion when she said, "Wow, I am so sorry that you had a sty on your first day of junior high. That could have ruined your whole life, so it was neat that you made it through the day. I would have had a cow!"

I thanked her, a bit stunned at her kindness, said goodnight, and turned out the light.

In the middle of the night, Marilyn woke to desperate sounds coming from another part of the house. She bolted out of bed and followed the sounds into Auntie Betty's room, and she saw our aunt clutching her chest and struggling to open her nitroglycerine bottle. Marilyn opened the bottle and put a tablet under her tongue, and then ran into our parent's room to get help. Marilyn ran back into the room to hold Auntie Betty's hand until the ambulance came and took her to the hospital.

Mom rode with Auntie Betty in the ambulance while Dad sat by the phone with us, waiting to hear how she was doing. Marilyn and I were each tucked under one of Dad's arms, softly talking about our aunt with genuine sorrow.

Was she my favorite person? No. But, I felt deeply for her because I knew how alone she had been and saw her humiliation at being dependent on our family for care and stability. I could get past my feelings and attitudes to love Auntie Betty, even if I did not like her very much.

Auntie Betty passed away that night. Most of the Mendelson family cried. Dad comforted his three girls and made salami and eggs for breakfast. Mom called Sinai Memorial Chapel to make arrangements for her funeral. Marilyn sat in Auntie Betty's room, wondering how long she should wait before she could ask for that room without looking like a buzzard circling her prey. I figured I would not have to go back to school until my sty disappeared and put the sunglasses away.

Chapter 17
Does Jackie Seem Odd to You?

The changes that I experienced in 7th and 8th grade were mysterious and unknown. Growing up meant change. My understanding of change started out to be myopic and quite literal. My legs were getting longer, and my shoe size was getting bigger. I noticed that I wanted to eat a little more at dinner time.

I no longer crushed my diaphragm on the sink when I was brushing my teeth, and I could reach the glasses in the cupboard without a footstool. At school, I made good friends, got involved in student government, got my menstrual period, and dealt with everything myself. My grades were average only because I was not that consistent with my homework; I was honestly interested in learning.

My dad taught me to dance during my childhood. He would hold up his thumbs and say, "lick them." I would, and then he would lovingly shape my eyebrows so they would have a perfect natural arch. He taught me how to be ladylike and polite. But that was it for growing up lessons, except for, "If a boy tries to take advantage of you, drop to one knee and punch up into his crotch."

What in the hell did that mean? What could a boy do to me that warranted that behavior? I didn't know, and I didn't ask. Mom was a Victorian prude. She never talked about sex, never was unclothed in front of us, and later, I suspected never in front of my father either. She would not talk about anything sexual, anatomical, or biological in nature, and if someone even started to make an off-colored comment, she would get nervous and flustered and shut it down. She never talked about puberty or body changes with us openly, so every change that happened to us during those pubescent years were assumed to be "abnormal."

Breasts were not breasts. Vaginas were not vaginas. Penises were not penises. There weren't even genitals, and when I first heard that word, I thought that meant Christians. All those body parts were called private parts.... genderless nameless bits not to be discussed. I was not sure what their primary function was, but I decided that the knowledge would probably dispel the white lie that babies come out of our mother's stomach much the same as the realization that there is no Baby Stork, Easter Bunny, or Tooth Fairy. It was at my first sock hop in the school auditorium when I experienced my first bodily sensation that evoked both fear and pleasure at the same time. I was slow dancing with Fred Pierce, and I felt him start to tremble. He got a sleepy, scared look on his face. I was hoping he was not bored or ready to throw up. He pulled me closer to his body, and I felt something hard against my pelvis and a slight rise in temperature coming from Fred's pants. Then I felt my own body react to that feeling and awareness as my spine started to ripple, my back arched, and I pressed myself harder into Fred.

I got a tingling sensation between my legs that I had never felt before, and I started to feel light-headed. Soon, that song ended, and both Fred and I hoped for another slow song to play, but the DJ played The Twist by Chubby Checker, and we twisted back to reality but with a newfound appreciation for slow songs. I was awakening in other ways, too. It was a beautiful fall day, and I was early for school, strolling toward Abbott Junior High, taking the time to look at the trees and birds that eluded me when I was usually running to beat the bell.

I saw a bird's nest in a tree and stopped to take a look when, out of nowhere, a huge black crow flew over my head, swooped down, and just missed clawing my scalp by inches. I looked up to see what was happening. Three more crows joined in, and they all started to dive down towards my head.

Our family had recently gone to the movies and saw *The Birds*, so I knew I would get pecked to death if I did not act quickly.

I took off, running and waving my hands above my head to try to keep them away from me. I was fleeing for my life!

Out of the corner of my eye, I saw a brown sedan pull up beside me. It was Mrs. Brewer, my homeroom teacher. She rolled down the passenger side window and screamed, "Get in the car now, Jackie!"

I flung open the door and jumped into the passenger seat, rolled up the window, and took a deep breath. I looked at Mrs. Brewer and said, "Thank you for saving my life. I promise I will behave in your class from now on!"

Mrs. Brewer smiled sweetly at me and said, "You are welcome, my dear. Let's just say you will behave in all your classes until you enter high school, shall we?"

I thought *that Mrs. Brewer drives a hard bargain.* I looked my teacher in the eyes and sadly agreed to be a good girl. We drove off to school.

Three hours into my classes that day, I was quite proud that I had caused not even a ruffle of a disturbance. Concentrating on being good in class and keeping a lid on outbursts and wisecracks took a lot of work.

At 11:40 AM, the intercom made a very loud scratching sound, and the principal of the school started to speak.

"Boys and Girls, this is Mr. Chapin speaking. I am afraid I have some very bad news. After I tell you, I would like you to pack up your desk, gather your belongings, go quietly out the door and go home. For those of you that take buses to school, please go to the pickup area, and they will be there shortly to take you home. For those needing to contact your parents, please come to the office."

There was a very long pause, and the children heard a cracked voice say, "President John Fitzgerald Kennedy has just been shot while riding in a motorcade in Dallas, Texas. It is not known yet if his wounds are fatal. We must all say a prayer for our President that he may survive this horrible act and make a full recovery. Now, go home children and be with your families. God bless America."

I instantly felt sick to my stomach and looked around the room in utter disbelief at what I had just heard. Boys and girls cried uncontrollably with deep sadness and pain. I couldn't slow my brain down to even think about thinking. I ran out the classroom door, through the schoolyard, around the cyclone fence, and down the sidewalk, blinded by my tears. As I fled past the high school, I thought, for one split second, about those black crows. Rage surged through me, and I thought, *let them try, and I will rip their heads off.* I kept running as fast as I could until I grabbed the front doorknob of my home, which had always meant that I was safe.

I was alone. Marilyn had not come home from school yet. Mom and Dad were still out at work. I turned on the television and started watching my President get shot over and over again on the Special Report. I could not bear to watch it, but I could not take my eyes off the screen. I sobbed and sobbed until I was exhausted. John Fitzgerald Kennedy was my first President. I was alive for other presidencies, but I was not aware of those men or understanding of that bigger world beyond my home and my family and my neighborhood. I knew that Russia was the enemy, but I had no real frame of reference that felt like it came from within. My admiration for Kennedy and the pride I felt that he was the leader of my country was palpable and intrinsic.

I loved his wife, Jacqueline, and especially because she was strong and smart as well as beautiful. I wondered what it was like to be Carolyn and John. I stopped whatever I was doing whenever I heard John Kennedy's voice. I started to believe in what he was saying where before, my willingness to believe was restricted to the voices of my parents, select teachers, and my Rabbi.

His death was a crushing blow to my bubble of goodness in the world. Then I saw Jack Ruby shoot Lee Harvey Oswald. I became aware of the world that I was living in. These concepts were coming into my consciousness hard and heavy, but I had no answers because I didn't know what questions to ask.

Just random hints of new realities and fleeting images of the vastness of the world, and somehow it all swelled to a crescendo of lost hope. My President was assassinated, and, for a time, everything good was bad. All hope was gone. I initially felt the swearing-in of Lyndon Johnson was a betrayal as if he had something to do with the killing. But then, I gave in to the fact that he was not my President, and I had no idea who he was but that someone had to step in, and that was why he had been the Vice President. I developed mistrust in who is leading my country for the first time in my life.

My parents and sister were also very distraught and bereft over the shooting of Kennedy. We talked about it over dinner and watched the funeral procession and all the coverage for four days straight. The many things left to discover were that sometimes, things just do not make sense. Sometimes devastating things happen, and the only requirement is to try to get through it intact and unharmed. I realized many things existed outside of my immediate universe that I did not control.

Being a good girl in school didn't seem so hard after that.

Chapter 18
High School at Last

The summer before high school at Camp Saratoga was magical. I could finally breathe. I was away from my parents at a Jewish camp for three weeks and could hang with my friends, make new friends, and have a blast! A high point for me was the Friday night Shabbat services. Sitting around the swimming pool, each camper dressed in crisp white blouses and t-shirts would light a Sabbath candle and float it in the pool. We would sing the prayer over the Shabbat candles while holding hands.

The sight of 500 candles bobbing on the water and lighting up the night sky was breathtaking. I could not remember a time when I felt so in love with Judaism, abundant with rituals steeped in tradition. I was connected to other human beings in such a spiritual way. My need to be cool disappeared and I allowed myself to be in that perfect moment as my authentic self. It was finally the day that I walked through the double glass doors of Hillsdale High School, and I was ready. I had been to five different schools before this day, and I knew how to adapt to the newness of almost anything. New clothes...check; new friends...check; new teachers...check; new locker number...check; new Jackie to fit into any situation...check.

As was par for the course, I was on my own, and Marilyn was nowhere to be seen. But, by the time I became a 9th grader, I had my resolve and knew just what my relationship with my sister was and was not and, even if I did not like it, it was what I had.

I had also identified my feelings of depression and found them, at most times, intolerable. I banked on high school being the panacea for my loneliness and isolation, and I went all out to make that my reality. I combed the landscape for all the important signs like who were the potential popular freshmen; who was on the football, basketball and baseball teams; who were the cheerleaders and pom-pom girls; where the good bathroom was; where to sit in the cafeteria, and, most importantly, who the established couples were to steer clear of any trouble.

The red flags were just as important such as the tough classes with strict teachers were, which kids were hoods, skags, and trouble makers; the behaviors that gave you a good reputation and the actions that would forever be a stain on your high school experience. My first rude awakening was that I had to take required college prep courses right out of the gate, so Math, Science, English, and Social Studies classes and the teachers were assigned. Tough class, tough noogies! Tough teacher, tougher noogies! There was no wiggling out for me.

On the bright side, that left Physical Education (which I thought would be no big deal) and two electives. Of course, one would have to be Study Hall so I could get some rest, and the other would have to be an Art class because out of all the learning experiences I really valued, that was my current deepest desire…to be a great artist.

I met my new best friend, Lizzie Fox, in the art class, and we became inseparable throughout the entire freshman year. Lizzie was a good artist, and she and I took that class very seriously. The teacher, Bill Snyder, was an extraordinary artist and very cool. Lizzie's sister Betty was a senior, very popular, the editor of the school newspaper, and also in the art class. I saw nothing but potential here.

Out of every fluffy cloud, a little rain must fall, and a monsoon hit me when I realized that PE *was* a big deal!

First, I had to take off my school clothes and change into a blue zip-up-the-front sleeveless onesie sack of a gym suit.

Second, I had to go outside and run around chasing a ball or run away from a ball until I broke a sweat, for God's sake.

Third, I sometimes had to put on a swimsuit that God only knows how many other girls had worn but certainly, enough that it hung limply to my knees and then had to swim in the pool with my suit floating all around my body as my hair got wet.

And fourth and worst of all, I had to go back into the locker room, take off any one of those costumes and walk naked into the gang shower, take a shower and walk naked past the PE teacher stating my last name, after which I was handed a towel the size of a facecloth to dry off with, re-dress and make it to my next class before the bell. NO!

My mission was to find a way to restructure my PE experience so that it would become more suitable to my liking. I discovered that when a girl had her period, she could get out of almost any activity and certainly the shower experience.

I developed the period that never ended so, at the start of class, during roll call when girls would say "here" or "R" (which meant regular; which meant you were on your period...go figure), I would yell, "R" as many weeks in the month as I could get away with. The teachers became very worried that I was bleeding to death!

Study Hall was my place of rest, and I did do my homework there, so I would be free to run around with Lizzie after school and not flunk out of my freshman year. Mom and Dad would have a cow if I did, and I did not want to spend any more time doing schoolwork at home than was necessary.

There were a lot of cute boys in the 6th period Study Hall, so I kept an eye out for a potential boyfriend that was cute but not too cute and popular but not too popular. I figured that I did not want the competition for the cute and popular boys, and the next level down would probably be nicer and not always looking for the next better girlfriend.

I did not know why I knew that, but it must have been my influence from the most important baby sitter I had ever had, television. Roddy Foster was a senior and always managed to sit across from me in the 6th period. I did not make the connection that he was doing it on purpose for months. Many times, when I would look up from my work, Roddy would be smiling at me but not in a creepy way, more in a matter of fact way. He had a great smile, good surfer hair, and wore madras shirts and jeans with blue Vans tennis shoes. Also, he drove a 57 Chevy. Roddy had a very bad complexion, and I thought that could be what made him a little shy and insecure.

One day in the 6th period, Roddy got up the nerve to say hello to me. I looked up from my books and smiled and said, "Hi Roddy, that only took you six months! Is it going to take you another six months to ask me out on a date?" I smiled.

He started laughing and said, "I didn't know you even knew my name!" He turned bright red, which did his ruddy complexion no favors. "Do you want to go to the YMCA dance with me on Saturday night? I know you do everything with Lizzie, so she is welcome to come with us too if you want her to, that is."

I thought that was so cool for him to include Lizzie, and I did want a little moral support on my first date, so I said, "Okay, that would be great. I want to go, and I will ask

Lizzie if she wants to go too."

I ran to Lizzie's house after school, and I told Lizzie about Roddy and the potential date. Lizzie said. "Is Roddy that cute guy with the zits all over his face? If I were you, I would not be caught dead with that pizza face. If you want to go to the dance, you can go with Craig and me."

I stared at Lizzie. I thought that was one of the cruelest things I had ever heard her say. Here, Lizzie was dating any boy, and every boy that asked her out and they were not all James Dean.

She never lasted more than three weeks with any of them, and they all seemed to line up patiently for their turn. They would all ask me how to get in good with Lizzie, and most of them ended up being my friends in the end after Lizzie dumped them. I decided not to take dating lessons from Lizzie.

"Never mind! I will go with him alone, like on a real date. I don't need a sidekick and certainly not one that calls him a pizza face behind his back. God knows what you will say to his face. He is a really nice guy, and I don't care if he has pimples."

We both shrugged our shoulders and went to the mall for a hot dog and a coke.

That Saturday night, Roddy came to the door to meet my parents, and we went to the YMCA dance. We stopped at McDonald's for cheeseburgers, French fries, and a coke. I thought *I could get used to this*.

At the dance, Roddy showed he was a really good dancer, and that hurdle was cleared handily. After the dance, Roddy took me to the Las Pulgas Water Temple, which was really not a temple but a beautiful cistern under a pagoda hidden up in the hills with spotlights all around. It was THE parking spot to make out in San Mateo County.

Roddy asked me for a kiss. I agreed, and Roddy leaned in and gave me the tenderest kiss I had ever felt. I held on to his chin, just like I had seen in the movies, and decided to breathe a little bit to see if that felt correct. It seemed okay and helped me to avoid passing out.

Roddy asked, "Did you like the way I kissed you?"

I said, "Yes, it was very gentle and sweet. Did you like the way I kissed you back?"

He said, "Yes, but I didn't like you holding on to my chin."

I felt embarrassed, and my face got red. "Well, I had to do something to hold your face from moving all over the place. I won't do that again!"

Roddy started laughing really loudly and said, "I really like you! You are cute, quick, and very funny! Let's go out again next weekend, okay?"

Roddy was my first real boyfriend, and we were inseparable from the first date on through the rest of the school year and all through the summer.

Mom and Dad loved everything about Roddy except for one thing...he was not Jewish. They did not give me a hard time about that because they knew Roddy was a senior and would be graduating and going on to college.

They were sure that the relationship would not be long-lived...at least to the point of being really serious, and they were confident that I was not in it for the long haul.

All that summer, we spent every day at Roddy's house while his mother was at work. We listened to Roy Orbison's records, ate bologna sandwiches on Wonder

Bread, and made out in Roddy's bed. Roddy had rules. If Roddy had everything off but his pants, I could be in my underpants. If Roddy was in his underpants, I had my pants on.

We were never naked but could touch each other anywhere. Roddy's biggest rule was that I could have orgasms, but he could never climax. We obeyed all the rules and had a great summer.

Freshman at Hillsdale High School

Chapter 19
The Straw That Broke the Camel's Back

The summer of 1964 was about to come to an end, and I actually felt sustained joy and happiness. This did not go unnoticed by my mom and dad, and nothing Marilyn could do knocked me out of equilibrium for months.

But all that was about to change. One evening, while scooping Bartlett pears and syrup into ramekins, Mom casually stated, "Your father and I bought a new house in Burlingame on the hill just below the Temple. You girls will be starting the fall semester at Mills High School with all your friends from Sunday school. Isn't that terrific?"

No sound could be heard. Not a creature was stirring. It was a cricket moment of monumental proportion. I made a sucking sound, and Mom glared at Dad. "Don't look at me! It was Jackie," he protested.

All the color drained out of Marilyn's face. Her eyes rolled back in her head, and she let out a bellowing sound that was indescribable, followed by, "I hate you both. I finally made some good friends at Hillsdale, and you are yanking us around again? What is wrong with you?"

On the night before our move up the food chain with the big fish in the fancy hills of Burlingame, California, Roddy and I went out on a date to commemorate the end of summer and to talk about what it would be like to not live within walking distance of each other anymore.

I felt guarded because I had grown to depend on Roddy and could count on him to always want to be with me. I thought about him when we were apart and got excited when he would call me on the phone or drop by unannounced. I cared about how he felt and what made him happy.

He was going to college, and I was going to another high school where I would, yet again, have to make new friends.

We went to McDonald's to pick up some cheeseburgers and drove to Coyote Point to park and watch the planes fly into the San Francisco Airport. I was nervous, and I could tell Roddy was too. We had never had a moment like this.

Roddy started. "I know you are going to a new school, and you will be making new friends, and I will be doing that in college. I know I should tell you that you are free to see anyone you want, and I should do that too. I don't want to break up just because you are moving 10 miles away. We can still talk to each other every day and go out on the weekends as we do now. So, I bought us tickets to see the Dave Clark Five in three months so that you know how serious I am."

He took a breath and stared into my eyes. This was my chance to let down my guard and tell Roddy how much I cared about him. I did want to keep going steady with him no matter what was in store for us after I moved. I mustered up the internal fortitude to be vulnerable and tell Roddy how I felt. I knew it was only fair to tell him because he took the risk with me.

In an instant, a wave of panic came over me, and I was strangling on the lump in my throat.

I don't deserve Roddy. If he knows who I am, he will not like me. He will find out and, when he does, he will dump me. Everyone I love finds faults in me or hits me, or ignores me, or says mean things to me or thinks my feelings are stupid or thinks I shouldn't have feelings at all unless they are always good. He will, too, so I better not go there! I don't know why everyone I love makes me feel so bad, but if this is how love feels, I don't need it.

I decided that it would fly in the face of the reason for me to soften to Roddy's confession of devotion to me.

"Okay! I love the Dave Clark Five. Thank you!" And with that, I jumped into the back seat and said, "Come on, let's make out before we have to go home." Roddy sprang over the seat of his 57 Chevy, and within 2 minutes, the windows were so steamed up you couldn't see in or out. I never told Roddy how I felt.

Getting used to the new house was the standard operating procedure for the Mendelson family. Mom set the kitchen up in the most logical way so that the silverware and dishes were near the dishwasher, as were the glasses. Besides being predictable, it gave a calm consistency to the chaos of constantly moving.

Marilyn was perpetually pissed and slammed around her room, putting things away. I could feel Marilyn's contempt for me, and that hurt more than her words or physical abuse. I was puzzled as to why I still loved her and wanted her approval. But I did love her and I admired her. I put my surfing posters and pictures of the Beach Boys on my walls. I hung the fishing net on my ceiling and placed my wicker chair at a perfect angle in the corner of my room. I opened my rattan screen with the multi-colored bubble gum in front of one of my twin beds against the wall. The other twin bed, intended for sleepovers with new friends, was piled high with stuff.

I looked down at the pile to assess what could be thrown in the trash. Mad Magazines and half filled-in Mad Libs books needed to be saved. Worthless confederate money needed to be saved just in case it ever became worth something. The "only once" used golf clubs went into the corner of my closet, marking a period of time when I had such negative feelings about the closet that I chose to throw my clothes on the floor rather than use it. Bubble gum trading cards could go… there, that's enough for now.

Whoa! My Dave Clark Five tickets! I will tack them up on my bulletin board so I don't lose them!

Chapter 20
That Loving Feeling

At Mills, I was quick to find the art class because I knew from experience that the art room would be my comfort zone. The first person that I met in my art class was Bob Riggs. He was the head yell leader for the varsity teams, and he was so cute that I got an instant crush and felt guilty that Roddy barely crossed my mind.

Bob and I felt safe around each other and became fast friends. I thought that I had hit the jackpot because he was a senior, and we had a lot in common even though I was a lowly sophomore. He had a car and would drive me to and from school on most days. Bob lived with his mother. His father had died when he was young. He was a bit of a mama's boy, and I could tell that he kept a lot of secrets from his mother.

As I went from room to room on my first days of school, I was delighted to find many of my Sunday school friends were in my classes. I sat down right next to Rip Miller in my English class. Rip Miller was a friend I had been going to Sunday school with since we were in the second grade. Laura Seigler and her boyfriend, Kevin Cornwall, were friends with Rip in that class as well. The four of us ended up spending most of our sophomore year in the same classes together, on breaks together and eating lunch together. After school, we went to my house to watch American Bandstand and Dark Shadows, ate grilled cheese sandwiches, and listened to records.

Laura and I would walk around the neighborhood, singing all the popular songs that were on the radio at the top of our voices in the middle of the street. We knew all the words, and we both had perfect pitch. Laura would always want to sing '*You've Lost That Loving Feeling*' by the Righteous Brothers.

I would take the high part, and Laura would take the low part, and we harmonized beautifully until Laura would start to sob as her sweetheart Kevin dumped her in the middle of the school year. I would then transition into my medley of "Don't Make Me Over," "Walk on By," and "Anyone Who Had a Heart," all by the schmaltzy Dionne Warwick.

Meanwhile, Roddy was working hard to prove to me that I was still the only girl on his mind and the only one he was still in love with. He would phone me almost every night after school, and we went to the YMCA dance on Friday nights, or to a movie, or for a walk around San Francisco on Saturday nights. He was always sweet enough to schlep all my new friends to the dances, and everyone liked him.

I liked him, but after a while, I found that I wanted to hang out with Bob and watch his band practice in his garage. I was also spending more time with Rip after school and began to look forward to those times more than date nights with Roddy. I had lost that loving feeling.

I felt very guilty, and I did not know how to tell Roddy that I thought we should stop seeing each other. Partly because I was unsure breaking up is what I wanted and because I did not want to hurt his feelings.

He was my first real kiss. He was the first boy that I gave my time to. But I stopped running to the phone at 8 o'clock, knowing it was Roddy. I let Marilyn answer the phone and manage the awkwardness for a few minutes before I came to the phone. I wondered what they were talking about for so long, and I was afraid Roddy was asking Marilyn what was wrong with me and why I was acting so distant. I felt under pressure to talk with Roddy because the Dave Clark Five concert was one week away, and I did not think it was fair to go with him knowing that I wanted to end the relationship.

I really didn't know what to do, and I really didn't know who to ask for advice because Marilyn hadn't dated much, and I just didn't talk to my parents about my feelings anymore.

After a while, I saw the Dave Clark Five concert tickets on my bulletin board and decided to stop taking Roddy's 8 o'clock calls for a couple of nights all together, to see what would happen.

Roddy called on both Monday and Tuesday night, and I chose to ignore him. I told Marilyn to tell him that I was doing my homework and that I would call him back later. But I did not. Marilyn was furious as I was continuously asking her to lie for me. Wednesday night at 7:30 p.m., Marilyn stormed into my room, screaming.

"I am not going to lie to Roddy for you anymore. He knows you're avoiding him, and you are hurting his feelings. You need to tell him what's going on. He wants to know what he did wrong so he can make it up to you. He was literally crying last night. Why are you so mean to him? Grow up and stop being such a little bitch!"

At 8 o'clock, the phone rang, and I did not pick up. It rang for two solid minutes before there was silence. Five minutes later, the phone rang again, and I did not pick up. My heart was pounding. No matter how hard I tried thinking, I could not come up with a good reason to break up with Roddy. I did not have the same feelings for him anymore, and that was the only reason. How could he be asked to understand something like that?

I was in the family room watching television, and Marilyn was in her room doing homework. I heard some strange noises in Marilyn's room, but I decided to ignore it because Marilyn had just screamed at me and I wasn't going in for more. The noises persisted, and I could feel cold air coming in through the window in Marilyn's room, which I attributed to Marilyn smoking in her bedroom and airing it out so our parents wouldn't know.

I went into my bedroom to get a blanket and looked up to find that the Dave Clark Five tickets were missing. I ran down the hall and threw open Marilyn's door to find her slamming her window shut.

"What did you do with the Dave Clark Five tickets?" I screamed. Marilyn just stared at me with the oddest look on her face. It was part terror and part anger with a big splash of self-satisfaction. I ran toward the window in the living room and threw back the curtains to see Roddy speeding away from the curb in his 57 Chevy.

I didn't say anything to Marilyn, turned off the TV, and went back into my room.

After a while, Marilyn walked into my room, holding her homework and a pencil. "I guess you don't care that you just crushed Roddy's heart and threw it to the street. You are such a little bitch. There was no way you were going to keep those tickets; you spoiled brat. I am so sick if you are getting everything that you want and not caring about anyone's feelings!"

She towered over me. I was going to tell her how awful I felt for hurting Roddy and that I just didn't what to do. Before I could get a word out, Marilyn slammed her notebook on the top of my head with all the force she had in her.

I literally saw stars and toppled to the ground. I rolled over and stood up to protect myself as Marilyn punched me hard in the stomach. I was bent over, trying to get air when I felt a sharp pain in my shoulder. I looked up to see that Marilyn had stabbed me with her pencil, and it was sticking out of my arm.

I looked down and saw the screwdriver I was using for an art project, picked it up, and stabbed Marilyn in the foot.

We were both bleeding.

This was by far the worst fight we had ever had, and both of us knew it. We knew we had gone too far.

"Come on, let's go into the bathroom quick and fix this before mom and dad get home," I said. "You are bleeding, and I am bleeding, and we have to make this go away. I don't know what just happened, but it can never happen again," I said.

Marilyn nodded, and we went into the bathroom and started wiping each other's wounds. We did this in dead silence. A dead silence that would become all too familiar to us.

Chapter 21
Adolescent Antics, Shenanigans, and Pain

I enjoyed high school. I understood it was my first community of choice. I could hang out with the kids that I liked and learned to like or tolerate the others. Even so, I could be running around the courtyard of the school during the break, talking to different groups of friends and laughing when a wave of melancholy would come over me, and I would feel sad and alone.

Then, I would shake it off by telling a joke or teasing someone I liked, and I would feel better. The more activities I immersed myself in, and the more time I spent with friends, the less time I felt buried in "the pit." I was able to adapt and shift to any situation to stay three steps ahead of my own dark shadow. I was the life of the party, and rarely did I ever have a falling out with anyone.

Rip was the only friend who was a challenge. He became my favorite person to spend time with because we seemed so much alike, but he liked to say no to me a lot, and that drove me crazy. I would go to his house after school to listen to music. I wanted to listen to the Beach Boys, and he insisted on Barbra Streisand. He handled his records like rare jewels, only touching the side of the discs with the palms of his hands. He would wipe each one before putting it on the turntable and would lower the needle down on the edge of the record with the precision of a surgeon. He never stacked his records on a spindle for the convenience of playing one album after another. No, that was brutal and lacked intent.

The drums would roll, the orchestra would start to play, and Barbra would belt out her first note. Rip planted himself in the middle of the room, imitating Barbra with his face and hands while singing every word to every one of her songs. Rip had no inhibitions when he was singing and acting out to his favorite singers, but he shyly stayed on the periphery of my friendship circles at school.

I went on dating sprees, but I would keep my feelings for the boys to myself. I discovered that when all my girlfriends shared their dating experiences and feelings about boys, the other girls would have opinions and start telling each other what to do or sharing rumors they may have heard about the guys. That was not for me, and besides, if they all knew how many dates I was going on, they would probably call me a slut or a liar. Either way, I was not doing anything wrong with my dates, and it was none of their business. Larry was a nice clean cut Jewish boy who had a motorcycle, and he would pick me up on Saturday mornings. We would ride up and down the Pacific Coast Highway from Half Moon Bay to Santa Cruz.

Larry gave me a turquoise blue hooded sweatshirt with the sleeves cut off above the elbows to match his yellow hoodie. We thought we were "all that and a bag of chips." I was singing on the back of the motorcycle with glee and stopped when bugs flew in my mouth and smashed on my front teeth. It was gross but worth the thrill of the ride.

Larry was getting close to thinking that he and I looked great together and were going steady. I had to consider if he was the boy that I wanted to be true to and not date anyone else. He was wonderful, but Larry wasn't that guy, so I tenderly said, "Larry, I love going out with you, but I am still going to be going out with other guys too. If that is alright with you, we can keep seeing each other, but I want you to know so you can decide."

Larry decided to move on, and I felt relief that I did not make the same mistake I had made with Roddy.

Derrick was a 6' 3" surfer dude from my rival school. He was really cute with a dark tan and longish blond hair. He wore bright white baggy pants that made him look like a milkman. My dad liked him, but I suspected it was more out of amusement to see the two of us walk down the street together, me being 5'1" and 97 pounds hand in hand with "the milkman."

Jeff was a not-so-nice Jewish boy from the "other" Temple. He would come over to see me after school because he knew that my parents worked and would not be home. We made out on the couch in the living room when no one was home. One day during our make-out session, I opened my eyes and saw that Jeff had taken off his jeans. I jumped up and ran to the other side of the coffee table.

Jeff jumped up and ran after me with this huge erection stretching the limits of his "tighty whitey" Jockey shorts. I ran back to the couch, picked up his pants and shoes, tucked them under his arm, and escorted him out the front door. I liked Jeff and his erection and was not angry at him. I just knew that I had to stop seeing him before something bad happened.

Neil was a boy that was in my Sunday school class that I had a mad crush on for years, and he had a crush on me too. We did not go to the same school, so we did not see each other that often. One day, Neil called to tell me that he just passed his driver's test and got his license.

"Neil, that is fantastic! You must be so excited. I am so proud of you!" I gushed.

"Des, and I am hoping you bite want to go out Briday night on a bate. Neil sneezed. "Ellow, can you hear me? My beers are plugged because of my cold. Achewwwww!"

I flashed on being out with Neil and him sneezing and coughing all over me. I could imagine his snotty nose and coated tongue, so I said, "I am so sorry, Neil. I am busy Friday night. But please call me back when you get rid of your cold, and we can go out for sure." Click. Neil never called me back.

The list went on and on with adorable young teenage boys courting me, taking me to school dances and proms, to concerts and movies, out to dinner and parking at the most popular make-out spots with the nicest views. A pattern was forming. If anyone liked me, I was open and present to them and felt happy and knew I was having fun. If I started to feel like they loved me, my walls went up, and I got high pitched penetrating danger signals, and I would shut down.

Rip was the exception. I loved Rip, and Rip loved me, but he never truly expressed how he exactly felt for me. I wanted to spend lots of my time with him, and so did he with me, but he never wanted to "take me out." He only wanted to "go out" with me. The big exception was when we went to the junior and senior proms. Rip went all out with a tuxedo, corsage, his father's borrowed Lincoln Continental, dinner at a fine restaurant, a flask of brandy, dancing around the prom, and the Tonga Room at the Fairmont Hotel in San Francisco after the dance.

Rip and I did everything together with a gang of kids that formed, all liking to do the same things. There was always some kind of mishap or adventure. By this time, I had discovered alcohol, and Rip and I got drunk almost every weekend. In the winter, the gang would go skiing at Lake Tahoe. Rip was great on the slopes, and I was adequate but fearless. I would ski right down the face of the ski run after Rip because I did not want to get left behind. It never occurred to me that those runs were for expert skiers. I would fly over the moguls with my knees in my chin, and when I would go way too fast, I would fall and start again. In the summer, camping was the activity of choice. Rip, Kevin, Jack, Smiley, and the gang on Hillside Circle and I would rotate between the Russian River, Big Sur, and Yosemite National Park. On a holiday weekend, we would go onto the river with homemade rafts. On top of the rafts were kegs of beer. Everyone had an inner tube tied to the rafts and a juice pitcher in hand. We would all drink and float until the kegs ran dry.

People on the banks would jump in with us on floats and in tubes and tie on to us. At the end of the "FLOAT," there was one pile of people in tubes on the river bank sleeping it off. One time in Yosemite, everyone was sitting around the campfire drinking rum and coke and cooking various food items on the campfire. I grabbed a pot and set a can of Franco American Spaghetti in it so it would not sit directly on the flame. All of a sudden, there was a huge explosion, and spaghetti flew into the air and landed all over Rip and our tent. I had forgotten to open the top of the can. Luckily, Rip was drunk and found the whole thing hysterical...until later that night. I did not clean the tent before we went to bed, as if the cleaning fairies would take care of it in the moonlight. Sometime around 3 AM, the tent started to shake violently. We woke up startled.

"Is it an earthquake?" I shouted.

Rip screamed, "No, something is out there! Look at the tent. Someone is touching the tent all over. What the hell?" Of course, our minds went to some serial killer until we heard snorting and puffing and scratching. We could see the impressions of great big paws on the tent and something going up and down the tent that could only be a tongue. We looked at each other and then back at the tent.

"Bear!" we screamed at the top of our lungs. The other kids sprang out of their tents and started banging on pots until the bear ran away. It was all my fault, and everyone knew it, but we also knew it was a mistake, one that could have killed us. I was no longer allowed to cook food on the campfire.

Although everyone in the gang loved having me around because anything they did was going to be much more fun with me there, I was starting to alienate myself a little from the group. I developed different interests. I was the only one in the group that painted and was going to art school after graduation. Kevin and I played guitar together and sang songs that were not being played on AM radio, so the gang was not too interested. Rip and I started going to rock concerts at the Avalon Ballroom and the Fillmore Auditorium instead of the Y dances. I did not sever ties with my friends; I just started to compartmentalize my life.

It was during that summer between my junior and senior year when I first smoked pot. A friend outside the circle asked me if I wanted to take the train to the City and go to the City Lights Book Store listen to Alan Ginsberg and Ferlinghetti read from their newest novels. So much was starting to bubble up in the City at that time that was extraordinary, and I wanted to be a part of it.

"Sure, let's go up there and get into some trouble," I said. We went to a beautiful Victorian San Francisco flat. The doors, jams and window sills were mahogany with crown molding throughout, and the hardwood floors were covered with Persian carpets. On the walls hung vintage Parisian posters and original oil paintings that looked like the work of the artists at the Art Institute. The lamps had

Tiffany shades, and a billow of patchouli incense was wafting through the air. I had just entered my first hippie pad.

A handsome guy came into the room with marijuana in a baggie and started rolling joints. This was his area of expertise because he rapidly rolled them with one rhythmic turn, lick, and twist, ...and they were perfect. He lit the joint, took a puff, and handed it to me. I politely declined. "No, thank you. I'll just watch."

"Oh, come on! I guarantee you are going to eventually smoke pot, so you might as well do it now with me. I am trustworthy and won't let anything bad happen to you." He meant what he said. After going back and forth for seemingly FOREVER, I finally acquiesced. I inhaled and held my breath. I did cough a bit, and it reminded me of taking a drag off my very first cigarette. I got a little dizzy, and that was all I felt for a while.

I did not remember how I got home, but I did know that I liked marijuana.

Rip and me at the Senior Prom

Chapter 22
A Blazing Candle at Both Ends

I escaped in my painting until all hours of the night and played my guitar and wrote songs by day. I enrolled in a Saturday course at the San Francisco Art Institute as a prerequisite for entering full time after I graduated. I entered the work program at school, which allowed me to work full time with modified school hours until the end of my senior year. I got employed at the San Francisco International Airport selling hot dogs in the International Terminal.

I made great tips because the hot dog stand was next to the bar, and the intoxicated would come in to eat something to soak up the liquor and stagger off without their change. Every Friday night, the troops that were coming home from Viet Nam landed there, and they made a beeline for a hot dog and a coke. I was the first friendly face they saw on American soil, so they gave me big tips, some of their medals, and more than a few marriage proposals. I saved my money and bought myself my first car, a very used

French Simca that was a little larger than a VW bug and, in my mind, the cutest car I had ever seen. I painted it fire engine red and, although it was just a puddle jumper, it was mine, and it got me to the City and back for classes and around town for fun.

I was burning the candle at both ends; keeping up with work, my activities, and my school schedule was taking a toll on me. And as for school, I was getting average grades in every class but physical education. I hated PE and PE teachers. I thought I was sliding by into home plate with a passing grade so I could graduate, but I was mistaken.

A student came into my English class and handed the teacher a note. "Jackie, please pick up your books and go to the principal's office." Everyone stared as I did the walk of shame. No one was ever called out to the principal's office to get praise or reward.

I sat down, and Miss Chapman cleared her throat. "Jackie, I hate to have to tell you this so late in the final semester, but you will not be graduating with your class. I have been informed by your PE teachers that you have failed swimming, and that means you will not have enough credits to graduate."

That was the worst news that a Jewish teenage girl living in the San Francisco Bay Area in 1967 could ever hear. Just imagining the looks of disappointment on my parent's faces made me nauseous. I ran to the gym to beg and plead for mercy.

"Miss Johnson, please! What can I do to change your mind? I will do anything you say. I have to graduate with my class. My parents will kill me!

"Jackie, I am sorry, but what did you expect? You have avoided PE for the last three years."

My heart fell into my stomach, and tears fell down my cheeks. I was speechless because I knew Miss Johnson was right. I was paralyzed in fear and hopelessness, and I could not move. I knew Miss Johnson was ready for me to leave, but I was stuck to the gym floor. I could not form a thought. I was exhausted in every way. My eyes were like faucets, and I did not flinch or utter one sound.

"If you swim every day after school until the last day of school, I will pass you so you can graduate. I do not want to hear any excuses if you miss a day. One missed day, and it is over! Do I make myself clear?"

So, every day I jumped into the pool and swam. I barely got out in time to dry my hair and get dressed and off to work. I did not tell my parents that this cloud was looming over me. My parents knew something was driving me, but they did not know what it was that was making me so obsessed. Marilyn and I were getting along better since she started college and made good "grown-up" friends, so I confided in her, and she sweetly told me to just do the very best I can and hope it is enough.

On Mother's Day, everyone filed into the family room to give Mom her gifts. Marilyn gave her a new bathrobe to go with the fifty other bathrobes that she had hanging in her closet. I handed my mom an oversized card but with no box to open.

My mom looked at me lovingly but puzzled as she opened the card and pulled out a folio with roundtrip airline tickets to Phoenix, Arizona, to see her brother Sammy. She was stunned!

"What is this? Honey, this is too much! This is your whole salary for months. That is so sweet, and I love you for the thought, but I can't accept this."

"They are not refundable! And you have not seen Uncle Sammy since Auntie Betty died. I want you to see him. This is tip money, Mom. I can afford it, or I would not have done it. Please go and have a wonderful time! Please!" I was adamant.

My mom was all packed and ready to go to the airport. Dad had her bags in the trunk, the car running, and Marilyn was already in the back seat waiting.

I was feeling extremely weak and every muscle in my body ached. "Mom, I don't feel very well. Do you mind if I pass on going to the airport? I think I better stay home." I was telling the truth, and she knew it.

She touched my forehead. "You do feel warm, honey. Go lay down. I love you and thank you for giving me such a thoughtful present." She gave me a big kiss and a hug and ran out of the door. The car pulled out of the garage, and I could barely hear the garage door close as I slid down the wall to the floor and passed out.

When Dad and Marilyn came into the house from the airport, my dad found me on the floor of the hall, burning up with fever. He took my temperature, and it was 104. He picked me up and laid me on my bed and tried to get me to tell him what had happened. I could only tell him that I could not move my right side, and I fell back away.

Dad turned white, carried me to the car, and rushed me to Mills Hospital, where they admitted me into the emergency room. The emergency staff prepped me for a spinal tap because of my extreme symptoms. They put me in the fetal position and rubbed betadine all over my back. The doctor was very careful not to let me see the size of the needle that he was about to stick into my spine.

The nurse came around to my line of vision in an attempt to keep me calm. They put a tongue depressor wrapped in gauze in my mouth so I would not bite my tongue if I felt pain. My head was face down in a pillow, and when the doctor stuck the needle in my spine, my shoulders started to shake uncontrollably. The nurse put her hands on my shoulders and said, "Hang in there Kiddo. It will be over before you know it. Don't cry."

I looked up, not crying. I was so delirious and in so much pain that all I could do was laugh like my funny bone had been hit by a lightning bolt.

The first week I spent in the hospital, my pain and paralysis moved from one side of my body to the other. I was wrapped in hot blankets because I could not stop shaking. I was non-communicative and just moaned. I was finally diagnosed with one of the worst cases of mononucleosis the doctors had ever seen. Marilyn and Rip spent all day at the hospital, and my sweet father spent every night until I finally broke my fever and started to come around.

Rip would sit at the end of my bed and tell me everything that was happening in school and who said to say hi. Marilyn was so sweet to me that I thought I should get deathly ill more often. Marilyn brought me milkshakes and told me any news about our mom and Uncle Sammy's visit from their daily calls.

"Doesn't Mom ever ask to speak to me?"

"I always tell her that you are at work or swimming after school. I think she actually thinks that you will be trying out for the college swim team at the San Francisco Art Institute!" Marilyn said, playing with me. We both laughed at the thought of hairy hippies swimming relay races. We decided it was a good thing that she had never gone to see the school. Dad was fit to be tied, and he was wrestling with whether to tell Mom while she was away with Sammy or wait to tell her until she came home. If he told her, she would end her visit and rush right home, and there was nothing she could do that he wasn't already doing. He decided to ask me what I wanted.

"I feel like I am getting better, and I don't want her to end her visit because it could be the last time she sees Uncle Sammy. Besides, you are taking perfect care of me, and, right now, you are all I need." He was relieved, and there was color in his face for the first time in a week.

After the second week in the hospital, I was no longer in pain, and I could move my arms and legs. The doctor wanted me to stay there another few days but only as a precaution. I remembered my commitment to Miss Johnson who had said, "No excuses."

I hadn't been swimming in two weeks! I still hadn't said a word to anyone about the stress I was under to graduate, although the doctor suspected something traumatic was happening in my life and had asked my dad about it since severe stress is a cause of mono. Dad replied that I was busy with my senior year and working full time and doing classes at the Art Institute on the weekends, but nothing out of the ordinary.

The doctor remarked that the activities he ticked off certainly sounded like a lot of pressure.

Dad stared blankly.

Mom asked for me when Dad Marilyn picked her up from the airport. Dad told Mom the whole story from start to finish and left nothing out. He told her it was my choice not to tell her while she was away, and he had to respect my wishes. Mom could see that he handled the whole ordeal brilliantly, and in some way, she knew that the bond that it must have created between him and me was very important at that time in my life and for him too.

As they were walking down the mustard-colored hall to me, he filled her in on the conversation he had with the doctor about the cause of the mono. Mom told him that she would get to the bottom of it. They walked into the room, and I saw my mom and just wanted to hug her for the rest of my life. After a few well-placed questions posed by her, I spilled the beans about everything. I took the blame for everything and knew I was wrong for sluffing off PE until it was too late. I told my mom that I tried to make it right, but I was too sick to go on. I was still willing to do anything to graduate but felt like it really was too late.

My mother marched into Mills High School the very next morning and asked to meet with Miss Chapman. They talked everything over, and Miss Chapman called Miss Johnson in to join the discussion. After sparring back and forth, she finally put her foot down.

"Miss Johnson, Jackie almost died trying to live up to her agreement with you. I will not allow that to happen again, and I believe she proved to you that she would do anything to graduate. Please allow her something she can do at home to finish up while she is re-cooperating."

I had to write a white paper on the history of women's participation in the Olympics, and if it were passable, I would be allowed to graduate with my class.

Staying home and recuperating was not easy for me. I missed my friends a lot and had missed so much work that I had to quit my job, and that made me very sad. Mononucleosis made me depressed. I was on strong antibiotics, making me quick to anger.

Marilyn came home from the College of San Mateo with a hippie friend named Al that I could hardly tolerate under the best of circumstances. He would walk into the family room and drape himself on the couch and change the TV channel no matter what I was watching, just to irritate me. His filthy, greasy, smelly hair was down to his waist, and it made stains on the throw pillows. His nails were long and dirty, and he talked really loudly with food in his mouth would spray all over the floor.

Al started teasing me about something, and I exploded, grabbed him by the hair and his leather fringe jacket, and physically threw him out of the house. Marilyn went to push me and give me what for, and I grabbed her and threw her out the door behind him, screaming at the top of my lungs. I went into my room, feeling totally unglued and unwilling to go on. I put a note on my door.

FINISHING MY HOMEWORK AND GOING TO BED. ALREADY ATE. SEE YOU AFTER ART CLASS TOMORROW. LOVE ME.

I got the bottle of Seconal that the doctor prescribed the day I got sick and put all the pills in my hand, threw them back in my mouth, and swallowed them. Done! I then laid down on my bed to die. It all just had to be over. I had not one more ounce of strength for fighting, for school, or for my future. There wasn't a closet dark enough or a touch gentle enough to pull me out of the depth of my despair.

Every Saturday morning, my alarm went off at 8:00 AM so that I could get to San Francisco in time for art school. That Saturday morning was no different. Some God awful song was blaring on the clock radio, causing Marilyn to slam into my room to make me get up.

She walked toward the pile on the bed when the covers flew off, and I slurred, "Alright, alright... I'm getting up." I was drugged out of my mind, to be sure, but I was alive. The pills were too few to do more than knock me out. I crawled out of bed, and, for my punishment for either failing to die or continuing to live, I made myself go to class. God help anyone else driving on the road that day because I was so loaded I could only see out of one eye.

I never told anyone about my attempted suicide.

Chapter 23
"Time Has Come Today...Young Hearts Must Go Their Way."

Rip, Kevin, and I had started taking LSD. We would go to Golden Gate Park on the weekends and "trip" and watch free concerts put on by the Grateful Dead, Quicksilver Messenger Service, and Big Brother and the Holding Company.

Then we would go to the Psychedelic Shop on Haight Street and look for new drug paraphernalia, float into Mnasidika to buy concert tickets, grab some fish and chips wrapped in newspaper, and head over to the Fillmore Auditorium or Avalon Ballroom to listen to more music!

Sometimes we would go to Aquatic Park near Fisherman's Wharf and listen to the conga drummers' pound out rhythmic beats while swaying hippie chicks danced, and we drank Red Mountain Wine out of a jug. At night, we would have a bonfire on the beach and smoke pot with the seemingly homeless hippies that were starting to flood into The City. The hippies would sleep under the Rowing Club on the sand, way at the back of the pylons so the cops wouldn't catch them. Several of the guys would hop the fence at Ghirardelli Chocolate Factory and bring back big boulders of chocolate discarded because they had too many wax chunks in them.

I was living many lives. I was Pat and Mel's little girl that sang in the Temple choir and sat with my family every night at 6:00 PM for a family dinner. I was a very independent, dependable, and hardworking girl. I slipped off to The City to smoke pot and take LSD with total strangers. I went to art class religiously. I was a compassionate friend and a loyal companion. I played guitar and wrote songs with lyrics that told it all.

One night when my mom got home from work, she saw me sitting in the living room playing and singing so, she asked if she could listen. I said sure and started over:

"Oh, how sad, that stained glass girl
She lived her life in a stained-glass world,
All she had she would gladly give
Until one day, she discovered how to live.

JACQUELINE MENDELSON

She left herself, knew not a friend
Built up her walls, lived to pretend,
Searched for no one's company
Walked life's lonely path aimlessly.

Once she laughed, once she cried
Now those hues she's thrown aside,
A new color shatters every day
She has learned to live her life that way.

Once a pure and loving heart
Is frozen now and torn apart,
Her aging road has gone one way
No turning back to find a better day.

Thinking back on loves she's lost
All her mistakes, her life it cost,
Knowing now that she's too late
Wondering if tomorrow's worth the wait."

Mom stared at me in disbelief. "Do you really feel that way, Honey?"

"No, mom, it's just a song," I sighed. I had a split-second decision to make as to whether to tell my mom that I did feel that way and that I even tried to kill myself and that I did not know what to do. But then I would need my mother to fix me, and I did not believe she could so, I kept quiet.

"Okay, Sweetie. Go wash your hands and help me set the table. Dinner is almost ready."

I put my guitar back in the case, gathered up all my songs, and went to my room. I sat on my bed, imagining my freedom, feeling both elation and fear for my life when I move out of the house to go to the Art Institute. I went into the bathroom and pretended to wash my hands and came out to set the table.

I could smell the tuna casserole, and it put a smile on my face. Food made by another was a safe and delectable combination for me. Every time my favorite meals were put on the table, I was overwhelmed with feelings of love and joy. The kind of love that I did not want to hide from or push away. Serving my favorite foods was not an accident, and I knew it! The Mendelsons ate, laughed, and talked joyfully throughout the whole meal.

"Tomorrow is a big deal, huh, Jackie?" Dad asked. "You have grad night, right?"

"Yeah, it should be okay. It's at the Millbrae Bowl, and I can't think of what we will be doing there until the morning, but, oh well, it'll be fun because all my friends will be there."

Grad Night at the bowling alley turned out to be an event to remember. Kevin, Rip, and I "dumped the lump" (that is what we called taking LSD because it was a drop of acid on a sugar cube), and it started to come on when we were bowling.

The pins at the end of the alley moved to the music blaring from the speakers, and the bowling balls connecting to the pins sounded like shattering window panes. The three of us found everything funny that night, and we noticed some fellow trippers that had taken acid as well because their pupils were as big as saucers, and their cheeks were aching from smiling.

I kept seeing a life-sized bunny rabbit walking around and tickling everybody. I was quite sure that I was hallucinating. I was sure it would go away when the drugs wore off.

The sun came up, and the party was over. A bunch of kids decided to go out for breakfast and drive to the beach to play in the waves and sleep. Everyone was lying on the sand, rehashing the night.

Louise weighed in. "I just loved it! I almost finished my pint of vodka and was feeling no pain. But I kept seeing this big rabbit and knew I was drinking too much, and I should slow down!"

Danny laughed, "You saw that rabbit too? I smoked a joint before I walked in the door and kept seeing a bunny rabbit, and I was sure there was no good reason for a rabbit to be at grad night, so I just tripped out on it and kept my mouth shut.

I smiled and laid down my head. I made it to grad night, I get to graduate with my class, I am going to look for an apartment because I am moving to The City, and there really was a bunny rabbit. I fell sound asleep.

The next day, my mom and I went with Lizzie and her mom to find an apartment near the Art Institute. We were both enrolled and passed all the pre-requisites, ready to start class in the fall. There was a big debate on whether we should be allowed to set up the house so soon before school starts, and we won, and the parents lost.

Lizzie did get a job in San Francisco and was going back and forth every day to work, while I was looking for a job and had several applications in. Our school was costing a fortune, so we had to earn some money to make ends meet. The parents would pay the rent and utilities, but Lizzie and I had to take care of the rest.

We found a fantastic two-bedroom apartment in a great neighborhood off California Street on Hyde, right on the cable car line that goes to the school. It was up the first flight of stairs at the front of the building with great sunlight from bay windows, spotless and freshly painted. The rent was to be $110 a month, so the parents would only have to pay $55 each.

Lizzie and I were dancing around in circles with glee at this great find when my mother turned to the landlord and said, "Do you have a vacant apartment that is not in the front of the building so close to the street? I am worried about their safety."

"I do, but it is two floors up, and it is only one bedroom. It is $100 a month."

The blood in my veins was starting to boil with every step I took towards the smaller apartment in the back of the building. We walked in, and I wanted to cry. It was a lot smaller, and there was no real sunlight except for the windowpane in the back door. The bedroom and living room had bay windows, but they overlooked an air gap separating the building next door.

I stomped my foot. "There is no way we are going to move into this tiny dark apartment when we can have that great two-bedroom apartment for only $5.00 a month more each. We both need a bedroom so we can study undisturbed and better light so we can paint. I will pay the extra $5.00 and, we are no safer back here than we are in the front.

Mom and Mrs. Fox signed the lease, and the landlord gave us the keys…to the tiny dark box up the stairs in the back.

"Okay, girls, let's take one last look at the apartment. You will have to toss a coin to see which one of you gets the bedroom and which one has to make a bedroom out of the living room. I felt something as close to hate as I had ever felt for my mom at that moment. We walked back up the three flights of stairs.

"Give me a coin, and let's get this over with!" Lizzie said.

My mother started to flip the coin, and I snatched it right out of her hand. "Not you! You have done enough!"

I flipped the coin in the air, and Lizzie called out 'heads' as it fell down to the hardwood floor. "Heads it is!" Lizzie yelped with glee and ran into the bedroom to start her imaginings. I stood in the living room, dumbfounded and furious. There was no door to my room. Anyone in the kitchen could look right at my bed.

I was moving away from my family home to my new found freedom with my mother's rotten decision wrapped around my neck. It occurred to me that my very "high drama" reaction was surely the separation rage necessary for me to get out on my own.

I was silent all the way home. I knew I would be gone soon enough, and I couldn't wait to leave home. I was just afraid I would not take good care of myself when I did move out. And I had good reason to be afraid. I had a lot of secrets. No one knew how much I was drinking. Or that I was smoking pot in San Francisco with guys that were going to be my teachers at the Art Institute.

I cut my face and my legs with a razor blade twice. I ate at Saint Anthony's bread line and smoked cigarette butts with some bums from the Tenderloin just to do it. Some guy asked me if I liked to ball, and I said yes but, I had no idea that it meant liking sex, and the guy tried to jump my bones. I flirted with the Mexican busboys at the mall food court, and they followed me home, and I had to wave scissors at them in a stabbing motion until they finally left my front porch.

I was lucky that I was still a virgin and had not been attacked because the boys at my high school were not at all like the men I was meeting in San Francisco. They thought I was a woman or experienced, and the boys I grew up with knew I was just like them…cracking out of a shell slowly and needing gentle gestures, not lunging and lurching. I knew I was entering exciting but dangerous times, and my instinct to be afraid of myself was not unfounded. It was the day to leave, and Rip and Kevin were going to help me get everything moved in and put away. Kevin was staying home to go to the College of San Mateo, so he would only be 17 miles away from me, and Rip was moving to Rohnert Park to go to Sonoma State, which was about 35 miles north of me.

The gang was breaking up, but everyone vowed to see each other as often as we could and to meet up and party when everyone came home for the holidays. Rip and I never acknowledged that we were not going to be in each other's lives every day.

I had gone to Cost Plus and bought Indian Madras bedspreads, which I made into curtains to close off my bay window for privacy. I also made huge over-stuffed floor pillows larger than a mattress to go on the floor in the exact dimensions of the bay window enclosure. I decided to make lemonade out of lemons and created the perfect little hippie pad of my own. The boys helped me hang pictures and mount my Harmon Kardon speakers, and we tried out my stereo blaring "Purple Haze" by Jimi Hendrix. Everything was balanced, and I was happy.

I said, "Let's go back to my parents' house to finish getting my clothes and some kitchen items my mom has boxed up for me. We can grab something to eat and make the final run." I thought about how weird it sounded to not say I was going home but that I was going to my parent's house.

Mom prepared lunch for us kids and packed a snack for later. When I was all packed up and ready to head off to my new life, my mom handed me an envelope. "I almost forgot! This letter came for you yesterday. It looks like it's from the US Post Office."

I opened it up, and it was a letter saying that I passed the postal exam, and I got a job offer to work at the post office. That was fantastic, a new apartment in The City, school in the fall, and a job at the post office. Then I looked at where the job was…APO/ FPO at Terminal Annex…. Half a mile from the Mendelson house at the San Francisco Airport.

I would have to come back within a mile of my ex-home to work every day. Perfect! Just perfect that I was always being showered with cosmic jokes.

My dad was at work, but I had an opportunity to say goodbye to him over our last dinner together, so all that was left was to say bye to my mom and Marilyn. I was still mad at Mom, but I was not about to leave on a bad note, so I threw my arms around her and gave her a long hug, and told her I loved her and not to worry about me. Then I gave Mare a side hug and told her to come up for a visit at any time.

As we pulled away from the house, I looked back to see my mother clutching the living room curtains and sobbing uncontrollably. Next to her was Marilyn, patting our mom on the shoulder and waving at me with a motion that looked more like a signal to keep going than a wave. 'Keep going…that's it…bye bye...and she's gone!'

ACT 2
Chapter 24
The Beginnings

Lizzie and I started setting up "Hyde Street" by going to Calla Foods on Hyde and California Street to shop for things I needed to make dinner, snacks, and munchies to have around when we got the cravings.

I waltzed up and down in my hippie bell-bottom jeans, my skin-tight yellow, purple and blue tie-dyed tee-shirt, and stacked-heeled black nun's shoes while pushing a cart with boxes of Kraft Macaroni and Cheese, Wonder Bread, cans of tuna, Best Foods mayonnaise, cans of Nally's Chili Con Carne, American cheese, peanut butter and jelly, potato chips, milk, Kellogg's Frosted Flakes, apple sauce, cans of creamed corn, and napkins. I stood back, looked into my cart, and said, "There, I think we got all the basic food groups!"

Then, upon rounding the last corner of the last aisle, I had an epiphany. "I can eat ice cream and cake, and it doesn't have to be anybody's birthday! I can even buy the cake I want to eat and the flavor of ice cream I like, and no one can say a word!"

Carrying all those groceries two blocks up the hill and then up three flights of stairs was an entirely different matter for me. Exhausted, I fell in the front doorway pondering my freedom to do my own thing and make my own choices but being responsible for what comes of that freedom can be exhausting.

The rest of the summer, Lizzie and I juggled work and play like there was no tomorrow. I took the same bus down to the airport APO/ FPO Post Office every day for work and made fast friends with the other hippies that worked there. Loren, Reuben, and Rita "cased" the loose mail with me, and they lived in a flat around the corner on Larkin Street.

Casing mail at a huge hub post office that was also the Military Post Office (APO is Army Post Office, and FPO is Fleet Post Office) during the Viet Nam war was no easy do! We had to memorize every zip code for every city and town in California and accurately throw the letters into the proper zip code slots at the speed of light to keep our jobs. I was quickly discovered as an asset, and I was moved to register packages coming in from the soldiers in Viet Nam. I learned the benefits of moving mail arriving from Viet Nam.

The soldiers would hide Thai sticks, which were huge marijuana cigarettes, in cassette tape cartridges. They were meant to be disguised as loving voice messages sent home to people in the States. When you shook them, the real ones would rattle, and the ones with drugs wouldn't. One day, I felt a package, and it seemed to contain pills. My tribe and I loved pills, so I looked around to see if anyone was watching me. When the coast was clear, I stuffed the package down the back of my pants to hide it from everyone's eyes. I decided to start small and see how it went.

I hadn't stolen anything since grammar school. I went into the lady's bathroom and hid in a stall. I tore open the package and in it were hippie beads and a love letter. I was relieved and freaked out at the same time.

I hid the evidence at the bottom of the feminine disposal can hanging on the wall because nobody would ever look into that can. I ran back to my work station. There would be no pills for me and no love letter for some poor girl who will never know that she was loved at that moment by that person in that way. I just hoped that he would try again.

After work, we would take the bus to Hyde Street, and I would make my signature dish for everyone; one piece of white bread topped with two slices of American cheese smothered in hot chili con carne. We would smoke numerous joints, listen to music, and pass out in various sitting and lying positions. In the middle of the night, Larkin Street would go home to sleep, and the next day, we would do it all over again. On the weekends, Lizzie and I would do laundry and other chores in the morning. We saw no reason to do dishes every time we used them, so they piled up in the kitchen.

When the pile got so bad that there was no longer a trace of counter space, we would run a hot bubble bath and wash them in the tub. After chores, we would go to Golden Gate Park, drop acid, and then go to the Fillmore Auditorium or the Avalon Ballroom. The concert we would choose to attend depended on our mood and our high. It was like choosing between the Beatles and the Rolling Stones, some people liked one group over the other, and some liked them both.

The Avalon was the Beatles. The venue promoted great bands and was easy to move around in, and they had Near Beer for the underage hippies. The Fillmore was like the Rolling Stones, grab an apple at the door, climb the stairs, and enter crowded chaos like the first mosh pit in history. My passion was listening to the bands from the front of the stage. Lizzie went to pursue her favorite hobby, which was being a groupie.

It was astounding to see the parade of drummers and lead singers from the most obscure to the most famous bands that crept through the Hyde Street halls, down the stairs, and out the front door. Even more astounding was how I ever got any sleep on Friday and Saturday nights. And if the banging and howling weren't enough, on most occasions, there was a wingman that I had to tolerate in my room until the couple stopped coupling.

Some of the guys were fun. They were also band members, and once they realized that I was not going to "give it up" just because they were there, we would make the best of our time together. The musicians would play my guitar, and we both would sing their hit tunes, or we would smoke pot and eat and laugh at the noises coming out of the other room. There were rock stars who became more than a one night stand. Lizzie and I would fly to Los Angeles on the $ 10-midnight flyer to hangout in Laurel Canyon to see the guys, and we also got to see what the LA scene was all about. One time, Lizzie's longer-term rock star love made the mistake of getting stoned and blurting out that he loved Lizzie in bed, but he had more fun with me all the rest of the time.

Sooner than we could realize, we were on the next plane back to San Francisco, and the summer fun ended. That was alright because school was starting at the San Francisco Art Institute, and it was time to settle down. I got my schedule of classes and room assignments, my bios on my art and humanities teachers, and the list of art supplies and books I had to purchase from the school store.

The Art Institute building was old and majestic with a tall bell tower and a view of the bay that could stop time. I went down to the classroom and was overwhelmed with the magnificent smell of oil paint and linseed oil. My love of art and painting was only matched with my olfactory bliss when around the medium. The canvases in the art rooms, in various states of creation, were enormous, and I soon discovered that I would be building my frames and stretching my canvases. The walls were 20 feet high, and the huge windows that let in the natural light were true signs that I was entering a new world. It was a make-or-break world that would only offer success to those with real talent and creativity. Fakers need not apply. On my first day of classes, I saw old friends from the classes I attended during high school and the teachers that I recognized. Lizzie and I ended up in different classes, and that was expected. I was into oils and sculpture, and Lizzie was into drawing and pastels.

As important in the curriculum to art instruction were the humanities. The Art Institute demanded that their students be well rounded, so I had classes on literature, art history, and philosophy. My philosophy class was taught by a very odd man who turned to have worked on "the bomb." I sat with a girl named Annie, who introduced me to some guys who lived down the street where people would hang after class. The first time we walked down to the house to relax and decompress, the guys had a book reading, and the author turned out to be Richard Brautigan reading from *Trout Fishing in America,* which was my favorite book and author at the time. Everyone shared wine and listened intently, giving him all the respect due to him. Now I knew what Lizzie must have been feeling for her rock stars. After the reading, the guys pulled out a huge barrel from the back porch and lined it with plastic. Annie and I just looked at each other quite puzzled.

Was this going to be some kind of performance art? They carried out at least two dozen huge pumpkins with various and sundry knives and summoned everyone to a pumpkin to start carving. The only requirement was that all the pumpkin innards were to be placed in the plastic-lined barrel. It was the end of October, so everyone got to it, laughing and admiring the faces people were carving and imagining where they would place their Jack-o-Lanterns for Halloween.

Annie carved her whole pumpkin with her camera dangling down around her neck. She never put her camera down and seemed adept at keeping it out of harm's way. I admired how serious Annie was about photography and saw that she would not do anything that would get in the way of her being successful at the Art Institute. We admired all the finished products and thought, "that is a wrap," when the joints and LSD came out. Annie passed, making some lame excuse that we were just about to leave and blah blah blah! Everyone else did partake in everything that was offered that night, but I only smoked some pot. Annie and I slinked to the periphery of the room to watch what was about to happen next. One of the guys took off all his clothes and slid into the huge barrel of pumpkin innards up to his neck.

He started rubbing the slimy orange goo all over his body and began giggling and moaning all at the same time. People in various stages of stonedom walked up to the barrel and started rubbing pumpkin on him, too. Then they started giggling and moaning, and some took off their clothes and started rubbing the goo onto themselves and each other.

Annie and I had to know what the weirdness was all about, so we both went to the barrel for a feel. We could see why there was such an attraction. It was quite sensual in a very odd sort of way, but it was not for us. Annie took a few pictures, and we left the building.

"They will be pulling pumpkin out of their orifices for weeks!" I laughed. We said goodbye and took off in opposite directions and didn't socialize with each other much aside from class after that. It wasn't until years later that I realized that I was sharing a bit of San Francisco Art Institute Esoterica with Annie Leibowitz.

It was not long before Lizzie and I realized that we were slacking on our responsibilities and seemed to be taking more LSD than art classes. I never seemed able to turn down drugs when offered and secretly knew it was having a dulling effect on my creativity. I would stand in front of the canvas at school and, for the first time, draw a blank. Nothing was coming out of me. I looked around at the art from my fellow students, and I had a visceral reaction.

Why are we all painting these baroque naked women in pinks and blues surrounded by grapes, floating in the middle of huge canvases? This is not my art. These are not my imaginings. I can't be an Art Institute clone, painting by number so I can learn color, form, and composition. My art comes out like fire and crushing pain from unexpressed longing, rag, and need...not pink Kewpie dolls.

I went to see a social worker at The Center for Special Problems on Van Ness Street. I was introduced to Mrs. May, and I was informed that she would be helping me.

Mrs. May looked like my Auntie Harriet, but I decided to give her a try and told Mrs. May that I found it very hard not to take LSD and smoke marijuana every day and that I felt it is interfering with my art school and work.

Mrs. May listened compassionately and stated that I was losing my ego to LSD. She said that if I did not stop, it would destroy my creativity and art completely. She gave me two manila paper pill packages: one of Librium and one of Chloral hydrate. She told me to take one each in the morning and at night and not to take pot or acid with them. They were to be taken in place of illicit drugs.

I took the pills that night, and they knocked me out for two days. I went to see Mrs. May religiously once a week for months, collecting the pills and stashing them for future use. I kept taking acid and drifted further away from my studies. I spent hours sitting in my closet listening to music with my headphones blasting while on acid. I always backed my antics by rationalizing that I was still young and had plenty of time to shape up.

Chapter 25
Of the End

I went on a leave of absence from the Post Office, stating that my Mononucleosis was still making me exhausted. After getting a note from my doctor attesting to that fact, I was allowed to go on sick leave for six months.

With zero income and money in my pocket, I decided to start selling LSD. I was getting it for free in full brown bags from people closest to the biggest manufacturers and dealers in the Bay Area. I was very discreet and only let a few people know what I was doing, but they knew the whole drug-seeking hippie population in San Francisco. I soon had plenty of money.

One day, I was walking down Polk Street, and there I saw a friend from the College of San Mateo wiping down the storefront windows of a clothing store. "Peter! What are you doing here?"

"I work here!" Peter replied.

He squealed and picked me up and twirled me in circles until we both were dizzy, "Rita Louise, I am so glad to see you! Do you live near here?"

All the gay guys called everyone Rita Louise or Mary at the time. Most of my male friends were gay, and my female friends were not, so we were called fag hags and fruit flies.

I told Peter all that was going on with me while we were standing in front of the store. He asked me if he could come and live with Lizzie and me. He had to leave The Haight because they were beating up gay guys over there. He thought he would feel safer in my neighborhood. He said he would pay rent and sleep on the floor if need be. He was sleeping on a couch in the store basement at the time, and it was extremely chilly down there. I gave Peter my address and told him to come visit me after work.

Running home to talk to Lizzie, I had a million thoughts running through my head. *I just love Peter. He likes guys, so he would be safe to live with. Where would he sleep? Lizzie would like that he wants to pay rent, and we are all from San Mateo County, so we have that in common. He is so cute...why do all the cute guys like each other? I wish I were not still a virgin. Lizzie won't want a guy around when she brings home her drummers. He is gay, and she won't care unless her drummer is...oh my!* I talked to

Lizzie, and she agreed to meet Peter.

Peter knocked on the door. I opened it. Peter walked in and kissed me on the lips and walked right up to Lizzie.

"Oh my God, it's you! You were on the swim team for Hillsdale, and I was on the swim team for Atherton, and our girls didn't stand a chance when you jumped in the pool! How in the hell are you?" It was love at first sight!

Lizzie allowed him to move in and agreed to let him even sleep in her bed unless she had company. They did their little happy dance, and I was pleased. I also felt a little jealous that Lizzie seemed to commander my friend as her own.

We all got along incredibly well and did everything together. Peter had his tribe back in The Haight on Cole Street, and we all merged into one big happy family. Peter sold clothes at the To Kingdom Come on Polk Street, and Pam from Cole Street (also from San Mateo) did all the tailoring at the store. Another surprise was that Bob Riggs, my high school crush that was in my art class and the yell leader of Mills High School, lived on Cole Street, so we were reunited at last. He was gay too. We all started going to the gay bars on Upper Grant Street to dance and drink. We had fake IDs made on Fillmore Street, and no one ever questioned them at gay bars. Let's face it; we were young, sexy, hip, and could attract a crowd.

One day when Lizzie was at school, Peter was at work, and I was selling LSD in Cala Foods, one of my regulars put his arms around me and said, "Let's go get it on." I started to squirm and pull away, and then I froze. *He is so cute, and I have known him for two months, and besides, I have to get this over with someday. I don't love him, but I don't hate him either.*

"Okay, we can go to my house. But, you need to know that I am a virgin." I confessed.

You would have thought that he had struck gold, won the lottery and fell into an ice cream sundae.

He slowly laid me down on the giant bed pillows in the bay window and pulled the curtains shut. Incense was burning, and he had put an Otis Redding album on the record player. He was romancing me, and it made me feel calm and cared for. He slowly pulled my tee-shirt over my head and laid it at my side. Next, off came my bell bottoms.

He giggled that I was still wearing a bra because those had pretty much gone by the wayside. When he took my bra off, we both gasped. He, because I was beautiful. Me, because I was naked in front of a man in this way for the first time in my life. And he was naked in front of me, which was also a first for me.

He knew it was time to slow down, so he began to kiss me, and from behind the curtain, he grabbed a bottle of Kama Sutra oil and began to massage my shoulders and breasts and stomach until I closed my eyes and began to relax. He slowly pulled off my panties and gently lay on top of me, sliding his body around on the oil slick covering me, and it felt so good to me.

I started to push my body into his and move underneath him as well. He reached down and positioned himself to enter me, and I felt pressure and then pain. Soon it seemed easier for him to move inside of me, so I knew that he had breached me and that I was no longer a virgin. A few more strokes and he was done. He kissed me gently on the lips and asked how it was for me.

How was it? It what? It hurt, and then it was over. Where were the fireworks, and wasn't I supposed to have my happy ending here? What the hell! There is a spot of blood on my homemade pillow here. Good thing I can get that out. It is on the red part of the paisley. He is cute, and I did like the first part a lot!

"For my first time, it was wonderful," I lied.

He beamed like a preening peacock and said, "I am so glad. I wanted your first time to be special. Well, gotta run. I have some selling to do before the concert. See you tonight?" He threw on his clothes and ran out the door.

I stared at the ceiling for a long time. At first, I could not land on any thoughts at all; my mind was just blank. Then they started to flow. *Finally, I had sex. I am so glad about my first time. It did hurt, but not as much as I thought it would. He was very cute, clean, and smelled good too. I wish it could have been with someone I loved. I wish it could have been with Rip, but he is a virgin too, and that probably would have been a fumbling mess.* I fell asleep in the wet spot.

The next day I went to visit To Kingdom Come to see Peter while he was working. It was cool to do that because the owner was Peggy. She was a wild woman who made a boatload of money selling clothing in The Haight and on Polk Street to Jimi Hendrix and Jim Morrison and all the local bands like The Grateful Dead. Peggy was best friends with Janis Joplin and had a house in Stinson Beach, two stunning Doberman Pinchers, and a Shelby Cobra. She was probably the most famous lesbian businesswoman in San Francisco at the time, and Peggy knew everyone from the real crazies like The Beast to Bill Graham and could talk to anyone about anything and sound like she was an expert.

There was a big antique chair at the side of the wooden counter where I would perch for hours just watching everything that was going on. Peggy would fly in and out of the back room where her office was, waving her arms and laughing and pointing orders to her staff. She was gorgeous with long straight brown hair, ample breasts, a tiny waist, and aviator sunglasses.

She wore low cut mini dresses with flowing skirts and tiny little slip on come-fuck-me heals. Her lover, Kimmie, was equally gorgeous in an androgynous way with a smile that could light up the world. They were the "IT COUPLE" of the San Francisco Hippie Elite. I wondered what it would be like to be them.

When I got home that afternoon and walked in the door, Lizzie ran out of her room and closed the door behind her with this sly scared, excited look on her face.

"Ralph and John are in my room doing something, and I am going to do it too," Lizzie said.

"What are you doing that is making you look like a big weirdo?"

"We are going to shoot heroin. They do it all the time, but I am just going to try it. Do you want some?" Lizzie was coaxing me so that she would not be so scared, and I knew it. It was something like misery loves company, but I wasn't buying it.

"No! I will never put a needle in my arm. I hate needles, and I do not need to try heroin, so go on and do it in your room because I ain't in it!" I protested.

Ralph, who was one of my favorite lead guitarists, came out a while later and tried to talk me into joining them. I lovingly declined, but he persisted for more than two hours.

We would banter back and forth, but I kept saying no until I didn't. I did not know why I agreed when I did. Maybe Ralph wore me down, but I said yes, and they all crowded around me, and this is what I saw. Ralph took a spoon from the kitchen drawer and laid it on the table. He pulled a little folded packet of paper out of his pocket and carefully opened it up. Inside was a white powder with tiny little brown specks in it. He took the corner of a matchbook and scooped some of the powder up and put it in the spoon.

John walked in with a glass of water and a cotton ball from the bathroom. Ralph pulled out an eye dropper with the nipple from a baby pacifier on top of it. He tore a thin strip of paper off the side of a dollar bill and wrapped it around the end of the dropper, and then wedged a hypodermic needle over it until it was secured.

He drew up some of the water from the glass and squirted it over the powder until it dissolved. Ralph took three matches from the matchbook, lit them, and held fire under the spoon until the liquid bubbled. He rolled up a tiny ball of cotton and placed it in the middle of the spoon. Then, he put the needle in the cotton bit and drew the heroin up into the dropper and looked into my eyes. "Are you ready?" I nodded, yes. John took my left arm and tied a scarf around it right above the elbow. Ralph started tapping on the large vein that came up and then slipped the needle into my vein. A small bubble of blood came up into the dropper, which was the signal for John to untie the scarf. Ralph squeezed the heroin into my vein, pulled out the needle, and wiped my arm with a piece of cotton.

What happened then was like nothing I had ever experienced before in my young life. I felt warm all over and noticed a strange but nice taste at the back of my mouth...kind of like cumin. I got the sensation of falling down and backward quickly but into a bottomless billow of clouds. It was as if the love of the entire universe wrapped around me like a warm blanket on a cold night, and nothing was wrong. Nothing disturbed me or stole my peace.

This must be what love feels like, I thought.

In the next instant, I knew I was in big trouble. I ran to the bathroom just in time to manage my projectile vomit as it arced into the toilet bowl. I had never experienced that before in such a way. It was not the least bit uncomfortable, like losing my cookies when I drank too much. No retching or gagging...no groaning or moaning and holding my head in my hands. Just up and out and over! After three episodes of that little bit of business, I walked back into the other room.

Ralph was laughing at me and finally got out the words, "Oops, sorry Kiddo. I forgot to tell you about that part. It happens to everyone the first time or so. You will get used to it, Jackie. Grab some paper bags just in case it happens while we are out."

My eyes were half-mast, and my face felt like all my muscles went to sleep. I could hardly hold my head up, and I was asleep and awake all at the same time. I could hear everyone, but it was like I was in a tunnel. I could talk, but my voice sounded like it went two octaves lower and like I had gravel in my throat. My nose was itching, but it wasn't, and it took my hand forever to get up to my face, just randomly rub it.

I did not know how long I was sitting on the floor in my bedroom...it could have been an hour, or it could have been a week. My head was like a bobble doll, up and down and all around. The faint voices in the background got more distinct.

"Come on, Jackie, get up! We are going to a party at Blue Cheers. Jerre just got out of jail, and we are going to give him a welcome home he will never forget!" Ralph picked me up by the armpits and walked me out the door. I mumbled, "Who is Jerre?"

We all climbed into John's van and took off for Noe Valley. Lizzie combed her hair and put on makeup the whole way there. Ralph held my hair while I threw up in my last paper bag. It was party time.

We walked into the house, and it looked like a hippie Who's Who. I saw Peggy and Kimmie, the doctor from the free clinic, famous SF attorneys, Haight Street store owners, and every local San Francisco band. The guys from the Grateful Dead, Mint Tattoo, Quicksilver Messenger Service, and Big Brother and the Holding Company were all talking, laughing, passing joints, and spilling beer. I looked around with one eye opened and thought I was in a Fellini dream sequence.

"Here is the man of the hour!" Ralph walked up to a cute little guy with a jailhouse haircut and said, "Jackie, this is Jerre Peterson. Don't mind his hair...this dude is out of sight! Come on in the backroom, man...I got something for you." Jerre looked at me and winked, "Don't go away, Sweet Thing. I'll be right back for you." I found a corner in the living room and nodded off.

Chapter 26
I Can Stop Anytime I Want

Jerre started coming over to Hyde Street every day in the afternoon to see me. Lizzie and Peter started to get their noses out of joint because I was spending a lot of time with Jerre, and they wanted my time. That was a familiar theme for me, and I didn't know what to make of it. My friends always wanted me around like I was a mascot. But in truth, I have always been the one to kept equilibrium in my friendships, whether it is by showing compassion or telling a well-placed joke to lighten up any tension.

Jerre would rap his signature knock on the door. Upon opening it, Jerre would glide in smiling, kiss me, grab my hand, and pull me into the kitchen. On the countertop farthest from the sink was Jerre's little shrine to heroin. On top of a Jimi Hendrix album sat a glass of water, a silver spoon, and matches. Sometimes there was a bit of cotton, and other times Jerre would use parts of his cigarette filter to strain the drugs through the needle. His favorite silk scarf was wrapped around the doorknob.

Preparing his fix was a sight to behold. He had the concentration of a surgeon slicing his portion of drugs from the paper packet and putting it into the spoon. His breathing would change. He would only breathe through his nose, and it sounded rhythmic and controlled, starting very slow and picking up the pace as he got closer to the finish of his prep.

He rolled up his sleeve and put the syringe in his mouth. Then he spun his arm around quickly in a clockwise motion to bring blood down into his arm. He quickly wrapped the scarf around his upper arm to trap the blood below the tie. His veins bulged so he could put the needle in.

After hitting up the "smack," he smiled and looked up to nothing because his eyes were closed. He sighed and breathed from his mouth. He let himself enjoy the rush for as long as it lasted as though it were a climax.

Jerre, like many men, could not get an erection when they were loaded on smack. I was so new to lovemaking that I was happy about that because it gave me a chance to be with Jerre and enjoy him in almost every way to learn who he was and to like him. And to eventually love him. Or was it his heroin? Because after his ritual, he would give me just a small portion of what he was using, and it would keep me loaded for hours.

The next part of the routine was when Jerre would say, "Come on, Baby. Let's go out and eat."

He had his predictable places like Miz Brown's Coffee Shop on Polk and Pine for a chicken dinner. Or we went to the Grubstake on Pine for a killer cheeseburger. If he ever wanted to travel outside of the neighborhood, we took a cable car to Tad's Steak House on Powell for their special $ 1.75 steak, salad, and a baked potato dinner that was excellent. But no matter where we went, Jerre always said, "I got it, Baby! My Old Lady never pays when she is with me."

I knew that he was strung out on heroin, but I didn't care. I liked Jerre, and he made it very clear that he liked me. He was a little scary, but funny at the same time, with his jailhouse hair cut growing out. He was getting cuter every day. Strangely, I felt safe with him in a very unsafe lifestyle we were creating together.

Every once in a while, I would get a wave of fear that would rock my soul. I knew I was doing something wrong.

When I would ask Jerre to stop for a while to make sure we were not addicted, he would smile and say, "I can stop anytime I want. No problem. Stop worrying and go with the flow, Baby."

Jerre smoked like a chimney, and when he would nod out on drugs, he would drop his cigarette on his shirt or his lap, on the mattress or the floor. He had burn holes all over his clothes and my blankets...because Jerre moved into Hyde Street. By the time he moved in, he had grown on Lizzie and Peter. They found him to be quite a character as long as he did not set the house on fire. And that was not far-fetched since Jerre had managed to get loaded, jump in the shower, and proceed to burn a hole in the shower curtain with his cigarette.

"Okay, seriously, Jerre! You are the only junkie I know that can keep a cigarette lit in a pounding shower and manage to burn holes in the plastic curtain," Peter squealed.

Jerre laughed, but I could tell that Peter had hurt his feeling by calling him a junkie. That was a really nasty label to pin on a hippie, let alone Jerre Peterson, one of the founders of Blue Cheer...the heaviest metal rock band to come out of San Francisco at the time. Jerre was silent for the rest of the night, and this was really unlike him.

Peter looked at Jerre for a long time and then went up to him. "I'm sorry, man, for calling you a junkie. That was harsh and rude, but I said it because I am worried about you. You are using a lot of smack lately, and it seems like it is wearing you down. Jackie is coming up right behind you, and she is way too young to be doing that shit. You need to get it together before you wind up in jail again or dead. If you stop, we will all help you kick."

Jerre and I talked about it that night, and we both decided to stop. It would be very hard for Jerre, but I was not addicted, so I only had to give up the ritual that was just as addicting as the drugs. Jerre shot everything he had that night. Normally he would save a "wake up" for the morning, but by 1:00 AM, it was all gone, and Hyde Street was preparing for a long week ahead.

He and I slept through the night soundly.

Halfway into the first day, Jerre got a look in his eyes, and everyone started to position themselves between him and the front door. He snickered because he knew what we were doing. He did not say a word and just tried to hang on.

His legs started to cramp, and he was sweating profusely. His nose was running, and his eyes were red and watering. He started to shake, and his smile was gone and replaced with gritting teeth and a sneer. He curled up in a fetal position and buried his head in a pillow as he started to moan. Everyone looked at each other as if to say, "We are out of our league here. What do three 19-year-olds know about helping someone go through cold turkey?"

I put a burn-holey blanket over him, lay down behind him, and wrapped him in my arms tightly to keep him warm and help him from shaking. Every nerve in his body was firing at different intervals. Lizzie and Peter took turns watching the door and preparing small meals to keep him somewhat nourished and hydrated for three days. He never tried to convince us to let him leave. He was trying to stop because he did not want to risk losing what he had with me.

After three long days and sleepless nights, things seemed to turn around. Jerre's eyes looked clearer, and his face was more relaxed. I suggested that he take a nice warm shower to rinse off the stench of stale drugs and sweat escaping out of every pour. He apologized to everyone, but he could not take a shower yet. He said, "When I kick, if water touches my body, it makes my skin crawl, but I am almost ready. Please bear with me." We all agreed and lit more incense.

Peter had a great idea. "Let's borrow the Cole Street car and drive up to Mount Tamalpais and drop acid. It will be just the thing to kick the last bit of heroin right out of your system, and we haven't done acid in days. Come on, Jerre…are you up for it?" He nodded and said yes.

We drove over the Golden Gate Bridge and out the highway towards Stinson Beach. We found a secluded field with views of the Pacific Ocean and beautiful trees. We each put a small square of windowpane LSD on our index figures, held them in the air as if we were making a toast, and let the acid dissolve on the tips of our tongues.

Within 20 minutes, we were hallucinating and running through the fields, each in our trippy world. I was talking to Peter and Lizzie when I heard laughter. We turned to see Jerre in an open field walking towards a giant ram with horns the size of a park bench.

I froze in a panic, "He has to be stoned out of his mind. Nobody move! If we make any noise, he may mow Jerre down and stomp him to death. What should we do?'

Just then, Jerre walked right up to the ram and grabbed his horns and started to wrestle with the ram. At first, the ram tried to buck backward and rise on his hind legs, but Jerre held on tight and rocked his horns back and forth and side to side. The ram started moving with the motion, and the two of them continued trading power plays for a long time. Finally, Jerre let go of the ram's horns, and they faced each other, staring. The ram slowly turned around and walked off into the field.

Jerre started hooting and howling and jumping up in the air waving his arms.

"Did you see that? Did you see that ram and me being one with the universe? That was totally outta sight! It was like I was struggling to hold my power, but I didn't want to hurt him or overpower him. We were the same, and he was telling me, okay, man, but if I wanted to, I could knock you right into the ocean." Jerre was exhilarated, and I thought he was so adorable, and the LSD did finish off his withdrawal with a memory he will never forget.

Peter screamed, "You are out of your mind. As a matter of fact, so am I. Let's go home."

That night everyone got a good night's sleep for the first time in days. Sometime in the night, Jerre rolled over and started making love to me. This was the first time we had been intimate because Jerre was always too loaded to perform. I was surprised at how tender he was and how he satisfied me before he climaxed. I only hoped that everything we had just been through would put the hard drugs behind us, and we could have something together.

That morning, when we woke up, Jerre turned to me and smiled. I smiled back.

"Hey, did you and I do something together last night? I don't know if we did or if I had a really intense dream." Jerre waited for me to answer.

I stared at him. I gave him an awkward smile and said, "Do you want some coffee?"

Jerre Peterson...my first man

Blue Cheer...in the beginning.

Chapter 27
Hyde and Seek

I missed the ritual of shooting dope, but honestly, I missed the high even more. My life without heroin was nothing but problems chasing around in my brain. What if my parents find out about my missing classes at the San Francisco Art Institute? How was I going to get money to pay the rent when they do find out and cut me off? What if they make me move home after being in the real world for over a year?

Where does Jerre go every day that when he comes home, his pupils are no bigger than pinpoints and he is breathing out of his nose, and he's nodding out again? Why isn't he sharing it with me? Why do I feel like I am sitting on Peter and Lizzie's last nerves? How can I feel so disconnected with so many people in and out of my world every day?

"Jerre, I know you are getting loaded again, and I am bummed out that you are keeping it from me!"

Jerre stared at little innocent me as if I were smarter than I looked. "Oh Baby, I know, and I'm sorry, but I didn't want you to think that just because I couldn't stay clean, I was a loser. I promise I'll stop again, and when I do, I'll fuck your brains loose. I promise, Baby."

I thought about that image and shuttered. "I didn't mean bummed out that you are keeping a secret. I mean, bummed out that you are keeping the drugs from me! If you are going to do it, I am too."

Jerre's jaw dropped. "We need to get some money flowing in because once we go at this together, the hill will get steeper and steeper to climb. Hey, that would make a good song, huh, Baby?" When Jerre would laugh and joke, it made me melt.

Hyde Street became heroin central. All drug seeking and money seeking plans were strategized at the kitchen table. Peter and Lizzie both worked all day and played all night, so it was a private place to do business.

We both began copping smack for anyone we knew that was strung out. Jerre would go to the dealers in cabs, and I would measure the drugs and get the product out to the buyers. After a while, Jerre started taking me to the dealers so they would know who I was and would trust me just in case I had to go cop the drugs for him. And he started sending me out to cop alone almost every day. I went into the darkest and scariest parts of the Fillmore District, and I didn't even know enough to be scared. It was as if I was untouchable.

I would go to the Booker T Washington Hotel, a notorious and treacherous shooting gallery inhabited by ex-cons and felons on the lam. I was a little white girl walking down Steiner Street at 3 AM to cop from a dealer on the watch list of every narc in the San Francisco Police Department (also known as "the heat"). The only adrenalin that could break through the drugs was the rush of making it through a risky situation without getting caught or killed.

I actually began feeling proud of my successful heat evading missions. I had to keep up certain routines so that Lizzie and Peter did not get suspicious about the activity at Hyde Street. I still went down to the clothing store on Polk Street to hang with Peter for a bit of each day. I would assume my position in the chair by the counter and try not to nod out in public.

And, true to the nature of routine, Peggy would fly into the store at about 3:00 PM, laughing and shouting orders to the staff while heading for the back room. This time, she looked right into my eyes.

"Hey Dahlin', it looks like you have something I want. Come on in the back with me right quick." Peggy grabbed my hand and led me into the back room. I could hear Louisiana in her sweet singsongy voice and was mesmerized and scared all at the same time. I was going into the inner sanctum. What did Peggy want?

Peter snickered as he watched me disappear into the back room as the door slowly shut.

The back room looked like a luxurious living room. Peggy's huge oak antique lawyer's desk was in the far corner of the room, and on it was an antique library lamp with a Tiffany shade. Along the wall was a long crimson mohair camelback sofa with wooden inlaid swirls on the ends of each arm and legs to match. There were large oak armchairs with mohair cushions around a 10'x 20' antique Persian rug and torchiere floor lamps place strategically for ambient lighting. The walls were covered with Maxfield Parrish prints and beveled mirrors.

Behind one door was a bathroom and shower that Peggy had built for when she stayed overnight because she was too loaded to drive to Stinson Beach. Above the bathroom was a loft with just enough room for a big bed on the floor and a small Tiffany lamp.

"Sit down, Dahlin' and tell me, are you loaded on smack?" Peggy smiled.

"I wouldn't say loaded. But... why yes, I am."

From that moment on, I added Peggy to my rounds, but I had to agree to inject the drugs into Peggy's vein because she did not know how to get herself off, and she refused to learn. I agreed and headed for the door. "I'll be back later with your order." What I didn't say was that I had no idea how to shoot drugs into Peggy's arm because I had never done it myself. Jerre had always done that for me.

I knew I had taken another step into the dark alley of addiction when I learned how to shoot drugs into my arm on the very first try. Jerre thought I was a star, but I felt disgusted until the rush of the drug came over me, and I felt rapture again. I drifted through the realization that this was as close to my being a doctor as I was going to get and then off to The Land of No Thought. I went back to the store to deliver the smack and get Peggy high. That night, the back room took on a very different feel, as if someone covered the room in a translucent layer of grey silk.

I shot Peggy up so expertly that no one would have ever known that it was the first time I had ever done that to another person before. In a most bizarre realization, I had discovered how instantly important I became to Peggy. I went from feeling like an interloper in the chair by the counter to Peggy's favorite new best friend.

I always thought that I was liked for myself because that was all I had. Now I felt appreciated for who I am and what I could do, and surprisingly, I did not hate it. It was like being in my closet, the perfect hiding place for my soul. As long as I had the drugs, I was accepted, and my true self could be hidden from sight.

When I got back home and started to climb the stairs, I heard yelling and crying coming from the apartment. As I cornered the landing and headed down the hall, I saw police in the doorway and Lizzie and Peter screaming Jerre's name. My heart flew up into my throat, and I feared he was on the floor dead from an overdose. I pushed past them and flew into the apartment to see that it had been ransacked. There were clothes all over the floors, drawers turned over, and my Harmen Kardon stereo was missing. My speakers were gone, and some of Lizzie's jewelry could also not be found. Peter did not have anything to lose, so he was at peace with the whole situation.

The burglar ate our food in the refrigerator and brought his bottle of wine, which he finished and jammed up onto the kitchen faucet. The apartment was an utter mess, and I could see that the point-of-entry was through a broken pane of glass on the back door window.

I became enraged at my mother! "God damn it! We had to get the one-bedroom at the back of the building because we would be safe. Well, just how safe are we now, Mom? Wrong again, Mom! God damn it." I flailed around the living room/ bedroom combo throwing my clothes in the air.

Lizzie, Peter, and the police officers just glared at me like I was a stark raving lunatic. Lizzie told me that her parents were coming up to get her and that she was moving out. Lizzie also informed me that her father called my parents and that they were on their way up to the City to get me as well. The Cole Street gang was coming to get Peter, and he was going to live there with them. Pam said to tell me that I could move there too if I wanted but that Lizzie couldn't because they didn't like her very much.

Jerre was nowhere to be found, so Lizzie and Peter decided that he was the one that stole all our things and said so to the police. I knew it was not Jerre, no matter what anyone said. Why would he break in the back door when he had a key, for God's sake?!

I got a phone call from Jerre's brother Dickie that he was arrested that morning for possession of illegal narcotics and was in the county jail on Bryant Street. As I was hanging up, in walked both sets of parents.

Mom threw her arms around me. "Oh honey, I am so glad you and Lizzie were not home when this happened. We love you so much, darling, and we don't know what we would do if anything ever happened to you, right, Daddy?" He nodded.

By the end of that weekend, everything was moved out of Hyde Street. The families were broom cleaning to make sure they got our deposit back, and there was a final stack of boxes and some plants downstairs on the curb to be placed in our Ford Falcon station wagon. I asked my mom to sit on the boxes and hold my plant while dad and I got the car, and I gave the landlord the keys. Mom smiled and put one beautiful tall plant on her lap.

Lizzie and her parents walked out to the curb. I told Lizzie goodbye by giving her a big hug and thought to myself that I would probably never be seeing her again. As we walked to the corner and looked back at the building for the last time, Lizzie looked at me and smiled.

"Does your mother know that she is sitting there holding a huge marijuana plant?"

"Of course not, silly!" I winked.

We packed up the car and drove off. I sat in the backseat, heartsick. I did not even get a chance to talk to Jerre, let alone say my goodbyes to him. What would he think when he gets out and can't find me? What will my customers think when they can't reach me? How can I go back home and live with my parents and Marilyn again? Then I thought, 'I guess it's a good thing I learned how to use a needle.'

Chapter 28
Behind the Hippie Curtain

I suffered living at home and having to account for my every move. I was back in my parents' house, and if I was going to use drugs right under their noses, I had to make sure they had no reason to scrutinize me.

One night, I asked to borrow my mom's car.

"Sweetheart, you have a horrible cough. I think you need to stay in for once and get better. All this running around is making it impossible for you to get well." She was truly concerned.

I promise I will be okay, and I will come home early. Please, Mom!" I was pulling out all the stops.

Mom handed me the keys to her car, and I drove up to The City and swung by Mop's flat on Steiner Street in The Fillmore (District). Mop was a heroin dealer in "the hood" that I met through Jerre. Mop liked me a lot, so he kept selling to me after Jerre "disappeared." Mop was an old pimp and a player selling to jailbirds and bottom feeders never having enough money to feed their habits. They were always working some deal or scam with Mop to get just enough smack to satisfy their desire without getting sick. Mop got his name because he wore a messy black wig of straight, stringy hair on top of his head that looked like an old dirty floor mop. It was always just off-center as if it could fall off at any second, but it never did. He wore tight pants that no man over 60 years of age should wear, rayon paisley dress shirts with two buttons too open, and see-through silk socks with open-toed slippers.

His house looked like the den of iniquity. The living room was decorated with old couches around the walls, and the couches were lined with old junkies and hookers scratching and sniffing with their chins on their chests. The dining room had one bare light bulb hanging down from the ceiling, and around the table were customers in various stages of shooting dope.

One guy was nodding out with a cigarette in his mouth; only the total length of the cigarette was ash, perfectly intact moving up and down to the rhythm of his breathing, within a millimeter of his flammable rayon shirt. Mop handed me two little red balloons full of heroin knotted up in a little ball. "Now, you be a careful little girl and don't get caught, and, if you do, don't be saying my name." Mop winked at me and closed the door behind me. I could hear two chains slide into place and three deadbolts secure, and finally, a button pushed on the doorknob. I laughed to myself. *A button on the doorknob...really? Now that's just overkill!*

I popped both balloons into my mouth and manipulated one into each cheek with my tongue. Drugs were put into balloons so that, if the police run up on you to bust you for possession, you can swallow the balloons, and there goes their evidence.

I drove over to Cole Street and shot a little bit of junk. I got a little too loaded and needed to get back home before it was too late, and my mom needed the car in the morning.

Driving in the fast lane on the Bayshore Freeway, I could no longer keep my eyes open and passed out on the seat of the car. The car swerved three lanes to the right and careened into the bushes until it crashed to a stop. I woke up to find the car surrounded by bushes. I looked down and saw a tree trunk coming up through the floor of the car right where my legs would have been. All the doors were blocked. I rolled down my window and squeezed my way out through branches of bushes until I fell to the ground and slid out onto the shoulder of the freeway.

My lungs were so congested that I could hardly breathe. I stood up and ran to a small clearing where I threw the rest of the heroin over the bushes and into the marshy field. I stumbled back toward the car, wheezing and coughing.

I was wheezing and seemed to be barely breathing. "Let's get you to the hospital, young lady. Can you tell me what happened?"

"I was driving home, and I was coughing and trying to breathe, and I must have passed out. When I woke up, I was in the bushes, and this nice man saw me crash and came to my aid. Please take me home. I do not need to go to the hospital. I need my mom and dad. Please take me home," I pleaded.

On my way home, in the back of the police car, I could not stop thanking God that I was not taken to the hospital. If they saw the needle marks on my arm or did a blood test, I would have been screwed for a lifetime. But the sense of dread was creeping in that I had totaled my mom's car. I felt guilty for being so irresponsible and thoughtless of my parents and the trouble I keep lying at their feet.

Once home, the policeman recounted the story to my parents, reassuring them that I was alright and very lucky to be alive.

The door closed, and Mom and Dad looked at me. I did look pitiful. Marilyn looked at me with an expression that read *what kind of cock 'n bull story is she handing out this time.*

I knew I had to make a change.

The next day, Rip came over to see me.

"Jackie, I'm not going to ask you what happened, but I want you to stay away from The City for a while. You need a break," Rip was firm with me, and I appreciated that.

He went on, "Smiley and Jack bought two Bentleys and a Rolls Royce, and they shipped them from England to the Port of Call in New Jersey. They just found out that they have cleared customs and they can pick them up. Do you want to go with us to get them and drive them back here?"

"Are you kidding me? Holy cow! I have to ask my parents...I mean, tell my parents but groovy! I need to get out of here in a big way before something terrible happens, and this is just the thing. Rip, you are saving my life! Thank you!" I gave Rip a huge hug and a kiss. "When do we leave?"

"We found a drive-away car. This guy wants a car delivered to him in Philadelphia, and we will take the train to New Jersey from there. We leave in two days." I nodded with delight.

I stuffed my backpack with clothes, books, sucky candies, and my own freshly washed and fluffy towel. 'You never know,' I thought. I strapped my sleeping bag to my pack and made sure my guitar was secure in its case. I was ready. My body was feeling the pain of the accident and the lack of substances, but I was determined to tough through it! That's it. I had enough. I heard a honk outside the house, and I gathered up all my belongings and started to move toward the car. I stopped in astonishment. There was Rip, Jack, Smiley, and Perry stuffed into a small Toyota Corolla. "Road trip! Come on, Jackie, this is gonna be out of sight!

It was 11:00 AM, and I was wedged inside a can on wheels in silent wonderment of how I was going to ride like this to New Jersey. We started into the Nevada desert, and I was in awe. I was starting to pay attention to the land and the foliage and the differences from California. I had never been out of the state. I saw the lines of demarcation on a map, but I marveled at how nature had made those lines so real. We drove through the Appalachians across the Alleghany River and I realized how beautiful the state was with trees everywhere and mountains, just like California.

I felt a little homesick while loving the adventure of being so far from home. I was thrilled to finally see New York and then it was time to meet up at the Empire State Building to get the cars and start the caravan back to California. Rip and I got to drive the green Bentley, Smiley drove the silver Bentley, and Jack drove his silver and maroon Rolls Royce.

People stared at the cars and waved to show their astonishment and approval. We got peace signs, thumbs up and okay signs. We pretended that we were in a rock band going from gig to gig across the country. During the whole trip home, the Rolls Royce kept breaking down, and it was nearly impossible to find any parts for an old Rolls Royce in Sioux City, Iowa or Missoula, Montana. We either had to jerry-rig a solution to get to the next breakdown.

The whole gang was getting irritated. We had exhausted the fun and the novelty of being on the road; everyone had their fantasies of what we would do when we finally got home. My fantasy never wavered.

When Rip and I pulled into Las Vegas, I jumped out of the car and found a payphone. I called Pam. "When are you coming home? Get right over when you do. We have dope for you, so you don't have to stop and cop. Oh, and we moved to 2468 Geary Street," Pam sounded excited to have me back, and I felt relief.

The caravan pulled up in front of my parent's house, and everyone jumped out of the cars to hug goodbye. My mom and dad ran out of the house to see the cars and started laughing with glee at what they imagined was an excellent adventure for all the kids. I gave everyone a huge hug and a kiss and told Rip that I would call him later.

Rip (may his sweet soul rest in peace)

Chapter 29
Those People Aren't Your Friends

Rip was angry with me. I got so caught up in spending time with my family that I totally forgot to call Rip. I hated it when he got mad at me. He had a habit of savoring his grudges like a fine wine, and I would stew in my guilt if I slighted him even the least bit...or anyone, for that matter.

I called him up and apologized for ...whatever...but he chose to pout and dismiss me. That was it! I was going to hitchhike to The City. I did my laundry from the road trip, stuffed everything back into my backpack, left a note for my mom and dad, stole $20 from the hidden compartment in Marilyn's jewelry box, and headed for the freeway onramp to hitch a ride.

Within two minutes of posing with my thumb out in my tight tie-dyed tee shirt with no bra, I was picked up by a band of long-haired freaks in a VW van and then dropped right at the front door of a gorgeous two-story Victorian flat at 2468 Geary Street. I was excited to ring the bell and see who was still in the gang. I was eager to know what this new place looked like and the mischief they were all planning next.

Pam opened the door and shrieked at the top of her lungs, "She's back!"

A chorus of cheers erupted from upstairs. Pam grabbed my hand and ran me up the polished mahogany stairs, where I saw everyone from Cole Street and some cute new faces. I kissed everyone I knew and was introduced to Bobby and Ricky (the Leone Brothers), and Brenda and Dennis Murphy (the married hooker and junkie) with their toy poodle Princess. Pam showed me around the flat, and I could not believe my eyes.

There were beautiful mahogany wainscoting and crown molding for as far as the eye could see. Persian carpets and runners covered the hardwood floors. Each bedroom had either a wrought iron bed or a wood sleigh bed. The living room had a wood-burning fireplace, Tiffany torchiere floor lamps, and over the hearth was a beautifully framed Maxfield Parrish print. There were pots of lush plants in every room. The commodes and the bathtubs were in different rooms, so it was perfect for communal living.

The kitchen was big with all the conveniences and, at the end of the room under a bank of windows, was a big wooden dining table. On that dining table was a Jefferson Airplane album cover piled high with brown Mexican heroin and the paraphernalia necessary to get loaded.

I looked at the drugs and smiled. I looked at Pam, "May I?"

"Be my guest!"

I prepared the drugs while everyone sat around the table, filling me in on everything that happened while I was away. We talked about who started using heroin, what Peggy was up to at the store, how they got Geary Street and why it was furnished to the nines like a "counterculture chic" spread in *Architectural Digest*.

I spun my arm around to force the blood down to produce a vein I could easily inject. I tied off my arm and injected the drug while telling everyone about my road trip adventures, "The cars were magnificent and weeeeeeeeeeeeeeeeeeeeeeee......"

Everyone started to laugh because they thought I was making a funny sound. They all looked closer and saw that

I had expelled all the air from my lungs and was in the middle of an overdose. Everyone leaped into crisis mode. This was not the first time that the gang had to bring someone back from an OD, but it was the first time it was me. I was the one that usually led the rescue brigade.

Bobby grabbed me out of my seat and slapped my face and called my name. He and Ricky hoisted me up by my armpits and started walking me up and down the hall to try to get me conscious and moving. My legs were like rubber bands as they struggled to keep me up. Pam ran cold water in the bathtub and tossed in two trays of ice cubes to make sure it would jolt me awake when they put me into the water.

Peter put a table salt and water solution into a syringe and ran to the hall, and injected it into my vein as best he could. He picked up my feet, and they hurriedly carried me to the tub. Pam pulled off my hiking boots, jeans, and top. They slid me into the icy cold tub and rapidly packed ice cubes in my armpit and crotch.

I bolted up in the tub and took a deep breath, and stared into space. "What happened?" My words were barely audible. "I OD'ed, didn't I? I was floating in white light at total peace, but I could faintly hear someone calling my name."

I started to nod off in the tub, and Pam shook me and said, "Oh, no, you don't! Get out of the tub and start walking the hall until you can stand and walk on your own. Now! Get moving, little piggy. That'll teach you to put too much in the spoon after a break. Now, let's go up!"

Everyone closely examined me as I walked the hall, dripping and half-naked. Within twenty minutes, I had come back around and could manage to walk into the living room and sit on the couch. I put my pants and shirt on while Brenda and Dennis watched me. I yelled out to anyone that was listening, "Thank you, everyone, for saving my life! I am so sorry. It wasn't intentional. I think I took too much. That shit was GOOD! I owe you guys big time!" From the kitchen, I heard, "We are just glad that we brought you back. Don't you ever do that again!" Pam, Peter, Bobby, and Ricky were taking a turn shooting up the rest of the smack. If it was that good, they wanted some too!

Brenda sat down next to me while Dennis nodded against the wall holding Princess under his arm. "I am surprised we have never met before, Jackie," Brenda said. "So anyway, Dennis and I saw your tits in the bathtub, and we think you would make a very popular and successful working girl. What do you think?"

I was too loaded to react, but inside I went from laughing at the whole idea of my ever doing something like that to being pissed that Brenda and Dennis took advantage of my nakedness to assess my body for a job pitch.

"Thank you for thinking of me but, Jeffrey, Michael, and I have applied to be a census taker, and I should find out any day if I got the job." Finally, feeling very sober, I breezed through the house saying goodbye to everyone and apologized again for falling out and said I would probably be back the next day. I was out of there!

When I got to the store, Peggy gave me the cold shoulder for leaving town so abruptly, as if I were supposed to ask for permission. Peggy felt she had the kind of power and control which she could use to manipulate other people's lives and boundaries.

Peggy allowed very few people around her, and those she allowed had to challenge her intellectually just enough to be stimulating, be good company, and willing to go on runs when she needed something. I provided all three requirements, which meant that Peggy needed me, making me a target for her occasional fussing. It was complicated, but I could live with it. It gave me access to drugs, food, and another place to sleep in The City when I didn't want to go home, or I felt I was wearing out my welcome with the gang.

I also liked Peggy and enjoyed every moment with her at the store and even at her house in Stinson Beach. I sat in the chair by the counter at the store for three hours without a peep from Peggy. I was getting ready to get up and hitchhike back to Geary Street when I heard bracelets jangling, and a high pitched giggle. It was Janis Joplin coming in to see Peggy.

"Tell her Pearl is here!" she said. Wayne grabbed the phone and rang the backroom.

The door flew open, and Peggy came out to greet her, "Hey Dahlin', what are you doing in this neck of the woods?" She escorted Janis into the inner sanctum and closed the door.

I stood up, "I am out of here, Wayne. I'll see you later."

The back office door flew open, and Peggy ran out and grabbed both of my shoulders, "Do you have any dope? Janis and I want to get high." I shook my head.

She handed me a $100 bill and said, "Please go to Mops and cop some smack and bring it back here and you can have some too, and we can have a party. Will ya, Dahlin?"

I hailed a cab to Steiner Street and told the driver to wait. I ran up to the door, rang the bell with my special ring so Mop would know it was me. He buzzed me in, and within 2 minutes, I was back in the cab and on my way back to the store.

I was bringing heroin to Janis Joplin, my idol. When I gave the balloons of dope to Peggy and Janis, they both kissed me on the cheek, giggled, and cooed. I got so lightheaded I thought I was going to faint, which beats the hell out of overdosing just hours before.

Janis sat on the corner of the mohair couch and prepared her fix. Peggy sidled up to me and batted her eyes, signaling that she wanted me to cook up her drugs for her and then get her off. I played along with the happy charade.

We stayed up all night in the back room of the store, I went on food runs for Janis and Peggy, the last one sending me into an abyss of guilt. While waiting for my order, I was leaning over the counter, nodding out with my head bobbing up and down.

An older man and his wife were eating at the counter, and they looked like they had been at the opera or some kind of gala affair. I could only see out of one eye when I was that loaded, but I did peek at the couple and thought they reminded me of my parents when they went out on the town.

The man looked me in the eye that was open and leaned in to say, "Young lady, do your parents know where you are? You are a disgrace to be out in public looking like you do, and you need to go home and get your life together. It is a sin what you are doing to yourself, and you are going to end up in jail or dead if you don't change your ways."

He and his wife stood up, paid their check, and walked out the door.

Tears started rolling down my cheeks. I was ashamed and embarrassed. Everything he said was the truth, and it made me sick to my stomach.

I brought the food back to the store and handed the bags to Peggy, careful not to look her in the eyes.

"There you go. I am going to go down to the basement to get some sleep, and I'll see you in the morning. Tomorrow is Mother's Day, so I will do a breakfast run, and then I have to buy my mom a present and hitchhike home. Goodnight."

I laid on the bed in the basement, feeling empty and devastated like never before in my life. That man trumped Janis Joplin and killed my high. No amount of heroin could fill the hollow space that his comment had pierced.

Strung out on Geary Street

Chapter 30
Was My Face Red?

I ran up the stairs to get ready for the day and see who was there. Janis was gone, and all she left behind was a memory and a couple of purple feathers that dropped off her boa. Peggy was up in the loft, sound asleep. I looked at the office desk, and all the heroin was gone, except for the nice, fat heroin-soaked cotton in the middle of a silver spoon.

I added some water to the residue and began to pound the cotton until I drained every ounce of the heroine-water solution. I drew the liquid up into the outfit and injected it into my vein. I could feel and taste it immediately and knew that would suffice until I got to Burlingame to surprise my mom for Mother's Day.

There was a trendy and hip shop on Polk Street run by August, a gay guy that Peter dated on the sly. I did not know what I would find there, but I was going to give it a try. I thought he could help me, as my mind was clouded with heroin. As soon as I walked into the shop, the guy greeted me with a hello.

"Hey man, Peter says hi. I'm going home to see my mom and I need to buy her a present for Mother's Day. Can you help me pick something out?" I looked straight into his eyes to see if he was a friend or foe.

August smiled from ear to ear, "Sure, Doll, step over to the accessories counter, and let's just see what we have for Mom. Does she work hard and need to rest her shoulders and feet at the end of the day?"

I thought, "Yes, I think so. She sells real estate and is either driving around all day looking at houses or sitting at a desk on the phone."

"Here is the perfect present! She can rub this wand on her shoulders and feet, and all the tension will leave her body within minutes," he held up a box that could easily fit into a backpack.

"I'll take it. Can you wrap it for me?"

I paid for the present, and August wrapped it like it was fine jewelry from Tiffany's. I thanked him for helping me and then ran out of the store, stuck out my thumb, and in no time, I was back in Burlingame like a good little daughter.

As soon as I walked into the house, I was hit with the aroma of salami and eggs. I walked into the kitchen, kissed my dad hello, and looked around at the tray he was preparing. Orange juice, check. Coffee with sugar, check. Rye bread toasted perfectly with just the right amount of butter, check. Linen napkin, check.

Hurriedly, I went to the garden and picked two beautiful red roses to put in a small bud vase. I tenderly laid the vase on the tray next to the orange juice, "There you go, perfect."

Dad smiled at me and laid a plate down on the tray piled high with delicious looking salami and eggs, garnished with a sprig of parsley, and pecked me on the cheek, "Go get your sister, and we will all go in together to treat your mom with this breakfast in bed."

I walked into Marilyn's room without knocking just to get a rise out of her. Marilyn punched me so hard in the stomach that I could not breathe and fell to the floor.

"Did you steal twenty dollars out of my jewelry box last time you were here?" she screamed.

"No! I did not do it!" I gasped. "I can't believe you hit me so hard in the gut for no reason. And, on Mother's Day! Can you please not get mom upset on her day? What is wrong with you?"

Marilyn stared into my eyes, and I could see her wrath.

"I took your stinking twenty dollars, and I will pay you back, okay? Mellow out, you bitch, and if you ever touch me again, I will rip off your arm and hit you with the wet end! Now, come and grab your present, and let's go, show mom how much we love her."

The three of us walked into the bedroom to find our "princess mom" all propped up on her pillows, waiting to be served breakfast in bed and to be acknowledged for being a fantastic wife and mother. It was one of her favorite "holidays" because it was all things, Pat, all day! She got three huge kisses on the lips and a HAPPY MOTHER'S DAY sung in unison.

Dad went first and handed Mom an envelope with the sweetest card and two tickets to the Curran Theater to see Westside Story.

Marilyn handed our mom a big, beautifully wrapped package and card. The card was from Hallmark, a mushy, floral, daughter loves her mother number, and the present was a new bathrobe and matching slippers. I thought it was a nice present, but it was predictable. I felt my gift was different and extremely thoughtful of my mom's stress and hard work.

I handed my mom the impeccably store-wrapped gift and said, "I am sorry there is no card. It must have fallen off on my way home."

She smiled, knowing there was never a card and that I was trying to pretend that I wasn't thoughtless.

She opened the box and pulled out a beige cylindrical-shaped wand. She looked at my father horrified, and then instantly changed her expression to puzzled and somewhat grateful. I could read her expressions and immediately began to explain.

"Mom, you come home from work so tired and exhausted, so I thought you could use this. All you need to do is turn it on at the bottom and rub it on your shoulders, legs, and feet. It relaxes you, and you can massage your own muscles! Isn't that cool?"

"Your present is lovely, Darling. Thank you," she quickly shoved the wand back in the box, closed the lid, and put it in the drawer of her bedside table. And that was the end of the gift-giving part of Mom's special day.

It was not until many years later that I learned that I had given my mother a vibrating dildo for Mother's Day.

I stayed at my family home for a few days catching up on my sleep and eating my mom's cooking. I did not have any drugs on me, so I decided to take a break for a while. I was on my best behavior and let down my guard. I felt safe at home and was actually thinking about my life and what I needed to do to earn a living and get on with it.

One night I was in my room, and Dad called me in for dinner. Not thinking, I ran to the table but forgot to put on my long-sleeved shirt. I was eating and yakking about something, and all of a sudden, I saw my mom glaring at my arm. Then my mom looked at my dad and nodded her head toward my arm. He looked at her like she was nuts as she grimaced and looked at my arm again. Dad looked over and was horrified!

"What is that on your arm?" he asked. He grabbed it and held it up to the light so he could get a closer look, "What are these marks?"

I turned bright red and drew my arm back, "Nothing! I got scratched in the rose bushes when I picked mom's flowers for her breakfast-in-bed tray. God, what do you think it is?"

My parents looked at each other. Marilyn looked down at her plate. I looked around the table at all of them, waiting for them to say something, anything. We all finished our dinner and went into the family room to watch TV. I sat and watched *Ironsides* with the family and decided to go back up to Geary Street the next day.

Chapter 31
Life's Small Favors

When I walked up to the stairs at Geary Street, I was met by an excited Lotta. Her real name was Lorraine; she was from San Mateo and went to school with Pam. Everyone called her Lotta because she had a lotta' brains and moxie for a natural blonde girl. She was as pretty as a model with a beautiful face and legs that went on forever. She was in a long-distance relationship with a hippie drug dealer/entrepreneur living in Michigan; therefore, she traveled a lot back and forth.

"Jackie, come in the back room with me. I have a favor to ask you," she yanked my arm half out of its socket as we ran to the back of the flat.

"Bruce needs, like, 50 kilos of pot delivered to a guy in Washington, D.C., and he asked me to ask you if you would be willing to do it. He will pay you, like, $250 when you return if everything goes as planned. He will meet you here with two suitcases lined with baby powder in case there are sniffing dogs at the airport. You just need to take a cab to San Francisco Airport, buy a round trip ticket to Dulles, fly there, and take a cab to, like, the nearest hotel. Then call a guy to pick it up. He will get the suitcases and give you an envelope of money; you stay there for the night and take the next plane home. Will you be able to do it?"

I stared at Lotta like she was out of her mind. That word "just" had a way of minimizing the most volatile of situations…just one shot of penicillin should get rid of it; just let me put the tip in; just become a drug mule, and if you get caught, nobody knows you exist.

"No, I will not do it. Not for two hundred and fifty dollars. That is just chump change for the risk I would be taking. Add a zero, and maybe then I will consider it!"

Lotta picked up the phone and called Bruce. She whispered back and forth and looked at me and hung up the phone.

"Okay, Bruce said he will give you $750, but you better not blow it. And you can't do any drugs from the second you leave for the airport until you get back here. If you agree, I have to call him back right now because he has to make the arrangements really fast." Lotta had the most adorable phony stern look on her face that made me almost burst out laughing, but I held it in so no boats would start rocking.

"I will do it. And, if what Bruce means by 'don't blow it' is, don't get arrested by the police in Washington, D.C. with 50 kilos of illegal drugs, let him know that I have 'like' no intention of getting caught," I proclaimed with a disingenuous frown on my face.

Two days later, I smiled sweetly as I stood at the ticket counter of TWA and bought a round trip ticket to return on the first flight the next day. I grinned as I checked in the two huge suitcases and tied my waist-length frizzy hippie hair back in a bun. I wore a white blouse with a Peter Pan collar, a grey wool skirt, and a navy blue blazer with a pair of sensible shoes.

I pretended to be a school teacher as my cover. The attendant took my ticket at the cabin door, and I found my seat on the plane. I giggled as the stewardess walked the aisle to make sure everyone had their seatbelt on. The engine started, and we took off. I eased back in my seat. 'So far, so good.'

When the plane landed at Dulles, I walked to the baggage claim area and stood back from the crowd to ensure no one was looking at my bags while they circled around the luggage belt. When I thought I was in the clear, I hoisted both suitcases off the belt, walked out of the door, and got inside the first empty cab I could find.

"Please drive me to the closest hotel. I am bushed!" The cab took off, and within 10 minutes, I was checking in at the Hilton.

"How long will you be staying with us, Miss?" asked the receptionist.

"Just for a night, please. I start another leg of my trip in the morning."

I slammed and locked the door to my room. I called the number on the small slip of paper that Bruce had given me, and a voice on the line told me he would be right over to get the dope.

My buyer showed up and opened both suitcases to inspect the product. A lovely scent of baby powder came wafting out. He was satisfied, gave me a big fat envelope of money, and went out the door with the goods. I let out a sigh of relief and headed for the minibar. Bruce told me not to have drugs, but he didn't say anything about alcohol.

The next morning, five assorted mini-bar bottles later, I got up, put my disguise on, and checked out of the hotel.

On the plane back home, I said hello to the entire flight crew that was working my flight the night before. I knew I would have to rethink my modus operandi if I ever did the mule thing again.

I got back to Geary Street and gave Lotta the envelope of money. Lotta took out $750 and handed it to me and said, "It was a pleasure doing business with you. And, oh, by the way, the guy thought your get-up was very cute, but you ended up staying at the hotel where all the FBI and CIA agents stay and where they hide their informants. The place is totally wired! He almost told you to forget it because he was not about to take two suitcases out of that place in the middle of the night!"

She cackled and walked out of the room. I stood there and just stared.

That money was burning a hole in my pocket, so I went by Mops to get some smack and took it over to Peggy's to get her high for a change. Wayne buzzed back that I was in the store, and I could hear Peggy scream, "Tell her to get in here, now!"

"Holy shitcakes, what did I do now?" I groaned. I walked into the back room and saw Peggy on the floor, slapping and shaking Terry Hallinan with all her might and strength. She looked up in stark terror, "Help me! I don't know what to do. Janis gave him a hit of smack, and he went out!"

I ran out of the office door, through the store, out the front, and turned a sharp right into the liquor store on the corner of Polk and Pine. I flew to the back of the store and grabbed a bag of ice. Throwing a five-dollar bill on the counter, I yelled, "I'll be back for the change!" and ran back into the office and slammed the door.

I ran over to Terry and threw ice down his pants and packed it around his balls. I then packed ice in his armpits to shock him back to life. Nothing.

I went into a bag of condiments from Miz Brown's Coffee Shop and found salt packets. I tore them open and put a pile of salt into a spoon on the desk and filled the spoon with water. I put the salt water into the syringe lying there and ran back to Terry. He was not breathing. I kneeled on his arm until a vein halfheartedly popped up and slammed the needle with saline into his arm. I got all the saltwater into his vein while Peggy was pumping his chest.

Janis was on the corner of the couch, loaded and completely nodding out. I looked over at her as if she were totally useless but did not utter a word in that grim moment. Terry coughed and gasped and rolled over several times, trying to get away from the ice in his crotch. The ice stuck to his skin and hair, and he had to quickly sober up to get the ice off his balls. He crawled on his knees to the couch, pulled himself up, and pulled off his pants.

"What the fuck?" he looked around as if someone had done something awfully wrong to him. Terry was a very high-powered young attorney in San Francisco, and it did not occur to him that he did this to himself. It was the second time he let Janis put too much heroin into his veins. How could he act so dumb and stupid?

I stared at Terry, Janis and then at Peggy. I tempered my fear and rage and said, "Y'all best not be doing something you are not big enough to handle! If you can't fix this shit when it comes down, then don't do it unless you are with someone who can rescue your asses. Peggy, learn how to get your own ass off or stop shooting smack. Terry, think about the headlines in the *San Francisco Examiner* the next time you think about shooting smack! Janis…hello, are you with us?"

I walked out of the office and slammed the door. I could hear a faint chorus of "Thank you!" as I stormed out of the store. I knew that the event could have been a horrible disaster, and I was shaking all the way back to Geary Street.

I explained the whole situation to the gang at Geary Street as we all walked around the kitchen, cooking dinner, and passing joints. We were a family, and some of our best times were spent cooking and eating together. We just loved each other.

Pam came home just in time for dinner with Jeffery and Michael. They had just received their letters confirming they had passed their tests to be Census Takers for the 1970 Census. They told me to go to my parents' house in the next few days to see if I passed my test too. We all took the test on the same day, and that would give us work and money at the start of the New Year.

Bruce and Lotta prepared and decorated the dining room table for everyone, and we all sat down to eat.

"Jackie, you did good with that thing you did for me," Bruce was awkward at giving compliments. "I have something else I need you to do. Lotta and I are going back to Michigan to hang out at the farm, and we want you to come back and hang with us for a few weeks…if you want to. You guys can ride horses and swim in the pond while I work, and we can go to groovy places on the weekend. You both can have a good time if you want."

I looked Bruce in the eyes, "And what exactly is it that you want me to do? I know it is not to be Lotta's playmate while you are at work."

"Oh, yeah. I just need you to carry a brick of cocaine on the plane for me…that is all."

Everyone at the table stared at Bruce as if he had lost his mind.

"Sure, no biggie, Bruce! Will we put the coke into condom balls, and I swallow them and then throw them up at the farm? Or maybe you want to shove the whole brick up my ass? Sounds like a plan! And, for that, I get to ride horses and swim in the pond?" I was blown away at his nerve. I also thought he was an idiot to concoct that plan at the dinner table in front of everyone. It was nearly impossible for me to seriously consider the proposition and negotiate with all those shocked eyes on me.

"No! This time I will give you $2000," Bruce coaxed.

"If you and Lotta are going to Michigan, one of you should be able to do it and save the $2000 for legal fees. I hear Michigan is hot and sticky at this time of the year, and it will make my hair frizz!" I joked.

After three days, I was back in my teacher disguise and was boarding a plane for Flint, Michigan. I had the cocaine hidden in my purse. I was going to put it inside the guitar case that I had checked with my luggage, but we all decided that I needed to keep that package on me at all times.

Lotta and Bruce flew first class while I flew in coach. They totally ignored me at the airport and on the flight. They made no eye contact whatsoever. When they landed, the master plan was for the two of them to get their luggage and go outside to the curb. I would get my guitar and suitcase and meet them out there when it was clear that I had gotten away without being arrested or followed.

Lotta and Bruce waited for a matter of 45 minutes for me to come outside, and Bruce started to panic. He couldn't help himself. He went back into the baggage claim area to check what had happened to me. He hid behind a post and could not believe his eyes.

I was arguing with an airline employee quite animatedly. He could not tell what was going on, so he inched his way closer behind another post. I could see him out of the corner of my eye, but I ignored him just as he instructed. He started to signal me to get out of the airport. He could see that I had my purse, so he could not tell what in the hell I was arguing about.

All of a sudden, a baggage handler walked up and handed me a guitar case. I smiled, thanked him, grabbed my suitcase, and walked out the door. I was hysterical inside at the thought that Bruce almost had a coronary because I ran the risk of getting caught with his precious cocaine over my cherished guitar.

His lips were flapping at me all the way to his farm. I was not fazed. I rode horses and swam in the lake, and eventually, Bruce felt at ease knowing that everything worked out well. He finally saw me for the little gem I was. He really started to like having me around and paid more attention to me. At that point, I asked to be driven to the airport so that I could go home.

I said goodbye the next day, knowing that they would miss my ass. My mom and dad picked me up at the airport, and we all went out to dinner. Mom and Dad were excited that I was home and could tell that I was healthy and happy. They told me I had gotten a piece of mail from the United States Census Bureau and that it looked important.

I opened the letter and saw that I had passed the test and would be taking the census in San Mateo County. That meant that I would be living at home for several months, and I would also be staying away from drugs for a while. I knew I needed a break, and so did my parents. I would give them some worry-free time because I knew they deserved it.

Chapter 32
A Little Tied Up Right Now

The comfort of home gave me the safety I needed and the peace of mind my parents needed. Living under the same roof with Marilyn was another story! I, now seen as an interloper, was instructed that the telephone was Marilyn's, and I could not answer it if Marilyn were at home. When Marilyn was out, I was to take thorough messages and hand them to her when she came home.

It wasn't until years later that I learned that Jerre had been calling the house looking for me from the day I moved out of Hyde Street. He would cry to Marilyn that he missed me and needed to find me. Marilyn told him that I moved to Hawaii and did not know exactly where, but still, he kept calling. Marilyn knew that Jerre would mean the death of me, so she spent hours on the phone talking to him and soothing his lovelorn heart but would not tell him where I was…ever. The family celebrated the eight nights of Hanukkah, and in addition to the obligatory socks and underwear, I got cash. It was the first time I could ever remember getting actual cash to buy something that I would like, and it made me downright giddy. It was Christmas Eve, and I put my Hanukkah gelt in my car coat pocket and drove up to Polk Street to see Peggy. The store was nicely decorated and packed with people doing last-minute shopping.

You could smell the leather jackets that she got just for the holidays, and they were flying off the racks. I imagined Peggy was going to have the best season ever. Wayne looked up and said, "Peggy asked me to tell you to go right into the office."

Peggy was back there alone, and when she saw me, she jumped out of her chair and gave me a big hug, "It's so good to see you, Dahlin! Where have you been? Wait, before we settle in, go to the cash drawer and take some money and go to Mops for some dope...my treat. Would you, Dahlin?"

I went behind the counter and went into the cash drawer. I grabbed a handful of bills and stuffed them into my pants pocket, and told Wayne, "I will be right back. I am running an errand for Peggy, and she told me to take the money."

Wayne winked and waved goodbye.

About an hour went by, and I returned with the drugs. I went to open the door, and it was locked. I thought, 'That is strange. The store should be open for another two hours, at least.'

I knocked on the glass door, and a strange guy with pants draped over his arm appeared and stared at me. I yelled that I was out running an errand for Peggy and that he had to let me in.

He opened the door and locked it after I entered. My stomach dropped as I turned to look at him. He took the pants off his arm, and I could see that he was holding a gun.

"Get into the back room, now!"

I took a deep breath and walked to the back, not knowing what I would find when I opened the door. Wayne and Peggy were seated on the couch, and another tall, hairy hippie guy stood across the room, holding a gun on them. I kept my head down but could see Peggy staring at me with a strange inquisitive look in her eyes.

"Where is the money, little girl?" Hairy asked.

"What money?" I replied.

"Don't fuck with me, little girl. We went into the cash drawer, and all we found were checks and credit card slips and a couple of one-dollar bills. People pay cash for clothes, and there wasn't any shit in the drawer!"

"I told you, man, no one really pays cash here anymore! That's a fact, man!" Peggy argued.

"Shut the fuck up! I am asking her, and if you open your mouth again, I am going to shut it for good!"

I chimed in, "I have no clue about the money in this store. I don't work here. I only run errands for Peggy. I have ten dollars in my car coat that my parents gave me for Hanukkah, and you may have that. But that is all the money I have."

"Fuck that! I don't want your Hanukkah money. Lie down on the floor, all of you. Facedown. Put your hands behind your back and cross your legs at the ankles," Hairy barked. "Tie them up tight and then stuff all the leather into bags and put them by the front door. I'll keep an eye on them."

My mind was racing. 'He did not take my money, so he won't go through my pockets now. They are tying us up, so they aren't going to kill us. They will take everything they can and leave, so we just have to lay still until they leave and then get untied and call the police. No, I have to get out of here, and Peggy and Wayne have to call the police. And a Merry Christmas to us!'

Peggy piped up, "Hey, man. My tits are too big for me to lay face down. Can't I lie on my back?"

He allowed her to get tied up lying on her back, but they ran out of rope and lamp wires, so her feet were free. Hairy stared down at Peggy for a long time.

"Hey man, I have to take a leak. Can I just get up and go pee in the bathroom right behind you? You don't have to untie me, and you can see it's just a toilet. There's nothing else in there. I'm not going to try to escape; I just need to pee,"

Wayne said, "Peggy, piss in your pants. Do not get up. Shut up and lie there."

Hairy grabbed her arms and pulled her up to her feet and walked her into the office bathroom.

Wayne and I looked at each other, shook our heads, and buried our faces into the rug.

Hairy tried to rape Peggy. We could hear everything. Peggy was coaxing him not to do it. They were struggling against the walls, and he was swearing. She stopped struggling, and it sounded like she was laughing, but he kept swearing. We figured he threw her against the wall and then onto the toilet.

"Go ahead and piss, you bitch! I didn't want to fuck you anyway!"

Peggy walked out and got down on her stomach, and no one made eye contact. Hairy walked out, and we could hear the two guys pick up all the bags, unlock the deadbolt on the store door, and then we heard street noises and then nothing.

I was the first to get untied, and I untied Wayne and then Peggy. I peeked out the office door and saw they were gone. I ran to the front, dead-bolted the door, and ran back to the office.

"Are you okay? What the fuck? Why did you get up to pee?" I stared at Peggy and then thought better of asking any more questions.

I pulled a wad of money out of my right front pocket and balloons of heroin out of my left front pocket, "I have no idea why I took all of the cash from the drawer. When I got to Mop's and saw what I did, I was sure it was going to be the end of my life as I know it. Now, I am so happy I did it. There must be three thousand dollars here!" I handed the money and balloon to Peggy.

A tear came running down Peggy's cheek. I could not guess if it was happiness, relief, fear, or shame, but I did feel like a courageous hero, and I still had my Hanukkah money! I hugged Wayne and kissed Peggy on the cheek and said, "I am outta here! You have to call the police because then your insurance can compensate for the damage. Hide the dope in the basement. Merry Christmas!"

I walked out the door and heard Peggy yell, "Hey Dahlin, don't you want to stay and get high?"

Chapter 33
Census, Sense and Cents Less

The New Year and a new decade all seemed so exciting to me. I started my job at the United States Census Bureau, and I was astonished to realize how much I enjoyed the work. I got to work from a fantastic home. I did not have a dress code, but I knew that I had to look pleasant in appearance. I was walking up to people's houses, and I was paid for every census form I completed. The job was a challenge, but just what I could take on.

The whole family got into the act. My folks asked how many completions I got each day at the dinner table. I finally had something to contribute during the show and tell, and that boosted my self-esteem. Mom even drove me around the neighborhoods I had to visit just to see what the job entailed. Mom would also see if there were any houses for sale that her buyers may like. She would have her eye out for someone who might be planning to sell, and then she would stop the car and pay a call to the homeowner. I got a kick out of her tenacity, which I called "brass beans."

"Mom, exactly how many houses have you listed while hanging out with me while I do the census?" I smiled at her.

"I am taking my third listing tomorrow, thank you very much," Mom puffed up with pride.

"Don't you think I deserve to get a commission or a finder's fee? After all, I am the procuring cause of all this good fortune," I started laughing at my own gumption.

After dinner, I would go into the dining room and spread all my forms out on the table to complete my part of the work. Then I would update a contact sheet that had to be turned in to the district office at the end of each week. I was one of the highest producers in the district.

Jeffery and I were spending a lot of time together, and that was a trip because he was ushering at the theater where the play Hair was being performed. He became part of the Hair entourage and we would hang out with the cast at their house on Lower Haight Street.

One of their after play parties was packed with a diversity of people all high on Angel Dust provided upon entry as a party favor. In the middle of the living room floor was a huge in-ground spa situated at the bottom of a spiral staircase. Very stoned hippies descended naked and stoned down the stairs to the beat of blaring music, then slipped into the warm, inviting spa. The rapid pairing-off of strangers occurred and Bruce, the star of the play, walked up to me with a large man in tow.

"Jackie, this is my friend Luca. He is a singer from Italy performing here in The City for a night or two. He does not speak English, but he let me know he would like to spend time with you. Are you up for it?"

I figured, *why not? I need something to do, and Luca seems mysterious, and we won't have to make boring conversation.* I took his hand and led him into the small powder room under the stairs, where we proceeded to make love for what seemed like hours. He was magnificent and surprisingly agile for such a big man and, as we stared into each other's eyes as we bid each other adieu, it registered that he seemed familiar. Years later, I saw those eyes again…on Luciano Pavarotti.

One night, I caught Michael and Jeffery huddled in the corner, whispering. I ran up and slid between them.

"What are you two queens cooking up? Come on, let me in on it. Tell me, tell me, tell me!" Their surprise turned to annoyance, to amusement, and then to laughter. This was going to be good because the boys were giddy.

Michael started, "Well, do you know how on the census form they ask you to ask neighbors if an occupant moved if there is no answer on the third attempt at the door? I did that today, and I found out that Rod and Irene Hendricks moved to New Mexico. The neighbor said he is a dentist and started a new practice in Santa Fe."

Jeffrey took over, "So, we want to put a telephone in here on Geary Street in his name and scam the airline for tickets to Hawaii. We put the phone in, order tickets to be mailed to the house, and when they come, take out the phone and fly away for as long as we want. We could get flights on Pam Am, TWA, and United Airlines, all leaving around the same time. We would get a first-class round trip ticket with an open return. I know we won't get caught because some guys I grew up with in Boston did it, and they said it was a piece of cake. They send the tickets with an invoice to pay, but by the time they would expect the check, you are gone."

"Pam would never allow you to do that! It just doesn't make sense," I protested, but I also got excited at the very thought of such a thing. Rip and his family went to Hawaii almost every Christmas, and I was always green with envy. Just thinking that I could bask on the beach for as long as I wanted was simply thrilling. I was a bit taken aback at how available happy feelings were to me, and then I realized that I was clean of hard drugs and actually had feelings other than pain.

Pam walked into the living room just at the height of giddy, and the boys told her the plan. I looked at her and held my breath.

"Groovy, Baby! It makes sense to me. Let's do it! Larry can be my Rod Hendricks, and you can be Jeffery's, Irene Hendricks. Who is going to be your wife, Michael?" Pam was in, and I was in shock. Geary Street was not in my name, so I had very little risk, but the lease is in Pam's name. Brass beans! That night, the boys ordered the phone line to be installed on Geary Street in the good dentist's name. Once that was done, the really scary part began. We made up a cover story that each one of us memorized. We were Rod and Irene Hendricks, and we were freelance photographers with *National Geographic Magazine.* We would be calling the airlines from a shoot in New Zealand, asking for the tickets to be mailed because we will have to land in San Francisco and turn right around and fly out for an assignment in Hawaii.

Their secretary would inspect the tickets upon delivery and then immediately send a check for the invoiced amount to the airline. We would apologize profusely for all inconvenience but express their assumption that this sort of thing frequently happens in this complicated and fast-paced world. And so, when the phone line went in, the boys went to work calling the airlines.

I sat back and watched in awe at how scandalous my boys were and the ease at which they slipped on that identity and played the role without hesitation. The date we left would have to be after we all finished working at the Census Bureau and when Pam could get time off from working at Peggy's store. This took great coordination of takeoff times and other logistics.

Every day when the mail was delivered, we all gathered around the stack to see if the tickets were in there. Pam would throw open her arms to form a barrier so she could at least get the first look at HER mail.

"My God, people! Mellow out," Pam protested and then giggled. We backed off, feeling slight shame and wondering if this caper was going to work at all. We all eventually put it out of our minds.

Three weeks after the calls were made, the mailman slipped a fat stack of mail through the front door mail slot on Geary Street. It sat on the hardwood floor all weekend while we went to Monterey for a folk festival. Upon our return, you could hear the squealing and hollering all the way to Golden Gate Park.

On that Saturday, three sets of tickets were delivered. All flights were leaving on the same day within 30 minutes of each other. All seats were in first class with in-flight dinners and free cocktails. We did it! Now, who was going to be Michael's Irene Hendricks?

The doorbell rang, and Peggy rushed up the stairs with a very young girl she had in tow. They were both loaded on heroin, and none of us were on drugs ever since we started taking the census. I got a horrible feeling that no good would come of this visit with Peggy.

"Hi, y'all! Whatch y'all doin?

Jeffery slipped up and told Peggy that we were all going to Hawaii. She made him tell her the whole story, and he didn't really mind because it was one big brag fest. Peggy homed in on the only part that she cared about.

"Who is going to be Michael's wife?" Peggy shyly asked. Not a word was uttered.

"Man, fuck you guys! I don't want to go to Hawaii with you. I want you to let Kimmie go to Hawaii so I can have Debbie hang out with me, and we can do our little thang. I will pay for her and Jackie to stay in a hotel and kick money in so you all can eat and have fun".

We all liked Kimmie, so Michael had his wife for the trip.

The day finally arrived, and we all met at the airport in the main terminal of SFO. Pam and Larry had their glam on. Larry had on tan suede from head to toe, a long burnt sienna scarf wrapped around his neck, and a wide-brimmed safari hat. Pam wore a long lavender crepe peasant dress, a flowered silk shawl, and strappy sandals. From everything Rip ever told me about Hawaii, I didn't have the courage to tell Larry that the minute he got off the plane with all that suede, he would be soaked in sweat, and they would have to peel his suit off in the emergency room just to hydrate him from heat prostration. I kept that to myself.

Kimmie and Michael were the androgynous Hendricks'. They both had long hair past their collars, crisp but unremarkable starched shirts tucked into slacks with clunky shoes.

Each had a messenger bag over their shoulders and sunglasses covering half of their faces. I was sure that Michael had already applied suntan lotion all over his face in wild anticipation of getting the best tan out of all of us.

Jeffery and I brought up the rear, wearing bell-bottom jeans, hiking boots, flak jackets, and each had a camera hanging squarely around our necks. We ran all over the City the day before shopping at the army/ navy surplus store and pawn shops for just the right look to be the counter-culture freelance Hendricks'. Call us Rod and Irene.

Kimmie handed all of us a plump white envelope, "This is from Peggy. She says, don't spend it all in one place."

We wished each other luck and walked off to different gates to board different planes where one, none, or all of us could get caught. Or we could sit in first class and drink champagne for 5 hours, eat gourmet airplane food, and listen to the artistic stylings of Ferranti and Teicher. We had no clue about what was in store for us, but we were willing to find out.

Chapter 34
Aloha and Mahalo

Rod and Irene Hendricks.... party of six...all arrived at the Kailua Airport within 30 minutes of each other.

Jeffery's friend Virginia and her cute young son Frankie pulled up in their VW Bus to pick us all up to take us to Waikiki. The first stop was the Hilton, where Pam and Larry were going to stay and lay all their envelope money down on some nice digs. I looked at Kimmie and said, "Let's get off here, too. It is right on the beach and looks quite nice, I must say."

"Peggy made reservations for us around the corner from Virginia's place, so we and the boys could be close to each other. It is supposed to be one block from the beach, and on a street which seemed great for an easy walk to anywhere on Kalakaua Boulevard," I nodded in agreement because beggars can't be choosers, and how bad could it be?

Virginia pulled up to the Koa Cottages, "Here you go, kids. The clubhouse is right around the corner. Just look for the VW in the driveway. Come on over after you get settled in." And they were gone.

Kimmie and I stared at the Koa Cottages. They seemed more like a dump. I decided that I would give Peggy a piece of my mind the first chance I got.

Kimmie walked up to the front desk and gave the clerk her name. He looked at her like he was trying to figure out whether she was a girl or a boy.

This often happened with Kimmie, and it was hard to tell who she really was because she either looked like a beautiful boy or a stunning girl, but in any case, a knockout.

"Do you prefer one double bed or two singles?"

Kimmie looked at me, "What do you want?"

Holy shitcakes! It never occurred to me that I was going to spend a boatload of time, day in and at night, with a lesbian. Not once did that cross my mind until now. I knew that there was absolutely no way that I was going to sleep with Kimmie, let alone SLEEP with Kimmie.

"Twin beds, please. I toss and turn all night!" There, that put an end to that little bit of business in my mind.

The cottage was a nice size with a kitchenette and a full bath. We could utilize some of our cooking skills to cut down on food expenses. When we opened the cupboards to see the pots, pans, dishes, and utensils that were available, cockroaches scurried out and ran all over the floor, up the walls, and under the beds. Kimmie ran out of the room to the motel office to change rooms. When she returned, she said, "Welcome to Hawaii!"

For the first several days, we all spent daylight hours on Queen's Beach. That was a real name that was taken literally by every gay person in Waikiki. The gang got very tan very fast and no longer looked like the pale and gaunt hippies we were when we arrived. We lived on teriyaki plates with two balls of white rice and shaved ice for lunch, and we would meet at Virginia's or "The Cottage" for dinner.

One night at Virginia's, one of the guys that lived there who was a waiter at the most exclusive restaurant in Waikiki, came home with a huge wooden crate. It was filled with Tasmanian lobsters. He put the box on the kitchen counter, "I stole this off the loading dock at Michele's after my shift. Kimmie and Jackie can take half to their Cottage, and we can keep the rest here. Come on, let's cook up some of these lobsters and feast!"

Days later, back at The Cottage, "Lobster again!" I groaned as I took a bite dipped in butter. We had eaten lobster every day for over a week in all forms: steamed, boiled, broiled, and fried. I was quite done and bored with the same meal. Suddenly, while in the middle of a bite, I looked at Kimmie and ran straight to the bathroom mirror. I was shocked to see red bumps on the corners of my mouth and on my face, just like the ones I just noticed on Kimmie's face.

"What the fuck are these sores on our faces?!" I screamed.

Kimmie came running, and we crowded in front of the medicine cabinet mirror in horror. We both had little red pustules popping out of our skin and rashes forming around our lips. They were starting to come out on our hands and fingers as well. What was happening to us?

We went to the Free Clinic the next day, sure that we were dying of leprosy. The hippie doctor took one look at us and said, "You both have a very bad staph infection! It is

292

in the air here on Oahu right now, and many people are coming down with it, but you two take the cake. What have you been eating? Certain foods make the infection worse."

We told the doctor the story about the lobsters, and he started laughing. "There is not one food on this earth that could have been worse for you to eat while this bacterium was incubating in your bloodstream." Not funny! Kimmie and I were given massive doses of antibiotics and sent home to the Cottage to heal. Kimmie decided she wanted to go back to San Francisco. After two weeks in Hawaii, she had eaten enough lobster, gotten enough sun, and could not see herself recovering in the roach-infested Koa Cottages. She called Peggy to tell her the news, and they had a verbal battle, the likes of which I had never heard.

Kimmie was screaming and throwing objects against the wall. She took all her belongings and stormed out the door, "I am paying the guy in the office for another month here for you. Sorry. I will see you back in San Francisco!" And she was gone.

The fact that the hippie doctor told me to stay out of the sun only made matters worse. Being holed up in cucarachaville made me burst out in tears. I was in grave misery without a drug in sight. Just as I was starting to convulse with sobs, there was a knock on the door. It was Michael.

"Kimmie stopped by Virginia's on her way to the airport and told us what was happening. What a bummer. You have to stay out of the sun, you know. I am going to get us tickets to fly to Kauai, and we can rent a car and live in the dry caves or at Taylor Camp until you get better. And when we get back, I will stay here with you until the rent is up. It is getting a little crowded at Virginia's. How does that sound to you?" Michael was my savior.

The two of us spent two weeks living out of a Toyota Corolla and sleeping in the back of a remote cave on the island with a few nights at Taylor Camp and a few nights in the car. We ate oatmeal and brown sugar every day because we only had one pot that we borrowed from the Cottage kitchen, we needed water anyway to stay hydrated, and oats were light and easy to carry around.

The only drawback was the frogs. There were frogs jumping in and out of everything, and they were squished all over the roads by cars that could not avoid them in any way. At night, Michael and I would walk barefoot, constantly feeling the ooze and gooze of frog guts between our toes. We had a wonderful time together, though, and really got to know each other and the things we each wanted out of life. We both knew one thing; we wanted to get back to Waikiki and get high. Back on Queen's Beach, fully healed Michael, Jeffery, and I worked on our tans by day and partied in the bars at night.

Every once in a while, I would call home and say hi to Mom and Dad. My cover story for being in Hawaii was that Jeffery won the tickets calling into KDIA Lucky 13 radio, and he asked me to come along. They thought that was a cock-in-bull story, but they liked Jeffery, so they let me go. I had saved up enough money from working at the Census Bureau to be able to take care of myself.

One day when we were sitting on a picnic table on the grass by the beach, we saw a friend from the Haight Ashbury. Richard used to come by Geary Street all the time to get loaded. He and his wife, Nicki, lived in an apartment behind the International Marketplace, and he invited all three of us to come over to smoke a joint, and Nicki would cook some dinner. That sounded great to us, so we headed over, walking up Kalakaua Boulevard. The Hare Krishna's were marching up the middle of the Boulevard singing, playing their finger cymbals, and I found the sound mesmerizing. I could see why some people would find that life inviting. We walked through a pretty seedy part of town, and I could see that the neighborhood was filled with gypsies. The hustle made me uncomfortable, and I made a note to myself to invite them to the Cottage next time.

We walked up the stairs to their apartment and entered a very nice setup. The furniture was new, and the house was impeccably clean. I liked Nicki already. I learned that Nicki was an accomplished con artist and that Richard lived off her scams. They were very much in love and had been married for years. In all the time we spent together on Geary Street, none of us knew about Richard's secret life in Hawaii.

Nicki cooked a gourmet dinner, and after that, Richard announced he was going to get the drugs. We expected him to come back with a bong and some Maui Wowie. He unrolled a satchel to display spoons and syringes and a large plastic bag of white heroin. "What you have here, folks, is China White. I get it from a guy who gets it from a guy who gets it from China. It is so pure; you can only do what you can put on the head of a match. You don't have to cook it because there are no impurities. Just squirt some water in the spoon and pull it up into the syringe. Far out, huh?" Richard looked down at the heroin with love in his eyes.

I was the first out of the box. "No, thanks, man. I am clean, and I am afraid that stuff would kill me if I shot some right now." Jeffery and Michael fell in line and said thanks, but no thanks as well. It was a banner move for all three of us, and it only took Nicki and Richard shooting the drugs in front of us and having a sublime look of bliss on their faces for Michael to feel the intense craving, "Just a little taste for me." Jeffery fell next, "Yeah, I'll have just a little too." And finally, I said, Richard, I only want half of what you gave them. I mean it, Man. I will fall out."

And it was done. We all sat for hours in the apartment, nodding and occasionally trying to strike a conversation. None of us made any sense, and it did not matter at all. Soon it was morning. The sun came up, and there was a knock on the door. Richard opened the door, and a really greasy guy stood in the doorway. He had far too many layers of clothing on to be in Hawaii, so that meant that he was really strung out and cold all the time. He had those tell-tale blemishes on his face that junkies get when they are half-conscious and start picking their skin coupled with the massive zit-producing candy bars that junkies live on.

"Hey man, what's happening? Come on in. Guys, this is Maurice. He is the guy that knows the guy I was telling you about. We had a good night here, man. Thanks!" You could tell Maurice was mad at Richard for calling out his name so loudly. You never do that in front of strangers, ever, especially if that guy is your connection. Bad move, Richard.

Maurice backed out of the doorway and said, "You have company. I'll see you around, man." Richard knew he blew it. He stared out at him as he disappeared down the street. It was time for the three musketeers to take our leave.

I told the boys that I was really disappointed in myself for shooting smack. I was proud of myself for staying clean in Hawaii, swimming in the ocean every day, getting healthy, and being one with nature. Now, I felt like a dirty dog with no self-control. They tried to talk me out of my feelings by telling me that I just slipped once, and it was no big deal. I don't ever have to do it again, and if I was going to slip, China White was at least worth the minor digression. I was sold for the moment.

It took a few beautiful beach days for me to feel better about myself. I could take a full breath again and was holding my head up…when I saw a familiar guy walking across the grass toward me. I nodded hello and acknowledged him. He nodded at me.

"What's your name?"

"Jackie."

"I'm Maurice."

"I know. I met you at Richard's."

"Where are you staying?"

"Koa Cottages," I was very worried about where this was going.

"Wanna get loaded over at the Koa Cottages, Jackie?" Maurice smiled warmly at me.

I looked out at the beach to see if Jeffery or Michael were watching over me. They were not; apparently, they were busy talking to two cute boys. I walked off with Maurice, and for two weeks, shot dope with him, sneaking around so the boys wouldn't know what I was doing until I could tell that I was becoming dependent again. I looked in the mirror, and even though I appeared tan and young and cute, the pupils in my hazel eyes were tinier than pinpoints. I was obviously a mess, and I needed to go home before something terrible happened. I had track marks on my arm, and all the sun in the world couldn't hide that.

I told Jeffery and Michael it was time for Irene Hendricks to go home. They wanted to tell me to stay, but they could see I needed to get off the island. They drove me to the airport in Virginia's VW and kissed me goodbye on the curb. Jeffery handed me the keys to his VW Bug and told me I could drive it while he was gone. He told me where it was parked and made me promise not to crash it into a tree. I appreciated the gesture and put on my best happy face so he would feel good about his generosity.

I enjoyed the first class service on my flight home, being grateful I was not stopped on the way to Hawaii or on the way home for flying with stolen tickets. I was just lucky that way.

Chapter 35
Recouping in the Chicken Coop

I decided not to go home from the airport. I went to a payphone by the baggage claim area and dialed Rip's number. I always went to Rip when I needed to re-enter reality and feel safe.

Rip answered and was really delighted to hear from me, "Hi, Kiddo! I was just thinking about you. I have an opportunity to go to Canada for a while, so I am going to go in about a week, and I didn't want to leave without saying goodbye."

My heart sank. I needed him so much in my life, and he was leaving. I faked excitement, "That is so outta sight, Rip! Are you leaving indefinitely? What about school? Are you dodging the draft? Tell me everything in detail!"

He laughed, "I am going to take a semester off and travel all over Canada and end up at Ruth's for a while. She just moved up there and said it was really happening, and I need to get the draft off my mind. The gang asked me to tell you to come up and stay in my room while I am gone and get some fresh air and communal living. Do you want to?"

I looked up to God and whispered, "Thank you." Then I continued, "Um, I just stepped off the plane from Hawaii, and I have Jeffrey's car. Can I just drive up right now, and then I will see you before you take off?" I didn't wait for a response. I told him I would be there in two hours and said a few other sweet things that I meant, slammed down the payphone and headed for the spot where the car was parked. I was off again.

I figured it would take me two hours to get over the Golden Gate Bridge and up the 101 Freeway to Penngrove. That also took into consideration my brief 5-minute detour to Mop's house in San Francisco to get just a little something to take the edge off.

There were to be no other stops because Rip was losing patience with my drug abuse, and he would be mad at me if I made it obvious that my drugs were more important than seeing him. When I drove to the farmhouse on Old Adobe Road, it was clear that it was party time.

All the lights in the house and in the chicken coop were on, and you could hear music blaring from the field behind the barn. I left everything in the car because I was too excited to bother with my stuff when there was fun to be had. I ran down to the sounds of drums and guitars and clinking bottles and other homemade instruments. I spotted Rip, and we collided with each other in a huge hug and kiss.

"Hey, what's happening? You got here fast! You look so tan and cute. Did you have a fun time?"

I felt safe again, "Yeah, I just needed to see you." There was so much more to say, but I choked up and grabbed his hand and pulled him to an empty space in the big circle of hippy freaks as the joint was passed our way. We got totally stoned, and all the roommates came up to greet me.

I felt loved, as if I belonged there, and believed that this was going to be a good move for me even if Rip would be gone. We partied into the wee hours, and one by one, people peeled off to their spaces on the land. The Penngrove Farm was built by Russian farmers. The main house had a huge kitchen with an old O'Keefe & Merritt gas stove, wrap-around tile counter space, two big refrigerators, an industrial juicer, and a walk-in pantry with barrels of flour and brown rice. There was every staple necessary to cook, bake, and feed a hungry hippie household. Off the kitchen was a large dining room with a big oak table that must have been twelve feet long.

There were two bedrooms and a bathroom in the house. Vulch (Michael) and Ray each had a room, and the big service porch in the back was converted into Larry's room. Down the path, behind the house, between the barn and the massive vegetable garden, was a long chicken coup.

Right in the middle of the wooden coop was a heavy wooden door on a track. Inside, the raised floors were built of thick weathered wooden planks, and the walls were made of old cedar wood slats. To the right of the center was a skinny hallway leading to the bathroom, and beyond that was Art's room.

The space was huge, like a loft where Art created his oil painting masterpieces. He was a brilliant painter, influenced by Gustav Klimt meets Andy Warhol. I could smell the oil paints, linseed, and turpentine mixed with incense and marijuana. It would turn out to be one of my favorite aromatic hideouts. On the other side of the big door was Rip's room. It was the perfect size with a big comfortable bed, oak dressers, an overstuffed easy chair, a room heater that looked like a fireplace, and nooks and crannies everywhere. Every inch of the room reflected Rip's personality. I could see myself being very cozy and comfortable in that space, and I let out a giggle.

On the other side of that room was another bedroom where Harvey lived. And behind his room was a wood-fired sauna that could easily fit twenty people. Rip told me about the sauna that the farmers built but, I could never have imagined what it actually looked like. Big hot rocks sat in the middle of the floor surrounded by double-decker wooden benches that were polished and smooth from use.

Over the barn (garage), just off the road, was an unfinished loft, and that is where Rocky (Mike) lived. He would sit out the loft windows with his legs dangling down for hours studying and heckling anyone who went by. And, to the left of the barn was a homemade teepee where Klamath (Steve) lived. He would sit in the opening of his tent in a lotus position with his eyes sealed shut, doing fire breathing. He wore his tee shirt as pants, tied at the waist with a rope. The neck hole was wide open, exposing what I believed was the tiniest thimble of a penis I had ever seen on a grown man. Now, I was not a penis aficionado, but I was fascinated with that little thing and made a note to self to see if it worked one day after Rip was gone. I was not big on nicknames, so I had to really work to remember what these guys wanted to be called. It did not go unnoticed by me that I would be the only official woman living at Penngrove amongst a minimum of 7 men at any given time. My curiosity was peaked as to how that was going to play out.

I helped Rip pack all the stuff that he felt he would need for his adventure. Having traveled that road together and, from what I knew of my best friend Rip, I piled up the dental floss, nail clippers and emery boards, lotions and hair products, neatly folded boxer shorts, blinding white tube socks, and pristine tee shirts.

The wine was flowing, the joints were fired up, and everyone was having a great time. Rip felt really special, and that made me happy.

Art came around from behind the chicken coop stark naked and screamed, "The rocks are hot! Let's get sweaty!" I saw people rip their clothes off right where they stood and then ran to the sauna with joints and wine in their hands. I looked over at Rip, a bit stunned. I had never seen or been in group nakedness before, and I felt painfully awkward. Rip shrugged his shoulders, stripped, and ran off to join the others.

I walked to the sauna and heard singing and chanting. People were tapping on bottles to some kind of rhythm and stomping a beat on the floor. Billows of steam puffed out of vents in the wall. I took off my clothes and folded them neatly on a bench by the door. I yanked open the door and jumped inside. I could not see an inch in front of me for the steam, and the heat was so intense, I could barely breathe. I felt my way to a space on a bench, touching various people's body parts along the way. There, I was in.

The steam would subside for a little bit, and everyone could see each other in the room, but by then, it didn't matter to me. Everyone else seemed so natural, including Rip. I had to chill out in that heat and get over it. Art threw more water on the rocks, and the steam filled the room again. I smiled. I knew something. I knew that I was ringing in the Year of the Cock. I was developing a fascination and had no idea where it would take me. Rocky had the longest penis I had ever seen. It hung to his kneecap—m*ore research when Rip leaves.*

Rip left the next day, and I stayed in bed sleeping off the party and getting the hard drugs out of my system. I was trying to recover from the hangover. Every once in a while, one of the guys would knock on the door to see if I was okay. I would yell out that I was groovy and just a little under the weather. I wanted to start my time in Penngrove, clear-headed and able to engage with everyone, so I tried to sluff off the drug stupor and be positive and present.

When I finally emerged, I was bright-eyed, freshly showered, and ready to find my way with the guys. I walked into the kitchen, and it was bustling. The guys had gone to Bodega Bay and brought back some big Dungeness crabs and freshly baked French bread. They were spreading newspapers on the table to start cracking the shells and separating the meat.

I saw a bucket of freshly picked blackberries on the counter, "Whose berries are these?"

"They are ours! Do you want to make something out of them?"

I yelled, "Yes! I am going to make pies for dessert." I washed the berries and added some honey and flour to them to macerate. I measured flour and salt, pulled the butter out of the fridge, and cut it into the mixture. I added water, and bam! I had my crusts rolled and formed in the pans. I filled the crusts with berry filling.

The pies went in the oven, and I started making a Crab Louie Dressing that I remembered from the Fisherman's Grotto Number 9 restaurant on Fisherman's Wharf in San Francisco. The guys were a little stunned at my whirling around the kitchen and quiet as it was kept, so was I. It occurred to me that I knew what I liked and was able to make it happen in the hopes that they would like it too. It seemed like a win-win to me, and in fact, it was.

The Louie dressing was just what the crab needed, and everyone loved how delectable the taste was. When the pies came out and cooled, they looked and smelled perfect. I was sated with a delicious dinner, filled with good feelings, and I actually felt happy.

Chapter 36
My True Debut

The free love generation was full of girls like me; we pretended to like the orgies and the "zipless fucks" because everyone seemed to be doing it and liking it. If you didn't, you would be mocked, called a frigid cock teaser, or just banished from the tribe. The free clinic was a revolving door of hippies with sexually transmitted diseases. Many of the chicks were having to get abortions, and those who had babies seemed to allow anyone and everyone to share in the raising of their children. That was just not a part of the deep values that still ruled my behavior and self-judgment.

I did not know if it was the fresh country air, some very attractive specimens of men with wafting pheromones at the commune, or my true time to experience my sexual debut, but I was now a willing participant and initiating interest and making my own moves. I also realized that the drugs that people were using there were much more conducive to physical expression, whereas my heroin was a retreat where I had no desire to connect with anyone but myself, so much like the solitude of my closets. I soon discovered that the guys at Penngrove were raised in families just like mine. They did not promote group sex, and they were respectful of the women and me that they dated and brought over for dinner and playtime. They did not kiss and tell, and their private rooms stayed private at night. The only outlier was Klamath. It seemed that inappropriate behavior was in his nature; his emotions would get out of control, and he would act out in disturbing ways.

After Rip left, Klamath started showing up around me a lot. He would also volunteer and help me pick berries by the railroad tracks. He tried to teach me how to meditate and perform his fire breathing ritual. He asked me to help him tend to the vegetable garden. He asked me what Rip and I had going on between us and if we were in a monogamous relationship.

I didn't know how to answer that question. Rip was still a virgin, but the Penngrove gang clearly didn't have a clue about that, and I was not about to let that kitty out of the bag.

"Rip and I have an agreement that when we are apart, we can do what we feel as long as we are mindful and do not discuss it with each other. That seems to work for both of us".

When I really thought about it, that was actually the truth. Rip does nothing, and what I do, I keep to myself. I made a note to self, *let Rip know about our arrangement so that he does not get blindsided when he comes home.*

Klamath went to my room that night, and some tender kissing led to "the deed." His thimble doubled in size to about the length and girth of my pinkie finger. He entered, made some frisky pumps kind of like his fire breathing, and it was over.

The next day, Klamath, the Conquering Hero, asked me to go to Oregon to camp on the river with him and his gypsy friends. He said we would be back near the beginning of June. That was three months in the northwest rain and snow.

"Thanks for the invite, but I need to stay here." He looked stricken as if I had just used him as my sex toy.

He turned on his heels and stormed out of the chicken coop, and the next day he packed up his teepee and set out in his old yellow pick-up truck for the Klamath River to hang with the gypsies.

Life on "the farm" in Penngrove was, for the most part, exciting and easy all at the same time. People dropped by to study or to smoke a joint and talk politics. We gathered at night to take a sauna, and every weekend was a full-tilt boogie of a party.

When things got too much or too little, I hopped into Jeffery's VW and drove down to The City to see Peggy, the Geary Street gang, Mop, or all of them. When my laundry piled up, I popped down to my mom and dad's house, sometimes still known as home, to spend a few days to regroup and feel the love. I had no idea how detached I had become. In my full world of people, places, and adventures, I was almost totally disconnected.

On a trip home, I made a visit to the dentist only to discover that I needed to have my wisdom teeth pulled. I decided to run up to The City to get some drugs and say hi to Peggy first. Peggy ran out of her office and gave me a big hug and a kiss, "Where have you been, you little rascal? I am honored that you have decided to squeeze me into your busy schedule."

We talked for hours in the back room. Peggy filled me in on Janis and all their antics together, and I told Peggy about the farm and the little thimble. I realized that it was the first time Peggy had ever seemed interested in what I thought and was planning to do. As a matter of fact, I had never told Peggy any of my personal stories before, and Peggy seemed riveted and asked me to tell her more.

"So then, this guy named Rocky knocked on my door one night after a sauna," I continued. "He was the most endowed dude I have ever seen. I agreed to have sex with him. I wanted to have sex with him, but I could not imagine taking him all in without an exit port on the top of my skull. He told me not to worry and that he has done this before, and he knows how to be careful. We laughed, and I said okay, but I don't want to look. Keep the lights out. It turned out to be quite nice and…"

I looked at Peggy, and her eyes were glazed at half-mast. She had a very scary seductive look on her face, and my gut flipped.

"Listen, Peggy, it's late, and I have to get home. I am having my wisdom teeth pulled in the morning, and I need to get some sleep."

"Nah, ah. You are going to stay here tonight, and you can leave first thing in the morning. You knew that this was going to happen eventually, didn't you Dahlin'? Don't be scared...I will be gentle with you just like that Bobcat was only better, much better. We'll get loaded first... you'll be fine, Dahlin'. Just fine."

I was curious, and I felt love for Peggy, but I didn't want to get recruited! Nevertheless, we got loaded, and, for the moment, my fear melted into a puddle.

Peggy walked me up the stairs to the loft. She took off my clothes and massaged me with body oil that smelled like jasmine. I decided to close my eyes until it was over. She handed me a lit cigarette and told me to smoke it if I was nervous. I took a drag and then another drag.

Peggy nibbled on my inner thigh, and I started to react and move. Peggy lit another cigarette and handed it to me and said, "Don't move!"

Oh, for the love of God! I have a lit cigarette in my right hand and a lit cigarette in my left hand on a mattress in a loft that could go up in flames at any second while Peggy has moved to my lady bits, and I am not supposed to move?!

And when it was over, Peggy smiled sweetly and looked right into my eyes and said, "That wasn't so bad, was it, Dahlin'? I have wanted to do that for a long time."

I looked at Peggy and smiled, "Listen, thank you for that. It was epic and very unexpected, but I gotta run." I threw on my clothes over layers of jasmine oil, slid down the loft stairs, and ran out the door.

I reached my home just in time to go to the dentist. Mom asked, "Where were you, Sweetheart? I was worried you would not make it home in time."

"I wouldn't miss this for the world!" I laughed.

When I came out of the heavy sedation after my teeth were pulled, the dental staff were laughing hysterically. I propped myself up on my elbows and garbled out through gauze and cotton, "What did I say?"

"Never you mind, young lady! It's just a good thing your mom was not in the room!"

Peggy Caserta...member of the Hippie Elite

Chapter 37
Nice Face

Dad would not stop teasing me because my wisdom teeth extraction left me looking like a chipmunk storing nuts in my cheeks. He kept saying, "Nice face," and it was getting on my last nerves. I was down to one pain pill a day, and I hated being teased, badgered, or baited.

"Hey, little squirrel, have you seen my daughter? Never mind, don't talk with your mouth full. Ha Ha. That's a face only a mother could love. Did you at least get one good punch in?" Dad was pulling out all the stops.

Rip called to see how I was, and I pleaded, "Please, get me out of here, Rip. I'll be your best friend. I must leave this place before I go insane. You have to help me!"

He told me to get some clothes together, he'll grab Kevin and his new girlfriend, and we could all go camping for the weekend on the Russian River.

When we got to Penngrove, we asked everyone if they wanted to go camping, and nobody wanted to take us up on our offer.

"Looks like rain, and I have to go down to my parents' house on Sunday for Father's Day," Rocky said. He was a good son, and we all felt like ingrates because we totally forgot about Father's Day.

Rip decided for all of us that we would go as planned and deal with the feedback later. So, we drove to the river, singing to the radio at the top of our lungs and smoking pot. We found a primo site right on a cliff above the water and set up tents, and put a pot of coffee on the campfire. I got food ready to cook dinner while we still had a little bit of daylight left. Hamburger sizzled in the big iron skillet, and when I added the onions, everyone came to the campfire to watch me create my masterpiece gourmet goulash.

I poured the tomato sauce into the meat, added a can of corn and some rice, and let it simmer while we continued smoking dope. We all grew hungrier by the second. Rip took a taste every couple of minutes to test to see if the rice was cooked. When it was ready, he proclaimed, "Dinner is ready! Get it while it's hot!"

Soon, thunder clapped, and rain poured down on us in buckets. We grabbed our plates and ran into the tents.

We laid in our tents, listening to the rain for a very long time. Water started to seep in, and our sleeping bags were getting soaked. We suffered until the first light, then gathered up all the soggy bedding and the tents and stuffed them into the trunk. We hippie chicks went down to the river to wash the skillet, utensils, and plates. It was still drizzling, and we were wet and cold to the bone. We looked at each other, and without saying one word, tossed everything into the river and ran back to the car.

At Penngrove, the place seemed deserted. We got into dry clothes and were sitting in the chicken coop, trying to decide if we were going to drive home for Father's Day or just call home later to talk to our dads.

"I really want to go home, you guys," I said. I felt guilty that I forgot about Father's Day in the first place and could not even imagine just calling my father later like he was an afterthought. And even though he was teasing me and drove me out of the house, I adored him and would just have to tolerate his sense of humor.

Then Amanda, one of the gypsy girls, knocked on the door and walked in. "Hey," she said to me. "There are two policemen up at the house looking for you. Are you coming up or what?"

I wondered if they came to arrest me for drugs or something. I paused a minute and then told Amanda to go up and tell them that I went camping for the weekend at the Russian River, and I told Amanda to ask what they wanted. Amanda walked out to do the deed.

She came back five minutes later and sat down next to me, "Your father died, and you need to go home right away. Your mother has been calling everywhere, trying to find you. I am so sorry, Jackie."

I stopped breathing and crumpled to the floor, shocked and paralyzed. Rip picked me up and ran me to his car.

I moaned all the way home. My eyes were wet, but I was not sobbing. I was groaning and whimpering like a wounded animal. I could not talk, so Rip did not even try to communicate with me. I was overwhelmed with grief. More so, I was stricken with guilt. A guilt that would haunt me for the rest of my life. I forgot about Father's Day. I was a selfish and thoughtless little bitch. I would never get to see him again. I would never get to tell him how much I loved and admired him. I would never get to apologize for all the horrible things that I did and all the horrible things that I thought. He would never see me get my pathetic life together and see me make something of myself. I was a miserable failure to him as the last awareness he had of me. I did not get to say goodbye to him one last time. I broke into a million pieces that day, incapable of letting myself off the hook.

I walked into my family home to the sound of my mom wailing in anguish. She saw me and ran to me and held me with the little strength she had left in her body. I walked her back to the couch and just held her while she sobbed in my arms. Marilyn sat down beside us, and we wrapped around each other for dear life. What were we going to do without our dad? How could any of us imagine our life without him? How could we even think of a life without him?

ACT 3
Chapter 38
Who Was Mel Mendelson?

I only saw one picture of my grandfather. He was standing with his hand on my father's shoulder while holding baby Stanley, my uncle, in his arms. I was drawn to his features and knew why my father was so handsome.

"Dad, please tell me something about my grandfather. I never got to meet him," I would coax. Every time I asked my father about him, though, there would be a sense of disconnected energy. The feel in the room would shift. Though the change registered on me, I never knew the reason behind it at the time.

It was decades later, when I was sitting on my Uncle Stan's hospital bed as he was actively dying, that I finally heard the truth about my grandfather Mannie and grandmother Hazel. Finally, learning the secrets of the family showed me how the pieces of such a puzzling family fit together. As it turns out, the same was true of the Siegel family on my mother's side.

Uncle Stan started, "Mannie was never home except for the occasional Sunday, and your father and I called him 'The Sperm Donor.' One day when your dad was 17 and a sophomore in high school, The Sperm Donor just dropped dead on Market Street in front of his store. He was 40 years old and had a massive heart attack, and that was the end of that.

"There he was, dressed to the nines, just got off the ferry where he would go gambling at lunchtime, perfectly pressed and as stiff as a board. He had nothing but a pair of dice in his waistcoat pocket and a small wad of dollar bills in his slacks."

I got that detached feeling again and felt the energy shift, just like I remembered with my father as clearly as if it were yesterday.

"In a chance meeting 30 years after your grandfather dropped dead, your dad met a guy at a business lunch that recognized his last name and asked if he knew Mannie Mendelson. Your dad said that yes, he was his father. The guy said that he worked with him years ago and that he was the most successful salesman he had ever met. He said that he assumed that we were left financially secure," Uncle

Stan recalled. Looking at me, my uncle continued, "Your dad proudly said that our father came home every Friday night with fifty dollars to support the family, and that was a lot of money back in those days! The man gasped and said, 'Fifty dollars? I saw his paycheck, and he made one hundred and fifty dollars every Friday!' Your dad thought this man must have been mistaken because we were left penniless and had to move in with relatives."

There was a long pause.

Uncle Stan started to cry uncontrollably, and I got very scared of what was about to come next. "Your grandfather had two families that he was supporting. Just blocks away, he had a mistress and another son that was the same age as me. We played together in school. We were in the same clubs, and I was in his wedding party, for God's sake!" he sobbed. "And if that's not horrible enough, he named his illegitimate son the exact same name as your dad.... Mel!"

I was left speechless. In that instant, so many things that had made no sense to me before began to fall into place. I knew that secret was only one tiny piece of the patchwork, however. All I could think about was how little I knew about the people I most loved all of my life

"Mannie gave your Nana Hazel fifty dollars every Friday and the mistress fifty dollars and the fifty dollars that were left he spent on the ferry drinking gin and gambling," Uncle Stan's voice came to me, as though he was talking inside a tunnel. My visit with Uncle Stan ended for the day, and I slogged out of the room. My head was spinning with thoughts of my dad and what a hard hand he was dealt with growing up.

My father was older than everyone else in his class. His mother was so lonely when he was a child that she kept him home to be her companion until the school board forced her to let him enter school. He was an extraordinary athlete, and, in his junior year, he was recruited to go away to training camp with the New York Yankees for the summer. He was sure to be picked up for his incredible catching and batting record.

Mel was tall and handsome with a great sense of humor. He was stalked by all the Jewish girls within a 20-mile radius. He was living the perfect teenage life until the day The Sperm Donor dropped dead. My father had to quit school and take care of the family. He never made it to training camp, and his dream of becoming a professional athlete was over before it even began. His life now revolved around keeping his brother Stan safe and tending to his mother and her strong will and frail disposition (also known as alcoholism). He supported the household by working for a tannery selling hides.

Uncle Stan also told me about Nana, my dad's mom, Hazel Laurence, who tormented me as a child. She was a third-generation San Franciscan, the daughter of a very successful businessman and an only child. When Hazel was 7, both her parents died in the 1906 San Francisco Earthquake.

She was taken in by a cousin and his family. Security felt precarious like a house of cards to Hazel; she barely knew the cousin she had to live with after her parents' death. Everyone was anxious all the time after the quake, so there was no one there capable of consoling little Hazel on her loss.

One day, as Hazel was walking home from school, she saw her new family driving away from the house with all their belongings loaded up in the cars. "Wait!" she shrieked at the top of her lungs. "Wait for me! Don't leave me.....please!" she screamed with all her might. There she stood, in the middle of Clay Street with just her pinafore, button-up shoes, and her book bag. She ran up the steps and tried to open the front door, but it was locked. Hazel ran back to school and found her teacher. She told her teacher that her family had abandoned her; however, in Hazel's mind, they were no family to her at all if they could leave her behind the way they had. They were worse than strangers to her. Her heart sank as she realized that she was made an orphan twice.

Hazel's teacher knew her deceased father by reputation and contacted James Hackett, his business partner, who had survived the earthquake. The Hackett's agreed to take little Hazel in that very day. They adopted her and took care of her basic needs but did not treat her as an actual member of their family. They were not Jewish, so she also lost her spiritual beliefs along with her bloodline.

She had a life much like Cinderella. She was privileged yet lived on the periphery. Though she was taken care of financially, she was emotionally starved. Hazel excelled in her classes in high school. Her academic accomplishments gave her a sense of personal pride, but really, the only enjoyment she had was when she, her best friend Clare, and their high school gang all met up at the Jewish Community Center and danced the night away. This was especially important to Hazel because she was able to re-connect to her Jewish roots and where she felt like she belonged.

One night, right before the last dance, Hazel looked across the room and literally lost her breath! "Who is that fellow standing over there?" she asked Clare. Clare said, "That is Mannie Mendelson. He is the most eligible guy in the City, but he won't give us high school girls the time of day."

At that very moment, Mannie walked up to Hazel and asked her if he could have the last dance of the evening with her. That ignited their whirlwind romance. It led to their eventual elopement against the strong objections of her adopted parents because Mannie was a 'Jew Boy.' They disowned Hazel, and she never saw or heard from that family again.

Mannie and Hazel had Mel soon after they were married. Ten years later, Stanley was born. They lived in a typical San Francisco duplex flat that they shared with Mannie's relatives. The Mendelson family lived in one flat, and Mannie's sister Elsie was in the flat on the other side.

Next door was Elsie's son, Milton, and around the corner was Mannie's other sister Maxine. They had Sabbath dinner together, but instead of saying the blessing over the wine, they said the blessing over the gin.

Pat and all her gang were at a dance at the Jewish Community Center when she looked across the room and saw Mel Mendelson. She turned to her best friend Marion and said, "I don't know who that fella is standing by that column, but I am telling you right now that I am going to marry him!"

And that did happen. Pat and Mel had a large wedding. Family came from all around to celebrate Bertha and Jacob's great fortune to see their youngest child get married to such a fine young man. The Mendelson family couldn't have been happier for Mel because it was clear that Pat adored him. The couple glowed with happiness. Mel could not wait to carry Pat over the threshold of their new home. Pat was excited about leaving her family home for the first time in her life. She couldn't wait to be with the man she loved.

Pat and Mel's wedding day

Chapter 39
And Who Was Pat?

I never met my grandpa Jacob, but when I would look at his picture, I could feel the generations of warmth and love he passed on to my huge family on my mother's side. He came from a small village in Romania, which was a Jewish enclave where everyone was either related or about to be related to each other. Jacob was a typical young village boy and was a baker by trade who had his eye on Bertha Bauman for many reasons. She was beautiful in his eyes and, as the oldest of six children, and kept a tight but loving rein on her siblings.

The Bauman family owned a small dry goods store where Bertha worked in the afternoons. Isaac, her father, came out from behind a curtain that sectioned off a small office at the back of the store to tell Bertha that Jacob came in him to ask for her hand in marriage.

"What did you say, Poppa?" she whispered. "I asked him if he loved you, if he wanted a big family and if he kept kosher," he said. "Jacob said that he had loved you from the moment that he first saw you. He said that the size of your family is God's will, so he has learned to work very hard to be a good provider. So, after he told me that he keeps kosher and that he observes the Sabbath, I now love this Jacob, and so if you love this Jacob, you have my blessing!"

Bertha and Jacob got married. They were blessed with one boy (Joe) and four girls (Sarah, Betty, Bessie, and Ruthie) in what seemed like no time at all.

One night, the extended family had gathered for Sabbath dinner. The men left the table and went outside to talk. There was word of a pogrom coming down from the north, and Jacob wanted to make a better life for his family while he could. He told the men that he wanted to go to America and settle there.

If any of them wanted to join him, he welcomed the company. He had also picked out a place in the US: Sioux City, Iowa. His cousin Benny had immigrated there and now had his own tailor shop and was earning a very good living. They strategized that the men would work and save up for a year, and then their wives and children would book passage to America and join them in Sioux City, Iowa.

That evening, the children were in bed when they heard screaming and the sound of horses galloping up and down the road. They could smell smoke. Jacob ran into the sleeping room and yelled for everyone to go out the back door and run into the barn because the Cossacks were coming! They ran as fast as they could into the cold, dark barn and dove under the straw. No one said a word as they heard men running and horses getting closer and voices yelling and wolves howling.

They could smell the terror in the air as the barn door latch shook. The family heard a muffled cry from somewhere in the straw and then silence. It was pitch black inside, and they were all shaking from the cold and fear when they heard, "Get back to the center of town. These wolves are attacking us from everywhere, so we will regroup and head south."

Jacob came to the barn and called for his family to come out. They were safe for the moment. The straw rustled, and one by one, figures emerged from the haystacks, all except for Sarah. They heard a whimper and a moan. Jacob ran toward the sound to find little Sarah's eyes staring out from the straw. He reached in and grabbed her, and Betty pointed to Sarah's leg, which was torn open. A wolf had gotten into the barn, found Sarah, and when she moved, bit her leg, and ran away. She was so afraid that the soldiers would find them that she held her breath and bit down on her scarf so she wouldn't make a sound. Sarah Siegel, without knowing, had saved her family from a terrible fate.

Jacob and a few of his cousins went to the center of the village to say goodbye to everyone they had grown up with and lived with for their entire lives. Eli stayed behind to protect the wives and children and would come to America and start a new life with them as well. The minute he arrived in America, Jacob drummed up an opportunity to start baking.

He had managed to open his own bakery in no time. Jacob saved every dime he possibly could for his family's passage to come over. He bought a modest home, found a synagogue, and discovered which schools the children would be attending – all while using a mixture of Yiddish, Romanian and broken English.

Exactly one year after Jacob left, the family climbed the gangplank of the ship and was led to steerage. Bertha got a long rope, and she tied every one of the children to her waist except for baby Ruthie. She kept that baby securely in her arms through the entire voyage to Ellis Island. The voyage was not easy by any means, but once they set foot on American soil, they vowed to never speak of the hardships that they faced when they were apart.

Who knew that there would be such a Jewish enclave in the middle of America? It seemed that the Siegel family, the Bauman tribe, and all the cousins made up a large portion of the Sioux City population. Once settled in, Bertha gave birth to Sammy, the first child born in America.

Seasons changed, years passed, and the children grew. Sarah married Seymour, and they opened a huge department store in Savannah, Georgia. Betty went to San Francisco to be a buyer at a very exclusive department store. Ruthie and Bessie were still finishing school and living at home. Joe married Mary Barnes, and they stayed in Iowa to start a family. Meanwhile, Bertha was not feeling well, so the doctor made a house call.

Ella (Pat) was born in Sioux City, Iowa, to Bertha and Jacob Siegel, who immigrated to America from Romania. The story goes that her feet did not touch the ground until she started school. All her older siblings in the house took care of her and carried her around like she was their baby doll. Clothing from her older sisters Sarah and Betty were shipped to her regularly and in quantities that Ella could never wear in one lifetime. She was smart, adorable, and talented – and she knew it. She was an avid tap dancer, played the drums, and had way too much energy for Bertha and Jacob to keep up with.

Ella was a good girl. She was respectful of her parents, her brothers and sisters, and the rest of her family. But was she spoiled! Ella hated her name because she got teased a lot for it. She had her father's ears, and all the kids got immense pleasure from calling her 'Elephant.' She decided to change her name to 'Pat.' That sounded like a modern name to her, so every time someone called her Ella, she threw a fit and would not respond until they all learned to address her as Pat.

Later, she also legally changed her name to Pat. I had heard every detail of the Siegel and Bauman family experiences in Romania and the arduous immigration to America. Every family member, living and dead, had told the stories to me in their unique way, and I never got tired of hearing them all. Interestingly enough, the stories remained amazingly accurate and consistent no matter who the storyteller was...except for one story, and that was about how they all ended up in San Francisco. Again, it would be decades later that the truth about this particular story came out. I really felt for my mother when the truth was revealed because all our cousins were talking about it and tried to ask her questions because she was the last living descendant who knew the real story.

Mom had made a pact with her immediate family that she would never discuss the truth. She did not care if they went to the library and got all the sordid details on their own – she would never talk to a living soul about it, and she didn't, and that was that. So, the story goes that Joe Siegel (her oldest brother) and his wife Mary owned the most popular nightclub in all the surrounding states.

It was "the" place to be seen, and all the elected political officials, from the governors to the mayors, made many of their backroom deals there. One night, at about closing time, a patron was drunk and started paying too much attention to Mary. Joe kindly asked the customer to leave his wife alone, finish his drink, and go home. The man refused to leave. More than that, he tried to put his hands on Mary. So, Joe pushed him out of the door and onto the street. Joe and Mary were closing up, and Joe had the bank deposit in a bag and his gun in his belt. All of a sudden, the man flew back in the front door and lunged after Mary. Joe shot him dead on the floor.

There was a trial, and Joe was found guilty of involuntary manslaughter. He went to jail, and shortly thereafter, the governor commuted his sentence. They were not going to let Joe stay in jail, but he did lose his license to run a nightclub. Sometime during all this upheaval, the Siegels decided to move to California to join other relatives that had already gone west.

They did not want Joe to think they were abandoning him because they would never do such a thing. So, with Joe's blessing, Jacob, Bertha, and Pat packed up and moved to San Francisco. Once there, they opened a grocery store on McAllister Street. Pat started middle school and began to make some wonderful friends with whom she went all the way through high school. Most of them ever knew her given name was Ella. In a perfect genetic déjà vu moment, Pat and all her gang were at a dance at the Jewish

Community Center when she looked across the room and saw Mel Mendelson. She turned to her best friend Marion and said, "I don't know who that fella is standing by that column, but I am telling you right now that I am going to marry him!"

And that did happen. Pat and Mel had a large wedding, and family came from all around to celebrate Bertha and Jacob's great fortune to see their youngest child get married to such a fine young man. The Mendelson family couldn't have been happier for Mel because it was clear that Pat adored him. Mel could not wait to carry Pat over the threshold of their new home.

Pat was excited about leaving her family home for the first time in her life. Soon after the wedding, war broke out in the Pacific. Mel joined the Navy. Jacob and Bertha asked Pat to move in with them while Mel was in the service, but she declined and said, "I need to stay in our house and keep the home fires burning."

The streetcar that Pat took to get to work went right by her mother and father's house, so, in the morning, her father Jacob would jump in the car and give Pat a lovely kosher lunch. On the way back home, Jacob would jump on the streetcar and give Pat a nice hot kosher dinner. Things continued in this manner until Mel came home. During the time he was away, there was never a moment when Pat did not feel loved and cared for in the way of the Siegel tradition – with good food that kept on coming!

Not long after Mel came home from the Navy, Jacob Siegel passed away. Pat took the loss of her father very hard. For the longest time, every day, when she took the streetcar to work, she would expect him to hop on with a container of food. Eventually, she chose to believe that he was still hopping on at the stop; only he was now feeding her soul instead of her body. That is how she healed her broken heart.

The "soon to be" Pat Mendelson

Chapter 40
There Were No Words

The family started coming into town from all over the United States when the news got out that Mel Mendelson had passed away at the age of 51. My aunts and uncles coordinated the funeral arrangements in gatherings, which took place in the rarely used living room.

Mom sat on the couch as family members and close lifelong friends entered the room silently, trying to guess anything she may need that they could provide for her. They saw the vacant far off look of a mortally wounded wife. We mostly sat in silence until someone would talk about the kind, righteous man my father was. Mom remained inconsolable. She rocked in her loved one's arms.

The suit was selected for Dad's burial. The obituary was written and sent to all the local papers. Mount Sinai Memorial Chapel prepared for the service to be held within 48 hours of Dad's death, just as Mom wanted and just as Dad would have wanted. The chapel had flowers coming in, and the guest book was being prepared. Every Jewish tradition was being respected in homage to a righteous man.

But there was one problem.

The gravedigger's union was on strike, which affected the entire San Francisco Bay Area. No graves were being dug for the deceased. No gravesite ceremonies could be held. There would be no funerals. Every departed soul would be held in cold storage throughout the state of California until the gravediggers got their 5 cent raises, or their extra day of sick time, or their desired dental plan. Nobody would be buried at Eternal Rest Cemetery until the strike was over.

This was as abhorrent a situation as could have ever been imagined in the Jewish tradition. This was a Shonda. How could this be? I lost my mind over this injustice. My wrath took over my guilt ten-fold, and I embraced that searing ire with everything in me. I was determined to put a stop to that nonsense no matter the cost. I grabbed my father's car keys from the counter and looked at Rip with an intensity that scared him to death.

"I am going to the cemetery to fix this sick shit right now. You can come with me or stay here. Your choice! But I am out of here!" Rip ran out to the garage behind me.

I threw a shovel in the trunk of the car and peeled out of the garage, almost running over my Auntie Marion carrying a kugel. I cleared the driveway by the skin of my teeth.

I pulled up to the entrance of the cemetery to see a parade of grave diggers marching with picket signs. I rolled down my window and said, "Excuse me. I have to get up to the office." Not one picketer moved aside. "Get out of my way so I can drive in there, or I swear I will run over all of you pieces of shit. Move your fucking asses, right now!" I pulled the car right up to within one inch of the line of men until they parted a way for me to get in.

I popped open the trunk and pulled out the shovel.

"What are you going to do I?" Rip said. "This is hallowed ground here. These people that run the cemetery are not your enemies. Please think about this, Jackie. No good can come of what you are planning to do."

I walked into the office and asked to speak to the cemetery director. I was ushered into an office to see a startled man in a black suit sitting behind a mahogany desk.

"May I help you, miss?"

"Yes, my name is Jackie Mendelson. My father passed away yesterday, and we are having his memorial service the day after tomorrow at Sinai Memorial Chapel. After the service, we will be having a graveside burial in the plot that my parents purchased from this cemetery. As you know, being the caretaker of a Jewish cemetery, it is unacceptable to wait to bury our dead. I am here to dig my father's grave if you will please show me where the plot is that *we own*." I leaned on my shovel and waited for his response.

"I am pleased to meet you, Jackie. My name is Mr. Shapiro. First, let me say that I am sorry for your loss. May your father's memory be a blessing to you and your family. I cannot let you dig your father's grave. The only people who are allowed to break ground in any cemetery are the union workers, and as you can see, they are on strike. As soon as the strike is over, we will have them dig every grave and see to it that all who have passed away get a proper burial. I am so sorry, but there is nothing I can do to get the grave dug any sooner."

My upper lip curled, and I sucked in the air as my rage started to well up, channeling Dad at that very moment. Rip fidgeted.

"Mr. Shapiro, I did not ask you to do anything but show me the gravesite," I said. "Show me the plot."

Mr. Shapiro stood up, "I am afraid that I cannot do that, Miss Mendelson. I am afraid you are going to have to leave, or I will be forced to call the police and have you removed."

"It is not your land, Mr. Shapiro. My parents bought that plot. It is our land! You say you are sorry? You are sorry…a sorry son of a bitch. I assume that you are Jewish, although you cannot prove it by your behavior. We do not believe in hell, so I hope to GOD you find your hell right here on earth and in this lifetime! This is far from over, Mr. Shapiro!" I locked arms with Rip, held my head up, and walked out of the office.

I threw the shovel back in the trunk and got in the car. I looked over at Rip, who was stunned. He didn't know what to say.

As I approached the driveway to go out onto the street, those on the picket line quietly parted to let my car go by.

I drove to the nearest gas station, where I found a phone booth. I made several calls. Then I jumped back into the car.

"I am going to drive to the City to get some dope," I told Rip. "I need to get loaded. If you come along, you can wait in the car until I come out. It is your call."

Rip chose to ride it out with me.

Everyone was waiting for me at Geary Street when I pulled up.

"Give me half an hour, and I will be back, and then we can go home." I had to hit and run because I had to get back to my mom and the house full of relatives. I also had enough sense to know that I had to be there for Marilyn, too. After all, Marilyn saw our father dead on the couch in front of the TV watching golf and would probably never be able to get that image out of her head. Rip folded his arms over his chest and nodded.

Pam met me at the door and gave me a huge warm hug, "We are all so sorry, Jackie."

The spoon and water glass were all set up. Pam handed me the smack folded up in a paper. I emptied half of it into the spoon and started to prepare my hit when Peggy walked into the room with her arms out, signaling me to pause for a hug.

Peggy wrapped her arms around me and whispered in my ear, "Well, you finally killed your father, huh?"

I pulled away from her, horrified. We all had that nightmare that we would hurt our parents so deeply because of our drug addiction that they would crack and break from sorrow.

"I'm just kidding, Dahlin'. You know that, right?" It was too late. The damage was done.

I went back to the table and put the rest of the smack in the spoon, filled it with water, and put the lit matches under the spoon until the drug bubbled up. I tied my arm with a silk scarf and tapped around for my vein. I had bad track marks and had already blown out one vein in my left arm, but I found another good one and slipped the needle in. I untied the scarf and pushed the drug into my arm. I could smell the heroin and taste it in my mouth as it surged through my body. I put my head back in ecstasy and stopped breathing.

Pam was the first to realize that I had overdosed. She screamed for everyone to man the battle stations and brought me back to life. Bobby walked me around, but I was limp and unresponsive. Peter ran the tub, and they did everything right, so I came around within 10 minutes.

When I had realized what had happened, I was filled with remorse but too loaded to do anything more than apologize and leave the house. The gang understood.

I went down to the car and opened the passenger door. I handed the keys to Rip and said, "You drive, okay?"

Rip obliged and slid over into the driver's seat, "Are you okay, Jackie?"

"Yeah, kiddo. I'm just a little loaded. Let's go home and see what is waiting for us." I nodded out, and Rip got us home safely.

I went right to bed, and Rip told the family the story of what I tried to do at the cemetery. He told them that I was tired and exhausted. They could ask me all about it in the morning.

Chapter 41
Before It's Too Late

Days turned into weeks, and weeks turned into months, and what was left of the Mendelson family was covered in a cloud of helpless, hopeless despair. It had been three months since my father had passed away, and the gravediggers union was still out on strike, and the relatives had long gone home, promising to return when there could be a funeral.

The mirrors were all covered, and Mom would not allow anyone to take the shrouds off until the burial. She sat on the end of the couch day and night, just rocking and crying. I did my best to tend to my mother, but I had never experienced anything that could have prepared me for what I should do or say to comfort her.

I went through every emotion. I was afraid of what life would be like without my father. I was enraged at the situation because I knew my father's soul could not rest until he was buried in the ground. I was ashamed of myself in every way; for being a junkie; for failing as a daughter by blowing off Father's Day; for every time I rebuffed my father's affections and treated him like a silly old man; for adoring my father and pretending like I didn't need him anymore. I was in agony over my loss and felt I had no one to turn to because my mother was so grief-stricken.

One day, I was in the garage filling glass bottles with gasoline and tearing rags to stuff in the tops. I had a dozen Molotov Cocktails prepared and was planning on setting the rags on fire and lobbing them at the picket line. I placed that last one in a cardboard box when Rip and my mom found me.

"What do you think you are doing, young lady?" she was horrified.

I very calmly explained that I could no longer tolerate this "religious" injustice and was going to firebomb the cemetery workers. I would rain hell down upon them.

Rip and Mom looked at each other in total disbelief. It would have been laughable in any other circumstance, but I was going off the deep end, and that was not funny. Rip told my mom that he was going to call Kevin, and they were going to have to get me out of town. Although she did not want me to leave in case the strike settled, she knew Rip was right, and we would just have to keep in touch for the day when we must return. The next day, Rip, Kevin, his new girlfriend Kathy and I left for Mexico for an indeterminate period. We all had loaded backpacks because we did not know how long we would be on the road. We took a train to Tempe, Arizona, and hitchhiked to Nogales to cross the border.

Kevin and Kathy crossed first and went right through to the other side. Rip went next. I was stopped and taken to a building where I was searched, along with all my belongings, for contraband. An hour later, I walked out of the building, crossed the border, and we ran to catch the train going south.

At each train stop, a woman with buckets of tamales and other homemade items would climb on the train and walk down the aisles selling food. We ate tamales with God knows what inside and drank beer, slept, woke up to more tamales and beer until we got off the train, and found a hotel. Next to the hotel was a cantina where we found other American hippie travelers. The next day, we walked all around the town until it started pouring rain, so we decided to take a bus out of Mazatlán to find a dryer climate. The bus was packed with people and chickens, and the seats were very uncomfortable. I felt a little woozy and crampy and itchy and all-around miserable as night time set in, and we had miles to go. Rip was leaning on me, sleeping, and I was fit to be tied. Hot and claustrophobic, I got up and found an empty row of seats at the back of the bus.

Just as I was settling in, a stunningly handsome man walked up to my row and looked down at me. We locked eyes for an almost uncomfortable moment, and I moved my feet off the seat to make room. Without saying one word, we very quietly made love in the back of the bus.

Then he, just as quietly, returned to his seat. I never said a word, and if any of my traveling companions knew, it was never mentioned. We pulled into Guadalajara and found a hotel. We were all exhausted and went right to bed to get some rest before going out to scout the town.

I woke up with a start and ran to the bathroom. My guardian angels must have been on strike because I had Montezuma's Revenge in the worst way while throwing up in a little trash basket only to find I had gotten my period and picked up some hitchhikers…crabs!

I went back to bed and told Rip the good news. He and Kevin went out to the nearest Pharmacia to find something for diarrhea, something for throwing up, some tampons, and Quell for "Los pinchos sequences."

Meanwhile, Rip would call home every few days to see if the strike had settled but always got bad news. He kept it to himself and told me that he would only let me know when he had something good to tell me.

We made it to Oaxaca and took a bus up a very windy road to San Jose del Pacifico at the tip-top of the mountain. We were so high up that the clouds were below us. We found a local who spoke broken English, and he directed us to a farmer's property with huts he rented to travelers. We found a big hut for all of us, and we strung up our hammocks to get ready to sleep.

The farmer came with dinner for the four of us, and we couldn't have been more appreciative. Then, there was a knock on the door jamb, and in walked five hippies to share a bottle of Mescal and stories about the quaint little town we happened upon that grew magic mushrooms that were sold at the local post office. We all got hammered and passed out. The hangover the next day was debilitating, but we made ourselves get up to go to the post office we were told about. We got to the little red hut and asked for "ungas" which was some kind of slang. The woman behind the counter presented large banana tree leaves. On each leaf was a line of perfectly placed mushrooms, and on the tip of the leaf was a perfect dollop of local honey. We found a secluded area behind the hut and dipped each mushroom in honey until they were all gone.

We had no idea if we got one serving or several servings, but we decided that we would soon figure that out. The gang was stoned for days. Everything around us was either pulsating or flowing in a rainbow of colors. I kept thinking, *I know nothing. I know everything. I know nothing at all. I know everything about everything! I feel my father's spirit all around me.*

We all felt wrung out and decided to go to Mexico City and get a 5-star hotel room on Rip's Bank of America credit card. It was there that Rip got the news that the strike had settled, and we could go ahead with the funeral. Rip told Mom that he would buy us plane tickets to get home, and we would be there within 24 hours. We had waited 120 days for this moment, so 24 hours seemed like a second.

The motley crew in Oaxaca, Mexico

Chapter 42
Busted

My world was caving in on me, and I was too depleted to even care. The gang on Geary Street was holding me up, giving me a place to live when I had to get away from my mother's endless grief. There was no stopping my runaway train of an existence. The stench of my life was in a parallel process to the falling of the City of Love. The Haight- Asbury was under a dark cloud of addiction, constantly hovering, and the freedom that was once there had turned into a perpetual trap.

Peggy was in the process of closing down the store after the armed robbery took the last bit of steam out of her ambition. I came over to Geary Street to get away from my burdens and reality for as long as the next hit would last.

"Dahlin', would you take the Shelby and go get us some dope over at Mop's? See who wants some and get it for all of us, will ya?" Peggy sounded defeated.

I agreed and took the money from Peggy, "I will stop at Cala Foods and get some groceries while I am out. We are out of milk and cereal and stuff, okay?" Everyone looked up in agreement, and I could see the hunger in their eyes, along with the dark circles of exhaustion and addiction. My attractive and hip friends and I looked like washed out junkies.

Peggy handed me the jacket she was wearing, "It's cold outside, so take my jacket and hurry back, okay?" Bobby and I ran down the stairs and out the door.

Mop had just scored a boatload of heroin, and he was being very generous with the balloons of junk he was filling up. I was starting to feel a second wind, and I wanted to hurry up and do the shopping and get home to shoot up. I popped the balloons into my mouth and drove to the market.

At some point, I could taste latex and realized that I forgot to fold the little tails around the balloons to make a ball. My cheeks were full of heroin balls the size of little marbles.

After checking out, I grabbed the grocery bags and threw them into the trunk, and started out for the house. Bobby turned up the radio and sang all the way loudly.

Addicts were always excited on the way home to get loaded. We parked and got out of the car and grabbed the groceries. Out of nowhere, the police ran up on us, with guns drawn.

"Step away from the car and put your hands in the air!"

I could not swallow the balloons, which was the whole purpose of having them in my mouth. I would choke on the dangling tails. I took my tongue and stuffed them way back into my mouth.

"What is your name, little girl? We followed you out of Mop's and all through the market. Thought you would never finish!"

All I could think of to do was to pretend that I was deaf and dumb because I couldn't talk. I began pretending to use sign language and charades to indicate that I could not hear or speak. I seriously thought that they would buy that even though they must have seen me talking in the market.

The cops grabbed me by the throat and started choking me until I had to spit out the dope. I took a deep breath and started to cry. Bobby stood there, stunned at my performance...even though I failed to get away. I tossed him Peggy's keys.

"Can I bring the food to my house before you take me away? I need to give it to my roommates." I was resolved to sinking to my lowest point in life. The cops let me drop the bags of groceries off at the flat, and I told the gang that I was being arrested and asked them to try to get me out. I drank down a half-gallon of milk and walked up the street in handcuffs.

"Wait! Please wait for a second!" Peggy came running after us. I was amazed. I thought she was coming to confess and save me.

"She has my jacket!" The cops uncuffed me. I slipped off the jacket. Peggy snatched it and ran away. The cops put the cuffs back on and took me to jail in short sleeves in the middle of winter in cold and foggy San Francisco.

The guard recited me the Miranda Rights, took my mug shots and fingerprints, and locked me in a cell with a little old black grandma. I sat on a bench in total silence for over an hour, trying to get my mind to stop spinning. It was evening, and I knew nothing would happen until the next day.

I was going to have to sleep in that freezing concrete cell in short sleeves until morning when I would be arraigned. I knew all this because I had watched so much Perry Mason with my dad.

Before lights out, the jailor threw scratchy grey blankets in the cell. When my cellmate walked over to get her cover, she sat down on my bench.

"Why are you in here, child? You don't look old enough to be in an adult jail. What did you do? By the way, my name is Ruby. What is your name, child?"

I said, "I am so ashamed! I bought narcotics for my friends and me, and the police caught me. I have never been arrested before, and if my mother finds out, I will just die! My father just passed away, and I can't lay this on her too. It is just too much! I don't know what I am going to do. My name is Jackie."

"Well, Miss Jackie…the Lord must have a plan for you. I guess he figures you need to stop what you are doing to start what he wants you to do. Sometimes we must get hit over the head with a frying pan before we get the message. Do you know what I mean?"

I sighed, "Yes, Ruby. That is one bad frying pan he's got there! What did you do to get your message?"

"Oh child, I am 85 years old, and the Lord has blessed me with a wonderful life. I have my children and their children to keep me company, and I lived with my husband in marital bliss for 70 years until he up and died. I expect I will be in jail for the rest of my life because I killed my grandson's school teacher. Come to find out, he was touching all the little children in a bad way, and someone had to stop him. I guess that someone was me. So, I supposed I got the Lord's message before I landed up in here."

I patted Ruby on the shoulder and went to the end of the bench to try to bundle up in the blanket to get some sleep.

All night long, the jailers were locking the hookers up. The rumble and the clanking of the cell doors were brutal. I was thankful that I was not in their cells because they were up all night screaming at each other.

The next morning, I saw a Public Defender; he plead me down to a misdemeanor, and the judge gave me two years' summary probation and sent me on my way. I hitchhiked back to Geary Street and picked up my belongings. I wanted to kick Peggy's ass for sending me to jail in short sleeves, but she was gone. I told the gang all about my night in jail. I also decided, while I was sitting in jail, that I was going to leave the Bay Area.

Jeffrey had moved to Los Angeles, and he called me to let me know that if I wanted to get out of the scene, I could go down to LA and stay with him. I knew my night in jail was the beginning of the end if I didn't get out of town.

I was worried about abandoning my Mom, but then, if I overdosed or ended up in prison, that would be a worse kind of abandonment. The one saving grace was that I knew Marilyn would stay with Mom and make sure that she was alright and support her through her grief and worry.

Pam gave me some of their heroin as a lovely parting gift and drove me home to Burlingame to tell my mom about my plan to leave. I may have to tell her I was arrested for getting my point across, but I would hold that back if I didn't have to use it.

Chapter 43
Another Slap of Reality

Timing is everything. The spectrum runs from 'this is the absolute best time' to 'there is absolutely no good time.' I hunkered down in my family home, waiting for a clearing or even an up moment to approach my mom with my need to leave the Bay Area and move down to Los Angeles. It was like playing jump rope... you had to wait for the right moment to jump in, hoping you don't tangle in the rope and fall on your ass.

Marilyn and I were pretty much ignoring each other, and, by some miracle, we were not fighting. Each had come to our conclusion that not getting along would drive our mother into her own early grave, so we mustered up the discipline to peacefully co-exist.

"Sweetheart, why don't you take Daddy's car and go up to The City and see your friends for a couple of days? You look like a caged animal. I am going back to work on Monday, and your sister is working full time, and then, when you get home, you need to think about getting a job yourself. Honey, it's time." Her eyes glistened with loving concern, and that gave me hope.

I seized the moment, "I do want to get a job, Mom. But I want that job to be in Los Angeles. Only, I don't want to leave you if that will only make you sadder. Jeffrey has moved to the Fairfax District and said I could come down and stay with him until I get a job and find my own apartment. I am just not seeing any future here for me right now, and I think I just need to go away and make a fresh start. But I won't do that if you need me here."

My mother smiled a sad smile and seemed to be lost in thought, probably thinking about what a disaster I was.

"Mom, say something. Are you mad at me?" I needed reassurance.

"You may be right," she said. "Maybe a change will spark the drive you need to find your way in this world. You have seemed lost for quite a while, and I think it is time for you to fly. If you feel safe with Jeffrey, I am for it, Sweetheart." She gave me her blessing.

Chapter 44
Pick Up the Speed

I made it down to Los Angeles with my suitcase and guitar in hand. The apartment was on the corner of Melrose and Martel, up the stairs and at the end of the hall. It was bright and very gay chic. Jeffrey sauntered around the unit showing me where everything was and gave me the guest room until I got on my feet and could get my own apartment. We spent sunny days on the sweltering tarpaper roof in small beach chairs working on serious Southern California tans.

The area we lived in was just shy of what the Height-Ashbury was like before the hippie invasion, a very trendy neighborhood where half the inhabitants were young adults, and the other half were old Jewish couples who had lived in their houses for decades. The street was lined with small boutiques, various eating and drinking establishments. People walked up and down Melrose day and night shopping, eating, gathering on the corners to talk, and slipping into the local bars.

Los Angeles (fast and perky) and San Francisco (political and strategic) could not have been more polar opposites. Above the waist of California were dark and broody, culturally astute and rightfully smug Cosmo – Urban stoners lucky to have lived in the right place at the right time. We were in the hub of the counter-culture revolution. Below the waist of California were the young aspiring beautiful people with agents and headshots.

They had bright white smiles and were taking acting classes while waiting tables until they were discovered. Or they were hippies spending all day on Venice Beach and all-night partying in various and sundry concert halls, bars and clubs. It was not long before I got the lay of the land. I found the laundromat, Canter's deli, Pink's Hot Dogs, and the Bacchanal, a gay bar to remind me of home.

I took a little downtime to make sure all the drugs were out of my system while pondering what I could make happen for myself in this new environment. I had lots of cousins in the area and got a kick out of reconnecting and eating home-cooked meals prepared by my mother's first cousins. It was not long before I went walking the neighborhood looking for work. Right away, I landed a job at Astro Burger on Santa Monica Boulevard and Gardner as a counter girl and 'sometimes' fry cook. The burger stand was owned by a big Greek family.

I was required to buy a white dress as my uniform and gently begged the manager to allow me to buy white pants and a white blouse, almost exactly like the scrubs medical staff wear in hospitals. After Nikko saw my outfit, he conceded that I looked the part and handed me a paper hat that looked like a boat to prop on top of my head of hippie hair hanging down to my waist.

I thought I looked hideous but expected to have to make concessions if I was going to live drug-free and meld in with the straight folks. It turns out that Astro Burger was the "it" place for all burgers all the time. I recognized famous actors and actresses pigging out on charbroiled double cheeseburgers while futilely hiding behind sunglasses and hats.

I started to become friendly with the young adults my age in the neighborhood, and they would all try to get into my line to order and chat...when Nikko was not around. I started to notice which ones looked high on pot, which ones I would swear were flying on LSD, and the tell-tale pinned pupils of heroin addicts. About four months into my job, I ran into Mrs. Schacter, the owner of the apartment building, and she gave me a sweet hello.

"Jackie darling, the one-bedroom in the front corner of the building is vacant. Would you like to rent it? I know a nice young girl like you would like a little more privacy, so it is yours for $150 a month if you want to take it. Just let me make sure it is freshly painted and clean, and it is yours on the first of the month." Mrs. Schacter was an angel!

I wondered how Mrs. Schacter knew it was time to move out of Jeffrey's and into a place of my own. I was surrounded by gay boys at Jeffrey's place, and I needed to branch out and meet more people. It did not help that all the boys were drop-dead gorgeous but did not play on my team.

My new apartment was right on the second floor over the shop on the corner. It had a very classic wall-to-ceiling French windows that opened out to the street. It was bright and airy, but the street noise would be something I would have to learn to tolerate. It was perfect for me, and I had a real bedroom with a door and a spacious living room and a step saver kitchen (you could touch every wall pivoting on one foot). I could not have found a better apartment in a better part of LA for the times. One night, I was working the window at Astro Burger, and a strikingly handsome Israeli man came up to order his dinner. He had white paint in his dark curly hair on his shirt and stuck to the hair on his arms. I tried not to stare, but he had to be the hairiest man I had ever seen. He was so hairy that his shirt puffed away from his skin from his wall to wall fur. I found it surprisingly sexy and noted bodily sensations.

"Hi. What will it be?" I was composed and coy.

"Hello. You must be new. Please, a double cheeseburger, fries and a chocolate shake for here."

"What's your name?" I asked.

"Oh, you want to know my name. Just so you know, when I am not covered in paint, I am really quite a good-looking guy. My name is Zev. And what is your name?" Zev was leaning in through the window to get a closer look.

I got flustered, "No, I need to know your name so we can call you when your order is ready. I'm Jackie."

Zev came back to see me every day that I worked for many weeks. He was starting to grow on me. We talked about different things between ordering and picking up food. I found out he had just come to the USA from Tel Aviv to try to make a better life for himself. He had been in several wars in the army and wanted a calmer existence. He lived with five other Israeli guys, and they all slept on the floor in sleeping bags. He was born one month before me, and he wanted to take me out on a real date. I agreed.

Zev picked me up in an old Ford Falcon station wagon full of paint cans. We went to Canters on Fairfax, where Zev proceeded to tell me what to order for dinner. Normally, I would push back, but I decided to let it slide to see where this infatuation was headed.

"I want to ask you a question," he said. "And I don't want you to get mad because I like you very much. I need a green card to stay in the country. If I pay you $2,000, will you marry me and help me get my green card? After I get it, you can get a divorce if you want, or we can stay married if you want. I mean, I would want to stay married to you because I think I am in love with you. All I think about is you all day, and I rush to Astro Burger after work just to see your face. I know this is not very romantic, but it is true how I feel. Do you like me even a little?"

Zev was so nervous. His mouth was dry, and he was stumbling over his words. His face was bright red, and when he took my hand, his hand was cold and clammy.

I was in shock and didn't know whether to be flattered, scared, insulted, or compassionate. It never occurred to me that Zev was marriage material. I had no intention of getting married for a very long time. I was still trying to stay clean and live past 22.

I did have a chance to run my hands over his fur-lined body, and it was a total turn-on. I could not believe that I was falling for him, too.

I agreed to marry him and to help him get his green card. I did love him, and I knew he loved me. I knew because he would practically climb out of his skin when he was around me.

The marriage had to be a secret. I did not want my mother or anyone else to know about it. I felt my family and friends would not understand. I also knew that my older sister was to be married first, and that was just the way it was in my family. Marilyn had been dating the same guy for a long time, and I was sure they would be making an announcement soon, so I told Zev we would have to elope and not tell a soul. The next day, we drove downtown and got a marriage license and were to be married by a justice of the peace. We thought the scene was straight out of a B movie. While we waited for the ceremony, this little old spindly lady tried to sell us plastic flowers for a wedding bouquet, her services as an organist to play Here Comes the Bride, a wedding book with a Polaroid picture of us after the vows, and a bottle of pink champagne with two plastic glasses for a toast to our long and fruitful marriage.

After we politely refused every offer, the Justice of the Peace came into the room. He was clearly drunk, had two days of stubble on his face, and had to hang on to the podium to stay upright. We both got a kick out of the scene and told each other that it was the perfect wedding.

Zev went to his apartment, and I went home and did the laundry on my wedding night. We had not talked about living together and planned on seeing each other the next day, but there was no talk about how we would be a married couple, and that was just fine with me. I was taking my life one day at a time and had $2000 in my pocket.

I thought, 'What is a girl to do with all this money?' I went to the gay bar two doors down from the laundromat, drank during my wash and dry cycles, and played pool with some lesbians.

Zev...my Israeli Warrior

Chapter 45
Well, That Didn't Take Long

I was happy in Los Angeles. I had freedom, my own apartment, a job with a living wage, some new friends, and a secret marriage, which seemed to satisfy my need for risk and excitement; so, my drug-seeking behavior was under control.

On my days off and before I had to go to work, I would hitchhike or take the bus to Venice Beach to meet up with my new pool-playing buddies and lay on the sand and get tan. Being tan was strangely important in Southern California. It meant you were healthy, attractive, carefree, active, and prayed to Our Lady of Leisure.

There was a routine. We spaced out our towels close enough to hear each other's conversations but far enough for personal space requirements. We would slather on oily suntan lotion, turn the radio to K-EARTH 101, distribute the Quaaludes and get loaded enough to pass out and cook like Hebrew National hot dogs. Thankfully, someone would wake up and tell everyone to turn over so we can cook our other sides. After the beach day, we would go home to shower and change for pool games and cocktails back at the Bacchanal.

I had stayed away from heroin for months, and my body was strong, and my mind was clear. My address book was full of new friends, and I enjoyed my job enough to stay there until I figured what I wanted to do when (and if) I grew up. I called my mom every Sunday to see how she was and to assure her that I was alive and well and holding my own.

It was my day off, and my friend Mark from Astro Burger and I were packing up to go to Venice. Mark had a car, and he would stop by and get me when he could get away, and we would go to the beach or to a movie or out to lunch.

He was sitting at my coffee table in the living room while I ran around to finish packing up. He went into the tin box on the table and found a baggie of the pot and rolling papers.

"Hey, do you mind if I roll a joint?" he asked.

"Go for it. I'm ready," I walked into the room with my beach bag when the phone rang.

"Hello? … Yes, this is me…yes, I know a Bobbi Taylor. Yes, I know where she lives, but I don't *know* her know her! Who is this? Are you kidding me? Why don't you do it? NO? I can't do that. You have to do it, and you are there! Hello? HELLO!"

I hung up the phone, turned, and stared at Mark without saying a word for the longest time.

"So?" he asked.

I told Mark that a woman with a very deep and raspy voice found my name in this girl, Bobbi Taylor's, phone book and told me that I had to go over to her house right now and take her to urgent care because she overdosed on drugs and was dying on her bed. She would not tell me who she was and hung up the phone.

"The woman said that she left Bobbi's front door open and propped open the door in the covered parking garage so we can get into the building. She told me her apartment number. Mark, we must go over there. We can't just let her die."

We ran to Mark's car, drove to Bobbi Taylor's house, and took a parking place closest to the door in the garage. We ran up the back stairs and found her apartment, pushing open the front door that had been left open. I yelled for Bobbi, but there was no answer as I tried to figure out where she was.

When we looked in the bedroom, Bobbi was lying on her side on her bed. One half of her body was grotesquely swollen and blue from lack of blood flow. She must have been lying there for a long time. She was barely breathing and non-responsive.

We covered her up in her bedspread and lifted her off the bed. She was dead weight. Mark took her arms, and I took her feet, and we struggled to get her down to the car. We laid her in the back seat and hoped to God that we could get her to help in time.

The urgent care facility was right up the block, just two doors down from Astro Burger. We pulled up to the door and screamed for help. Two attendants came running with a gurney, pulled her out of the car as if she were as light as a feather, and they wheeled her into the building, shouting, "Stay there! We need information!"

I told the admissions nurse everything I knew but explained that I had only met the girl once, I didn't know who called me and I didn't know what she took. I gave the nurse my contact information, and Mark and I went back to the car and drove away. When I went over in my head what I had just told the nurse, I thought it sounded lame and unbelievable…but it was the truth.

Mark and I decided to call it a day, and I went back to my apartment to try to calm down. I put some records on the stereo and stared at the phone. I wanted to tell someone what had just happened, but I didn't know who to call. The doorbell rang, breaking my stupor. I opened the door.

"Jackie Mendelson? We are the police investigating the circumstances leading to your bringing Bobbi Taylor into urgent care today. Do you mind if we come in?"

I stepped aside and motioned them to enter my apartment.

The officers started asking me questions, and I tried to answer them as clearly and honestly as was possible. I noticed one of the officers looking around my home, and it made me very uncomfortable. I was just about to tell them that I had told them everything I knew when the nosy cop walked over to my coffee table. There was a corner of a plastic bag sticking out of a metal box. I started to panic. It was the pot that Mark had pulled out to roll a joint, and he did not put it back in the box.

The cop bent over and snatched the baggie out of the box and held it up for his partner to see.

"Well, would you look at this? It looks like our little rescuer is going to need a rescue of her own. Put your hands behind your back, Jackie. You are under arrest for possession of marijuana, and we are taking you to Sybil's house. You have the right to remain silent. Anything you say may be used against you in a court of law. You have the right to an attorney. If you cannot afford an attorney, one will be appointed to you. Do you understand what I have just told you?"

I nodded and hung my head, thinking, 'No good deed goes unpunished. How could those pigs be so cruel?'

As they walked me out in handcuffs, Jeffrey was coming into the building. He looked stricken at the sight of me getting led out to the police car.

"Call Zev or my mom and ask them to bail me out. I will be at Sybil Brand," I called out to him in my most pitiful voice.

They drove me directly to Sybil Brand Institute for Women, where I was booked. They took my fingerprints and mug shots and directed me into the back room where a matron was waiting to process me in.

"Take off all of your clothing, shoes, and any jewelry you have and put everything in this evidence bag. If you have any money, I will put it on the books for you, or you can get some candy and cigarettes in the vending machines on the way to your cell."

I complied.

"Open your mouth and stick out your tongue... Run your fingers through your hair and toss it around... Let me see behind both of your ears...Show me the bottoms of your feet, now raise your hands over your head."

I complied.

"After I put on these gloves, I want you to bend over and spread your cheeks. I am going to put one finger in your anus to check for drugs and then another finger in your vagina. When I am finished, you are to go over to that shower stall and stand, facing me, with your hands over your head. Is all that clear?"

I cried and complied.

I was sprayed with some kind of disinfectant...front and back. I was handed some new granny underwear, a very used faded limp blue dress, an old stretched out a blue cardigan, and a pair of flip flops and was told to get dressed and walk into the next room where I was handed a pile of bedding and a small towel. I was led into a holding area, and I would then be escorted to my cell.

The jail was like a big cement tomb. The bars were grey, and the walls were a pale yellow with scuff marks all over. There were long narrow windows letting light in at the very top of the hallway. My cell was the size of a closet with one bunk bed, a corner table with two attached chairs, and a steel toilet in the back corner.

The bunk beds were both made up, which indicated to me that there was no 'room in the inn,' so I stood outside the cell. I felt a slight push at my back, signaling me to go in.

"I'm not afraid to go in there, you know! I just don't know where you expect me to put my bed if the only two bunks in here are already taken. It's not like I know the ropes, but I don't know what you expect me to do!" I was getting a little pissy.

"You'll sleep on the floor under the bottom bunk. You missed dinner. Your cellmates will be back after the meal. Lights out at 8:00, and you will wake up at 6:00 and go down for breakfast. Now, go on and get in there. I have rounds to make." The matron slammed and locked the gate and walked away with her keys clanging on her belt.

I threw my bedding on the floor under the bunks and squeezed onto a seat at the table. I felt inside the funky pockets of my dress just to make sure my candy and cigarettes were still there. I pulled out a cigarette and lit it with a prison stick match.

My cellmates came back from dinner and saw me sitting at the table, smoking and eating a Snickers. They looked to see my 'bed' on the floor. They introduced themselves and told me what they were in for. I remained stoic when I realized that one of my roomies was one of the Manson Girls. I told them my story, and they all agreed that the pigs that arrested me after I saved that girl were full of shit!

I was feeling a little brave, "I'm not sleeping under that bed. That's bullshit! Anyway, I am going to get bailed out before the moon sets. My friends won't leave me in here."

"That's what they all say, friend. And somehow, we see them in the mess hall day after day waiting for all their friends to come and get them. Ain't going to happen, Jackie. Give me your cigarettes and candy now!"

I stared at Leslie, the ringleader, trying to judge if I was being tested or if I was really in trouble.

I took a leap of faith and said, "No, I'm not going to give you my stuff. I have had far too much taken away from me today, and I'll be damned if I am going to give up my cigarettes and my dinner. That ain't going to happen!" I lit another cigarette and gave each of them one to see if that would do the trick. It did for the moment.

All of a sudden, we heard a voice yell, "Lights out in five minutes. Lights out in 5, ladies."

"So much for all your friends bailing you out," was muttered from a bunk above.

My heart sank as I crawled under the bed, and the cell went dark. Two minutes later, I heard the clanking of keys coming down the hall, "Mendelson, you have been bailed out. Get your stuff together and come with me." What a wonderful sound to my ears.

I stepped outside of the cell, and it was slammed shut behind me. I reached into my pockets and pulled out the rest of my candy bars and threw some onto each girl's bunk. I turned on my heels and said, "See you on the upside, cellies!"

I was processed out and changed back into my own clothes. When I got outside of the secured area, I saw Mark and Jeffrey standing there. Mark looked traumatized, and Jeffrey looked smug. I did not need his facial judgments.

"Your husband, Zev, bailed you out. Why didn't you tell me you were married, Jackie? I would have bought you a toaster for a wedding present!" Jeffrey laughed without even knowing the story.

When I told Mark what happened, he turned as white as a ghost. It sure sounded to him like it was his fault I got arrested because he did not put the pot baggie back properly. And, in fact, it was but knowing that would not change anything that happened that day. Mark would do whatever he could to make it up to me, but I would hold out for the big favor at a later date and time.

I knew I had to go save that girl if I could, or I would feel horrible guilt for the rest of my life. I had buckets of that atrocious natural-born guilt at play already, and even just a little more would surely do me in.

Chapter 46
Yet Another New Leaf
Turns Over

The Superior Court of Los Angeles appointed two young lawyers to represent me in my upcoming court appearance. They told me that they would only work with me if I tried to stay clean throughout the entire process. Of course, I agreed.

I was scared and desperate. I was still on probation for my misdeeds back in San Francisco. I kept myself busy and distracted doing laundry and going to the beach with friends until one day, I made myself late for work and got fired. Zev will come around to see me, and I won't be there. He will think I am such a loser when I see him.

I could not stop myself from self-destructing. That night at the bar, I was telling my tale of woe to the beach gang, including Debbie, Peggy's L.A. playmate.

Two women at the next table overheard what I was saying and turned their chairs toward me.

"Hi! My name is Beth, and this is Linda. We both drive catering trucks, and we are looking for a helper to work the routes with us. We will pay you cash every day after we finish cleaning the trucks, so you would be working off the books. You would have to help stock the truck in the mornings at the catering house in Mar Vista and then ride with us to help sell and refresh the stock during the route. There is a cleanup at the catering house after to prepare for the next day, but it is no big deal. The only thing is, you have to show up for work at 4 o'clock in the morning to get the coffee brewing and the hot food in the oven so we can make our first stop in Manhattan Beach by 6:00 a.m. You can wear shorts and a t-shirt."

"Take a breath!" I laughed. "You start work at 4 o'clock in the morning? Holy shitcakes! That is when I am just going to sleep." "I'll do it!" Debbie chimed in.

They said both of us could have a job, and we would get twenty dollars a day. That would pay the rent on Martel and my other expenses with some leftover to save for a car.

I woke up at the crack of dawn and made my way to the catering house using public transportation. I was shown the truck and learned what went onto the ice on the cold side and on the shelves. The hot ovens in the back were for the hot foods and the coffee spigots, the shelves for condiments, plastic utensils, and napkins. The other side of the truck housed the huge coffee urn and storage shelves. It was an all-around tight truck with a place for everything, and it was spotless.

We went into the massive warehouse to shop for the food for the day. Beth had me put all the food on a huge cart, so I would get a feel for what had to be on the truck each day. It was apparent that this business was not for the faint of- the heart: heavy lifting, crack-of-dawn at a crazy fast pace, perfectly dispatched and systematic, and 99% dominated by men who looked like they came straight out of a mobster biopic.

They joked on the lot but, when they pulled out to hit their first stop, it was every man for himself. Beth and I packed the truck and peeled out for our first stop at Metlox Pottery in Manhattan Beach. Beth talked non-stop about the route and the things I would be doing at each stop. My head was spinning with words, and my gut was flipping with excitement. After the first two weeks, it became clear that getting out to the catering house from West Hollywood was untenable. Beth lived in a huge 2-bedroom apartment in Marina Del Rey just six blocks from work, and she offered to let me rent the second bedroom for next to nothing. I had a decision to make.

Zev and I had been spending weekends together on Martel, and he stayed on the floor with his work buddies during the week. Talking to Zev about the job and moving away was going to be a challenge. He was already starting to try to tell me what to do and was asking about my whereabouts.

I chalked some of that control up to his fighting in several wars in Israel, and he was only 22 years old himself. But he was trying to hem me in, and it put me in fight-or-flight mode.

In truth, I did not feel worthy of having Zev for my husband. My abstinence from heroin was more like a medication vacation in my mind. I was managing myself, but I knew that could only last so long. I was already convincing myself that Zev would have a better life if I were not in it. He seemed so normal, and I was so abnormal.

I was not going to tell him about my drug use and my chronic dependency. After all, I had not used heroin since I moved to Los Angeles, and the Quaaludes on the beach was technically an appropriate use as a sleeping medication.

The fact that Zev had already started shaking his head and calling me "fucking Jackie" should have been an indicator that he knew I was as slippery as mercury. What I could not deny was that I was crazy about Zev.

I asked him if he wanted to take over the rent and stay there while I moved in with Beth to figure out if catering was for me. He agreed and helped me pack my clothes and other items. Beth pulled up outside the apartment in her huge, bright yellow Dodge van. We ran down and threw my things in the back of the van, kissed each other goodbye, and agreed to talk during the week.

"Who was that guy?" Beth asked.

"Oh, that is Zev. He is my husband," I said matter-of-factly.

"Whoa! I thought you were a lesbian!" Beth was stunned.

"No…is that a problem?" I said and stared out the window.

Chapter 47
Crazy? You Wanna See Crazy?

I loved working on the catering truck. It was physically hard but rewarding. I was gaining stamina. I learned how to anticipate the flow of money and product by the day of the week and by the numbers of people on the shifts at my stops. I was doing everything from shopping to stocking to taking the money and driving the truck. I learned where the clandestine shops were to get cigarettes and other items at a lower price than the catering lot store.

Beth told me that the route net had picked up since I started working, so she threw in extra money as a regular reward.

I was saving my money to buy a metallic copper 1970 Firebird convertible that a guy on one of my stops was getting ready to sell. I was able to buy some new clothes and go out to dinner without counting my change first. I got along very well with Beth. I was always happy and upbeat, and that made my mom sleep well at night. It also helped reduce my guilt. Guilt for slighting my father. Guilt for being a junkie. Guilt for dropping out of the San Francisco Art Institute. Guilt for leaving my mother. Guilt for being a selfish bitch and stealing from my sister. Guilt for being secretly married. Guilt for knowing there would be future guilt for hanging out with lesbians and for knowing that I would probably use heroin again if the opportunity should arise. Guilt for just being me.

It wasn't long before I recognized patterns that did not have to do with selling food on the food truck. After watching carefully, I discovered action at certain stops where certain guys would meet Beth at the storage side of the truck and then walk away with their hands in their pockets. I knew what this behavior suggested, so the next time it happened, I ran around to see what was going on. I saw Beth hand over a baggie of pills and take a wad of money. When she saw me, she looked panicked.

"Busted! What in the fuck are you doing, Beth?"

"This is called monetizing all opportunities available in the course of a workday, Jackie. They need beans (amphetamines) to stay up and pull double shifts to meet their quotas and pot for the weekends. I have what they need—simple supply and demand. We all do it. Ed sells hot cameras and stereos on his dry side. Willy makes book at all his stops. Ike supplies prostitutes to the owners of the stops on the company leased routes. Everyone does a little something extra on the side in this world, baby doll. That is how this stuff works. You help me sell from the dry side, and I will give you a commission. Are you in?"

"Are you popping beans, Beth? Is that how you run around the truck like a crazy woman from four in the morning until two in the afternoon, non-stop?"

"You bet, baby doll. How do you think I keep up with this crazy pace? I am older than you, and I need my energy. Eating Wheaties in the morning is not going to do it for me. Do you have a problem with that?"

"I guess not," I said.

So, I added peddling drugs on the side to my catering repertoire. It was astounding to see the amount of cash that was changing hands at that truck every day. The Dynamic Duo (as we became known in the catering lot) was making a killing! We went from one cart to two brimming over carts in the warehouse checkout line every day, and it was obvious to the other caterers that we were raking in the dough. They started to give us the stink eye on the lot.

After saving up one thousand dollars, I bought that Firebird convertible and had enough left over for the insurance for a year, several cassette tapes to listen to while driving, and storing money in a savings account. I sped back to the apartment to show Beth my car. That car could go from 0 to 100 MPH in 2 seconds flat!

I ran up the stairs and bounded through the door to find Beth in the living room with a woman I had never met before and one of the most unusual looking men I had ever seen.

"Jackie, this is my friend Juanita, but everyone calls her Juan. This is her friend, Joe, from New York. This is my roommate, Jackie. Joe is going to be visiting here for a while, and Juan asked if Joe could stay here because her apartment is too small," Beth looked sheepish. It was not her normal "Alpha Dog" demeanor.

My mind was flooded with questions. *Beth and Juan look like old friends, but I have not heard her name before. Juan has track marks on her arm. Who is she? What is Beth up to? Why does she look like the cat that ate the canary? Who is this, Joe guy?* I signaled for Beth to go back to the bedrooms with me for a little chat.

"Who are these people, Beth? She has fresh needle marks, and he doesn't look so good. He must be 6 foot 8 and has to weigh at least 400 pounds. He is sweating profusely, and each one of his legs is the size of a telephone pole. Something is wrong here, and you want to bring this into our house?" I was genuinely concerned.

"I owe her. I had a serious cocaine habit, and she took care of me until I could get it together. She owes him. He is her supplier, and he is running from some very bad men back east. He needs to kick a ginormous coke habit and hide somewhere he can't be found. That would be here," Beth turned on her heels and walked out before I could say another word.

When I went back into the living room, Joe was sitting on two chairs at the dining room table with a pile of cocaine on an album cover in front of him. He was making long lines of coke using the side of a playing card. He rolled up a one-hundred-dollar bill and snorted up one line in each nostril like a Hoover vacuum cleaner, then threw his head back and held his breath. He made a guttural sound and turned his head to stare right into my eyes.

"So, here's the deal, little girlie girl. I have to hide out here for a while, and there is no way that the guys that are looking for me would ever find me here. I have a coke habit that would kill an elephant, and I need to kick it here because I may not have access to any more drugs for a long time. Those white specks that look like lint that you see all over me, my clothes, and the floor all around me are actually cocaine crystals that are coming out of the pores of my skin. I cannot just stop, or I will die, so I am tapering down. See? This, here, is me tapering down," With that, Joe snorted two more lines.

"My legs are this big because I have, what do you call it, lymphedema. You can poke them, and it is like knocking on wood. It looks worse than it is, but it makes it very hard to walk, so I mostly sit all day. I suppose if you gathered up all these little shards of coke all over me and the floor, put them in a spoon and shot 'em, you would probably overdose. Don't do that, girlie girl, okay?"

I smiled at Joe. I liked him. He was very intuitive and seemed like a nice guy.

Joe also pulled a wad of money out of his pocket and told us that he eats a lot and so he will pay for food for everyone while he is there. He liked to cook Italian, but he also liked good food from good restaurants and will pay whatever it takes for it.

Joe settled in on the huge couch in the living room. He bathed several times a day to keep the crystals down. He slicked his black hair back gangster-style. He wore white slingshot undershirts and tighty-whity underwear day and night and nothing else unless he went out or strangers came in. Then, he would put on his large suit pants.

Juan came over every day to visit Joe while the Dynamic Duo was out working, and she was rarely there by the time we got back home. I could tell that she was loaded on heroin when I did see her, but I chose not to say anything. I could also tell that Beth was dipping into the powder pile, but it did not seem to affect her at work, so I kept my mouth shut.

One fateful day after work, I got home early from running a route in Santa Monica. It was the first time in weeks that I had the house to myself. Joe and Juan were gone, and Beth would not be home for at least two hours. I started vacuuming the cocaine shards and cleaning up around the apartment.

When I went into the bathroom, sitting on a dinner plate on the countertop was a pile of white heroin, a new syringe in a sanitized wrapper, a silver spoon, and a note on the mirror. It was from Juan.

"Thanks for being such a good sport and helping Joe. He thinks the world of you. This dope is for you because I know it is your drug of choice. Enjoy, and there is more where that came from. Love, Juan."

Love, Juan? Who in the hell does she think she is, bringing that into this house? I know Beth would not have told her I was an addict. That is really cold-blooded, leaving smack here for me. I am not even getting loaded anymore. Does she think she can get me hooked and add me to her client list? How fucking insulting! My righteous indignation was wearing thin, even on me. I walked into the living room. *If it is that big of a deal, I could just go and flush it down the toilet, and that would be the end of this obsession!*

I walked right back to the bathroom to toss it away. I picked up the dish and involuntarily sniffed the heroin and got instantaneous cell memory. I thought, maybe just a little hit wouldn't hurt. I would throw the rest away.

I took a small bit of the powder in the spoon. Unwrapped the syringe and drew water into it from the sink. When I put the water in the spoon, the drug dissolved immediately into a clear liquid, that was a sign of how pure it was. I paused to rethink what I was doing.

I pulled half of the liquid into the syringe and shot it into the vein on my right arm. I felt a rush like the first time I had ever shot dope.

Just like that, I was shooting heroin in the washrooms of the gas stations by my stops in between the morning break and lunch. I was driving the truck loaded, and my customers started asking me if I was feeling alright. Some even asked me why I had changed all of a sudden. I kept smiling and thanking them for their concern.

Then, the guys at the catering lot started noticing my "shut down" behavior. Beth always defended me and said hard work made me more serious, but I was kidding the kidders. Those guys lived in the belly of the beast and knew an addict when they saw one. Everyone was concerned for "that youngster," but nobody said a word to me.

Beth picked up a cocaine habit of her own again, and we both started using drugs out in the open, inside our apartment, with no shame. Beth would snort coke and clean everything in the apartment. I would shoot up some smack and talk to the toaster. One time, I tried to smoke the telephone receiver. We were crazy and out of control, all while showing up for work at 4 o'clock in the morning

One day, Beth decided to confront me about my addiction. I told her it was the pot calling the kettle black. Beth was so coked up; she could not control herself and started screaming. Beth was jumping up and down on the floor and stomping her feet. She hopped up onto the antique oak dining table, pulling her hair and screaming, "Jackie, look at you! You are crazy on drugs! You are crazy strung out and have to stop it immediately. I mean it, Jackie, you have lost your mind!"

I looked up at Beth out of one eye and said, "I have lost my mind? I am crazy? You are running around the dining table with cocaine rings around your nostrils, and you call me crazy? You wanna see crazy? Look in the mirror!"

We both stopped our commotion dead in our tracks, looking at each other with despair. Beth climbed off the table and sat down on the couch and started to cry.

"What are we going to do now? We are going to lose everything we have built," I started to sob.

"We have to stop before it is too late."

Chapter 48
What's the Use?

It seemed as though Beth and I were near the end of our ropes. But that did not stop us from continuing to use and abuse drugs. I had started making regular trips to Hollywood to buy my heroin so, my premonition about Juanita wanting to add me to her customer list had turned out to be quite true. As a way to thumb my nose at Juan, I also started buying dope from George, who was the go-to dealer for the stars in Hollywood.

One day, I got pulled over by an unmarked car when I was on my way back home. Unfortunately, I had a lot of heroin in my possession at the time, along with other drug-using paraphernalia. There was no possible way that I could have hidden it before the detectives stepped up to my window.

I pulled my beloved Firebird over on the side of the road, and soon, tears rolled down my cheeks. I knew that it was over for me and that there was no way I could avoid getting arrested. That meant I was not only violating my present probation in San Francisco but whatever else would become of me when I would be presented in front of Judge Ritzy again for my arrest in Los Angeles. My goose was cooked.

"Step outside, Miss, and put your hands on top of the hood of your car. I am going to have to pat you down. Do you have any sharp objects in your pockets at the moment?" the narc told me with a no-nonsense tone of voice.

"No, I don't, Sir. Everything I have is in the car right now. Please, do not bust me. I will do anything to not be arrested and get thrown in jail," I was pleading for my life. If my mother knew how much more of a failure I was becoming, it would surely kill her, and I could never live with that.

The other undercover cop searched my car and pulled out the drugs as well as the paraphernalia out of the passenger seat of my car, holding it up in his hands, "Look at what we have here, Nick. Looks like we're going to have to take Miss Firebird down to the station. Let her know that we are going to park her car around the corner and lock it up. We're going right now."

They put me in handcuffs, placing me in the backseat of their predictably grey Crown Vic, and then drove me to the police station in Hollywood. It was exactly the kind of stuff my nightmares were made of. The cop led me by my arm into an interrogation room, then placed a chair on one side of an old funky looking table that had coffee cup rings and other unidentifiable stains on its surface. I couldn't help but feel like I was in an episode of Dragnet, acting out a horrible scene, only I could not switch the channel.

"Hello Jackie, I am Detective Nicholas Trameno, but you can call me Detective Trameno. I am in a benevolent mood today, so I'm going to give you an opportunity to make this right before I charge you with the possession of narcotics and drug paraphernalia. That means you are going to have to give me the name and location of your dealer or connection.

"And then, you are going to make a purchase from this dealer so that we can arrest that person. At that point, we will not be pressing any charges against you, and you will be able to go on with your life as a free woman. But, do know this, there will come a time when you will be pulled over and not be allowed to give up your dealer. You will be sent to jail after awaiting trial, and you will have no chance of maintaining your freedom. Is that clear?" Trameno was clearly driving his point home.

"You want me to snitch? I can't do that. They will know that it's me and kill me. What else can I do?" I was desperate.

"That's about it, Jackie. Give up your contact or go to jail. It's that simple. You were arrested alone so, no one knows that you have been taken into custody. If you don't tell anyone you were arrested, it is unlikely that your dealer will connect you with the following drug bust. But it's all up to you, Jackie. What are you going to do?" the Detective asked me.

"If I tell you that I am going to snitch on my dealer, will you let me go right away? I can't go back and buy more drugs from them because that would be too obvious. But I do have someone else in Venice Beach that I also buy drugs from. I will tell you who that person is. I could buy the drugs from Joey because he hasn't seen me in a while. Please, let me go home. I promise I will do it another time. Also, since you are not arresting me, can I have my drugs back?" I pleaded.

"What are you, nuts? No, you cannot have your drugs back! But because I still feel benevolent, I will let you go home. However, we expect you to be working on this tomorrow. If you agree, we will take you back to your car, and you can be on your way. Make sure you answer the telephone tomorrow, or there will be hell to pay. I will personally hunt you down," the Detective seemed as serious as a heart attack, and I knew that I was out of any wiggle room.

I was shaking like a leaf on the drive back home. During the whole ride, all I could think of was how I could possibly get out of the trouble I had suddenly found myself in. I would not give up Juan because that would mean certain death. There were too many terrible people that she was affiliated with.

The only person I could think of to give up was Joey, but I really liked him and didn't want to bring this down on him in any way, shape, or form. Alas, I also knew that I had no choice. I called my young attorneys and informed them of what had been going on in my life since the last time I saw them, and they expressed their disappointment in me.

We all sweated through my latest court appearances because I was still using drugs, and Judge Ritzy was not one to be easily fooled. Even though they threatened to abandon my case, they kept working for me all because they cared so deeply for my mother. Mom was still in the dark about my twists and turns in Los Angeles, but it was only a matter of time before she would be dragged into my train wreck of a life.

They told me that I had to tell on my dealer, and I had to do it when the Detective called. They told me that I had to stop using drugs immediately, whether it meant going cold turkey or not. We all agreed to postpone any upcoming court appearances before the Judge until that little bit of drama was completely resolved.

Since they no longer trusted me to be able to do the right thing, they got the name and phone number of the detective that had arrested me and said that when I would inform them that it was all done with, they would call him to verify whether I was off the hook or not. And so, down went Jackie into the pits of my own personal hell. I could not tell anyone that I had been busted again. I had managed to land in the worst possible predicament for any junkie; I had to turn in a friend to save my own ass. It was going to break one of the most important codes out on the streets, and my guilt for doing it was eating away at me after just thinking about it. I came back home to an empty apartment. I had the urge to call Zev and tell him everything and beg him to rescue me, but I felt too disgusted in myself to even let him see me.

I stood in front of the huge picture window, staring out into space. A commotion at the USA gas station right across the empty field in front of my building caught my eye then. I saw lines of cars backed up as far as my eye could see. They were three lanes deep, coming all the way from three banks of gas pumps. 'What is going on over there? Did something happen while I was detained?' I thought to myself.

I ran to the television and turned on the news channel. The commentator was reporting that there was a gas embargo in place, and that meant that a shortage of gas was to be anticipated. In Los Angeles during 1973, that meant that the sky was falling since the city's name had become synonymous with heavy traffic. The price of gas increased by over 50% in one day. It was then revealed that until it was all over, drivers had to follow some kind of odd and even plan where car licenses ending with an odd number could only buy gas on odd-numbered days and so on. That seemed reasonable enough to me, but I believed that the whole embargo routine was just a ploy to raise the prices of gas and gouge consumers, which made me mad. I started cooking up a scheme to get my mind off of my current tragedy.

I changed into a white shirt and dark pants. I found a plastic badge holder, printed out 'STAFF' in huge block letters on a 3x5 notecard, and pinned it on my shirt. I grabbed a small receipt book that I used to keep track of customers that had charging privileges on my catering route. The last and most important item to top off my official ensemble was my beautiful leather changer belt filled with coins and four-rolls.

Carefully crossing the field so that none of the drivers would see me, I went up to the middle of the lines of cars and started knocking on the windows.

"Hi! My name is Carol, and I work for the USA Gas Corporation. It would speed up the process of you purchasing gas once you get to the pump if you were to pay now and hand this receipt over to the staff waiting to serve you at the station. I am sure that you know the rule that each car is only allowed to purchase $20 worth of gas on each odd or even day. Can I make this inconvenience a little easier on you?" I could not have sounded sweeter.

The first driver said, "That sounds like it will help move things along, but I was going to use a credit card. On second thought, though, that might muck up the process if we all started holding up the line waiting for our cards to get approved. Okay, here is twenty dollars. Do I just give the receipt to the guy at the pump?"

"Yes, Sir. He will take the receipt and pump your gas so you could be on your way. Thank you, Sir, and have a nice day," I put the twenty-dollar bill between my fingers so the other drivers could see it to help them believe that I really was a station employee.

I weaved between three lines of cars, taking the money and writing receipts until I realized that the first driver who paid me would be pulling up to the pump by then. I hurried down Glencoe Avenue and Allah Road at a fast pace to get away, but not in a way that would draw attention. I ran up the stairs, slipped inside my apartment, and bolted the door behind me. I was stunned and felt smugly proud when I looked out the window to see the riot that ensued at the gas station. The first set of cars had reached the pump, and the drivers were screaming at the cashier inside the glass booth. Arms were flailing, receipts were flapping, and the rage spread like wildfire all the way back to the last car. People were standing on their door jambs, trying to see what was happening at the pumps.

Drivers were leaving their cars in line to march up to the station to give anyone a piece of their minds. There was nobody, but the lowly cashier, available to hear their rants, and they believed her when she said that she had no idea what happened or who Carol was.

I had seen enough by then, so I thought better of standing in the window as the police pulled up to the station and began trying to calm the crowd. A slight twinge of guilt flowed through my body, but I justified my behavior in my mind until I realized that I had done the same thing to those poor drivers that I accused the oil industry of doing; ripped them off.

Bad Jackie! Bad, bad, Jackie! I am nothing but a blister on the ass of society! I am more criminal and derelict than

I am honest and upstanding. My good parts have been ruined. All I can think of is how to stay loaded. I feel trapped and like I am about to chew my own leg off. Even my thoughts are disgusting. I was in full-blown self-sabotage mode. The only thing that made me lay off myself was counting and recounting the three thousand and ten dollars I had collected from the gas embargo line.

I could hear Beth's changer belt jingling as she came up the steps, so I ran into my room to hide the money. No one could know anything about the arrest or the rip-off at the gas station or Joey or anything about me from then on. I withdrew even deeper into myself.

"Hey, Jackie, how did you do on your route today? Mine has been down a little since you have been running the Santa Monica stops. Listen, I have a pound of cocaine here that I am hiding for Rusty out at the Metlox stop. He will come here and get it within the week so, if he comes and I am not back yet, I am putting it in the garbage bag drawer in the kitchen where the gun is," she said.

"Gun?! You didn't tell me there was a gun here. What the fuck, Beth? I don't want anything to do with any of this. Leave me out of it!" I screamed.

I had seen the landlord walking around over the past weekend, and he had told me that the one-bedroom apartment on the other side of the landing was going to be vacant soon. He had asked me if I knew anyone looking to rent or if I wanted my own place. I had the money to move now, and I knew it was time to get out of the den of iniquity that I was living in. I decided to tell Beth I was moving out after I had secured the new place.

It was now or never.

I called Joey and started with a little bit of small talk, "Hi, Joey! Long-time no see. How is everything over at the beach? Great! Yeah, I am good, and I love driving the catering trucks and earning a living! Listen, have you got anything? I am flush and want to get a small supply real quick. Great, I'll be right over!" I hung up and started feeling nauseous. I was going to have to start becoming a regular with Joey again if I was to earn his trust so I could then smash it to smithereens.

Joey was glad to see me and gave me a big hug. I handed him one hundred dollars, and he gave me a nice sized balloon of smack. Leslie, his old lady, walked into the living room and gave me a hug, "Wanna stay for dinner, Jackie? We are having spaghetti and meatballs, Joey's favorite!"

Saying yes meant that I was lower than the belly of a snake but, if I didn't, it would be completely out of character for me, and they would wonder what was wrong with me.

"You bet! Thanks for the invite. I love your cooking!"

Et Tu, Brutus? I thought to myself.

My very cool copper Firebird

Chapter 49
Nowhere to Run...Nowhere to Hide

The more pressure that Detective Nick poured on me every day to lead them to Joey, the more I felt like I was falling into the abyss. I had started running out of excuses for not getting the deed done. The detectives had started giving me money to get dope and had even begun driving me to what they thought was Joey's apartment.

I would carry balloons of baking powder in my pocket, and when I would return to the car, I would hand over the phony dope and tell them lies about which building and apartment Joey was in, or that he was not home, and his girlfriend had given me the drugs. I needed an escape, and the perfect one had just fallen right into my lap.

I had to find a way to string Detective Nick Trameno along until I could get out of town. One day, Mom called me with some great news. "Hi, sweetheart. Are you sitting down? Allan just asked Marilyn to marry him, and she said yes! They are going to get married fairly soon because

Allan got an offer from a firm back east, and they are almost sure he is going to take it. Marilyn wants you to be her Maid of Honor! Isn't that fantastic?"

"What a great surprise, Mom! Do I need to come up there and help plan everything? I could stay with you until the wedding, right? What does a Maid of Honor even have to do? This is so exciting!" I really was excited, but it was mostly because I could see a way to get away from Nick for a while before I inevitably would have to wear the "snitch jacket" for the rest of my life.

"Oh, no, honey. I will be taking care of everything with Marilyn and the wedding planner. Even the things you would have been doing as her Maid of Honor if you were here. It will give me something to do, and you have responsibilities there in Los Angeles. It would also be very nice if you could bring Zev to the wedding since I know he is your boyfriend. Did you think I would not find out that you two were living together? Every time I call the apartment, he answers the phone. We have built a very nice relationship, no thanks to you! Anyway, Allan wants him to be included in the wedding party, as well. I love you, sweetheart, but I've gotta run now. There is so much work for me to do!" And then my mother hung up. Confounded. That's what I was feeling, confounded. I could not think straight. Everything was starting to pile up on me, and I had no idea what I was supposed to do. Now, I had to call Zev and ask him to be in my sister's wedding party, when we were hardly even talking anymore. He had grown tired of my addictive behavior. All the secrets and the thin veil of normalcy I had worn when we were together was irreparably frayed by then.

The doorbell rang, and I was waiting for Beth to answer until I remembered that she had gone out hunting for cocaine.

Oh, bother. Now what? God, can I just get some peace for at least a few minutes? I thought as I stomped through the hallway to go and open the door.

As I twisted the doorknob to open the door, the force of someone pushing through the entryway threw me back against the wall opposite the door, and I fell down to the floor from the impact. I was overwhelmed as three men wearing ski masks and holding guns surrounded me on the floor, making sure I could not move.

"Where is the cocaine you are hiding?! We know it is here somewhere, and if you tell us, we won't tear this place apart, and you might get to live another day. We aren't messing around here, you dig?" I recognized his voice from my days of copping drugs back in Hollywood.

I had no idea how he knew about the pound of coke, but it had to be because of Jerry or Beth. I hadn't said a word to anyone. It had never occurred to me that I could have just told Detective Nick about Jerry and his pound of coke instead of the two-bit dealer, Joey. It could have all been over relatively sooner.

"Quit your daydreaming and get me that coke! I am not jiving, ya hear?" I looked at him right through the holes of his ski mask.

"Shit, George, I know it's you under that mask. I can recognize your voice and those shoes of yours. I don't know who told you about the pound of coke, but you can give up the charade now. I will give it to you, it's not mine, and I don't give a shit about it. Just don't tie me up like this and stuff me inside the closet. As soon as I give you the damn coke, you get the fuck out. Got it?" I had had enough; my exhaustion and hopelessness had emboldened me to act even more recklessly at that moment.

George said, "I don't know who this 'George' is, but it ain't me. Just get us the shit, and we will get the fuck outta here."

I stood up and went to the drawer in the kitchen. I peeked in and saw the gun inside. For a split second, I thought about shooting the intruders for breaking in and entering my apartment. I could justify it, and I knew how to shoot a gun. Oh, for Christ's sake. Had I turned into a killer now, too? I took a pause that was too long.

George pushed me out of the way to reach inside the drawer, pulled out the gun, and tucked it into the waistband of his pants.

Then, he proceeded to pull out the pound of cocaine from the drawer, stuffed it inside his backpack, and threw it back over his shoulder, "Go on and walk to the bedroom in the back, then count to one thousand, Jackie."

"Ha! Fuck you, George! I knew it was you!" I yelled at the gang of intruders as I watched them leave from my place at the end of the hall, then ran back and bolted the door tightly.

Later, when Beth came home from work, and I regaled her with the story of what had happened, she freaked out. She then accused me of lying and said that I had taken the coke for myself and had sold it to feed my heroin habit. We continued to battle back and forth until we were both hoarse and exhausted from the screaming match. Beth refused to believe that it wasn't me, and if possible, she had become even more upset when she heard about the gun being stolen.

It had turned into a hopeless situation for me, so I decided it was the perfect time to announce that I was moving out and taking the one-bedroom apartment across the landing. Our great catering partnership and friendship had gone bad, all thanks to drugs and paranoia, and it was past the point of saving, so it was time to call it quits.

I did end up moving next door, but Beth and I avoided each other as much as possible at home and on the catering lot. I got a new telephone number, which gave me a much-needed reprieve from Detective Nick's daily dose of harassment. To make things easier on myself, I started running routes out of the rival catering lot in Culver City. It was a whole new gang of thugs, but I had built up a good reputation. I was welcomed warmly and shown the ropes by the other caterers I had come to know there. The owner, Louie, loved when he got good drivers that had broken out from Ike's band of thieves.

A few days later, Mom called me to fill me in on the wedding plans and asked again, for the umpteenth time, if I had asked Zev to come to the wedding as part of the wedding party. I was finally able to make my mother happy and quickly put that nagging to rest.

"Yes, mom. We are driving up in the Firebird, we will come early to get his tux fitted and my dress taken in. If it's okay with you, he could stay with us at your house. Are you happy now?" I was short with my mom, and it didn't go unnoticed.

"You can lose that attitude, Jackie. This is your sister's big day, and I will not have you doing anything to ruin it! And whatever you are taking down there, stays down there. I don't want to have to worry that you are going to be high on drugs in front of all our guests. Do you understand me, young lady?" She let me know that I had gotten on her last nerve and that she was not going to tolerate my selfish behavior any longer. When the time came, Marilyn's wedding went on beautifully, and as expected, she turned out to be a gorgeous bride. The whole family had come in from all over the States to join in celebrating her big day. Mom danced with all of her brothers and cousins; she hadn't looked that happy in a very long time. Zev was getting to know the entire family, and he was loving it. I felt comfortable with him, and it was obvious to my family that we both loved each other very much. And then, the moment that I had been dreading all along arrived. Uncle Joe put his arms around Zev and me to give us a tight hug.

"Now, when are the two of you going to get married?"

Without even thinking, we both said in unison, "We are already married!" The couple gasped in horror, and Uncle Joe gasped with disbelief. "Uncle Joe! Please, don't say anything. Mom doesn't even know. I wanted Marilyn to get married first, and we tried to wait, but circumstances happened, and…" It was too late.

"Everyone! Family! I have a huge announcement to make! Jackie and Zev are also married and, out of respect for Marilyn, wanted to wait until she was married to tell us. Mazel Tov to Marilyn and Allan as well as to Jackie and Zev! May they have all the blessings of a wonderful life together!" Uncle Joe started clicking champagne flutes with everyone around him. The guests were miffed; this was not what normally happened at most weddings.

I wanted to crawl into a hole and die. Mom glared at me with that "we'll talk about this later," stink eye I had grown accustomed to while she walked over to Zev to kiss and hug him. Zev seemed to have become paralyzed in Mom's arms. Marilyn and Allan looked very confused and hurt, then went back out onto the dance floor along with their close friends. Uncle Joe came over to slip a crisp one-hundred-dollar bill into Zev's jacket pocket and winked at him.

The other older male relatives then proceeded to do the same. I felt so ashamed of myself for letting that important piece of information slip out like that. However, I wasn't positive that I did not let it out on purpose, just to gain some attention for myself. Either way, it had felt like a betrayal for sister, a mortifying display of jealousy and selfishness. I was starting to get sick of myself. The next day, I expected my mom to tear into me for what had happened at the wedding, but she did not say a word to me. She fluttered all over Zev as only a loving mother-in-law could.

Somehow, she had turned it all into something wonderful in her mind. I imagined her talking to my dad in heaven, telling him that The Girls were with wonderful husbands and that they did a good job of raising us. That now, they could pray for wonderful grandchildren to complete the family as they dreamed of together for so many years.

Zev and me at Marilyn's wedding

Chapter 50
The Jig is Up

When we got back to Los Angeles, Zev went to Martel, and I went to Alla Road. Life spun on.

I managed a few months of equilibrium. My new route at the beach was trending up in net income. Nick had not found me yet, so all was quiet on the western front. Beth was keeping her bad vibes down to a dull roar; the only constant I had to deal with was the giant monkey on my back. I was shooting more smack than ever.

This time in my life was becoming unbearable. I thought of ending my misery more than once. I was alone in my apartment most of the time; no one would bring me back if I went out on a lethal dose. That is why I never let down my guard to cook up just the right amount of dope. I did not really want to die; I just didn't want to live my life anymore.

Many drug addicts are never too stoned for introspection. A flaming list of indictments is available to us at a moment's notice for self-loathing. We choose drugs over loved ones, friends, work, play, and certainly spirituality. I had done all that choosing. When I acknowledged the absence of my spiritual underpinning, I was left with despair that no amount of drugs could cover.

On my way out to work one morning, I noticed an unopened pile of mail. I tossed all the advertisements and opened the envelope from the Superior Court of the County of Los Angeles. It was my final court date to be held before Judge Ritzy. In bold letters, it said **THIS DATE IS ABSOLUTE, AND NO FURTHER POSTPONEMENTS WILL BE GRANTED**.

Great, now I have this to fret about all day. Is there anything else, God? Any other tragic turn of events you wish to bless me with? Lay it on me, Baby! This is how I knew my spirituality was in the toilet. All my life, I had never blamed God for anything.

I was always reverent and thanked God when I was blessed – for allowing me to graduate high school to my getting accepted to the San Francisco Art Institute to the dealer having drugs when I knocked on the door. I snickered at the idea that most of my misfortune I blamed on my mother. Mom did not force me to shoot heroin nor to steal Marilyn's thunder at her wedding nor to squirt glue into Diana Slavic's mouth. I had my very own demons that I had to accept, and they could not be laid off on anyone.

Driving in the dark to my first catering stop was my time to contemplate and problem solve. On this particular morning, all of a sudden, I felt a jarring bump and heard the crashing of metal on metal. I looked up to see the front end of my catering truck raised up onto the left fender of a Toyota Corolla. I was driving in a fugue state and did not see the car in the middle of Manhattan Boulevard, in the middle of a median lane turning left into a driveway.

I jumped out of the truck in a panic. I was going to be late for my stop. As I walked up to the car, I saw Texas license plates. The other driver was sitting in the driver's seat, staring in disbelief.

"Hey, are you okay?" I said. "What are you doing in this lane? Do you want to get killed? This truck fully loaded could have flattened you!"

"I'm sorry, ma'am. I have only been here for a few days. You can do this in Texas, but I guess not here, huh? I ain't hurt, and you hardly have a scratch on your bumper. Please don't call the cops because I don't have insurance." The man was almost in tears.

"Of course, I won't," I said. "I am just glad you aren't hurt. I can't say the same for your car. Be careful out there. I have to run, or I will be late for my stop. Take care!" I ran to the truck and backed up. I got to Valcor Electric and set up my table, flung open my cold and hot stainless-steel doors, and was ready for business just on time. All day, I felt like a dirty dog.

At the end of the day, I went home. There was just one flight of stairs to climb, and I would be back in the safety of my own home. In my tiredness, I didn't notice my door was partially open. Walking into my apartment, I looked around and gasped. I had been robbed.

Items were thrown around in every room. My Yamaha twelve-string guitar was missing. My beautiful mahogany Gum Bop Conga Drums were gone. My antique wooden hand-tooled picture frames with prints of loving mothers and their infants were stolen. My favorite blouses were missing and some random shoes. How odd that only my favorite things were stolen. I still had my stereo system and television and other things that could be easily hocked for drug money. I ran to the album cover piled high with heroin that I had hidden under my desk shelf in the living room. It was there, untouched. I was relieved that they did not find my dope but could not shake the feeling that someone I knew must have broken into my house. Only someone close to me would know what would really hurt me. I figured it was Beth.

People who dance with the devil do not call the police for any reason. I looked back at the date for my court appearance. I called my attorneys to confirm that I would be there and told them I was running from Detective Trameno. They told me to make sure I was clean when I entered the courtroom and that I should pray that the detective does not show up as well.

I called my mom, "Hi, Mom! I am okay, but I have a favor to ask of you. I have to go to court for the final decision on that charge of possession of marijuana. You remember when I saved that girl, and they came and arrested me? Anyway, can you come down here and be with me in the courtroom. I will be a lot less scared if you are there."

After a slight pause, Mom said, "Tell me when you need me, and I will fly down the night before so we can spend some time together. It is time you told me what is really going on in your life. I may not like what you are doing or who you have become, but I love you with all my heart and will always support you."

We both hung up and sighed.

Chapter 51
All Rise for the Fall

The gavel cracked with force on the judge's mahogany bench, and I jumped out of my skin.

"All rise. The Superior Court of Los Angeles is now in session, and the Honorable Judge Ritzi is presiding. Anyone having business here today, please be prepared to address the court when your case is called." The bailiff meant business.

Richard Sherman, my attorney, turned to look at my mother sitting behind him. My mom was silently weeping and bereft at her current predicament. "Mrs. Mendelson," he said to her. "I am not sure what will happen today because every time we have come to court, Jackie has been dirty, and the judge has gotten angry and told us to leave."

"What do you mean dirty? My daughter may be a hippie, but she has always bathed and washed her hair!" she exclaimed.

"No, Mrs. Mendelson! That means that she comes to court under the influence of drugs, and it is obvious to the judge. But I can see that she is not stoned or loaded right now, so this may conclude today." Richard and his partner Michael have been through two years of legal wrangling to keep me out of jail, and they both fear they have reached the end of my rope.

The bailiff called, "The County of Los Angeles vs. Jackie Mendelson. Please step forward and address the court."

"Richard Sherman representing the Defendant, your honor."

I stood, shaking by his side.

"Miss Mendelson, you have been a frequent visitor to my court for the past two years. Each time I gave you an opportunity to get clean and start taking your future seriously, within six months, you have ended up back here before me. I am going to put an end to this cycle today. I am going to give you a choice to make right here, and right now. You can go to jail for a period of not less than two years, or you can go with those two people at the back of the room to a residential drug program to get your life together. It is up to you."

I looked behind me at two scary-looking people; a big serious black man and a slight and wiry black woman who went from a smile to a frown to a smile in a split second.

"Your honor, with all due respect. I am a nice girl. I cannot go to jail for two years! That is hardly a choice," I whined.

"Young lady, our jail is full of nice upper-middle-class Jewish girls like you. Do you want to sit in jail in suspended animation for two years, or do you want to finally take the opportunity to change your life and become someone? Make your decision right now. We must move on. My court docket is full."

I looked back at my mom, and the picture image of my parents, Marilyn and me smiling in one of the moments of joy we shared so often as a family wafted through my memory and then broke into shards in my mind.

"I will go into the drug program, your honor. I have my mother here in town to help me pack up my things and find a place for my belongings. Can I enter the program on Monday morning, please?"

"You are hereby remanded into the custody of the representatives of Tuum Est to enter into their Therapeutic Community for a period of 18 months. They will escort you to your home to get your belongings, and you will be admitted to the program today. I will see you in this courtroom in six months for a progress report. I hope you will take advantage of this last chance. Good luck to you, young lady."

Judge Ritzi slammed down the gavel and called for the next case.

I slumped down into my seat with my head in my hands. My attorney yanked me up by the arm and walked me to the back of the room, where I met Alan and Diana. They drove us to my apartment in Marina Del Rey to collect the clothes that I would need to start my time in recovery.

I felt sorry for myself but even sorrier for my mom. Here was my sweet broken-hearted mother in Los Angeles, trying to do anything to help me while managing her own health issues and grieving the loss of her husband every second of every minute of every day. That was all too much for her to bear and withstand, and yet, I felt a relief that I was finally going to be in a place to get help if I was at all capable of accepting it and improving. My mother did not know what kind of environment her daughter was going to enter, and honestly, she did not want to know. In this case, ignorance truly was bliss.

Elmer and Diana were nice enough, but they were getting impatient with me. They told me just to throw a sheet onto the middle of the floor, get the clothes and shoes I wanted to take, and toss them in the middle, tie the ends up and say goodbye to my mom.

I had a pile of heroin hidden in the bathroom, and I was planning to get one last shot before I surrendered. Every time I went into the bathroom, Diana would follow me in. Then I would go into the bedroom, and Diana would follow. I could not shake her to get at the drugs. I ran into the bathroom and tried to slam and lock the door, but Diana and Elmer blocked it before it closed.

"Jackie, we can do this all day, or you can give us the dope so we can flush it down the toilet. You had your last shot. You are just adding to your mother's pain. Give us the drugs and get on with it," Elmer spoke with authority, and I knew he was right.

I handed Elmer a balloon filled with heroin, and he emptied the contents into the toilet and made me flush it. I watched my drugs circle the bowl and disappear into the sewer.

Elmer and Diana each took an arm and led me up to Mom to kiss her goodbye and then out the door and down the steps into the Tuum Est passenger van. That time I did not look back to see my mother.

I remembered the day I moved to San Francisco, and my mom was clutching the living room drapes and crying hysterically. I could not get that image out of my head for months, and I was not willing to see my mom grieving my departure. Not this time.

When we got to the program, I was led to a private office and told to sit down and wait. Diana started to walk off with my huge bundle of belongings.

"Hey, where are you going with my stuff? Hey, Diana! I'm talking to you!" I was pissed.

"Chill out, Jackie. No one is stealing your stuff. We are going to search everything for drugs and items you are not allowed to have here. Then we are going to wash everything, and you will get it all back, clean. We are also going to do a full-body search on you, and then you will shower and change into clean clothes, and that will be the beginning of the first day of the rest of your life," Diana nodded as if to punctuate her declaration and walked away to get busy searching my clothes.

Shame started to well up from my toes to a fiery heat in my face. They were going to touch my dirty clothes. A woman came in and introduced herself as Roseanne. She looked like a school teacher, and I just couldn't trust her. She asked me a zillion questions and wrote all my answers down. Then she explained all the rules.

"Jackie, I know this is a lot to digest, and you are going to feel very upset about it. I know. Believe me, I have been through it myself. But this is the most important thing you have to remember while you are kicking drugs and scheming to find a way out. *There is no way out*," Rosanne looked me right in the eyes.

"We are here to help you help yourself. We will guide you and kick your ass when you need it. We will give you all the tools you will need to stay clean, but it is up to you. You must decide if you are worth saving or a lost cause.

You must decide to value your life. You have to surrender to the fact that the sum total of everything you know got you here...into a drug diversion program as your very last chance."

Rosanne held a document close to my face so she could read it meticulously. "Here are the rules that you will follow, and if you don't, you will get kicked out of here to fend for yourself.

- You will not use drugs or alcohol while being a resident of this program

- You will not commit any act of violence or make threats of violence

- You will not steal

- You will not have any contact with anyone outside of the program for the first 90 days

- You will have an older resident with you as *Strength*, 24 hours a day for the first 30 days

- You will attend at least three group sessions a week

- You will attend family meetings

- You will attend a daily seminar every weekday

- You will read assigned books and write reports

- You will work on one of the assigned work crews every weekday and sometimes on the weekend

- You will not enter into a sexual relationship with anyone for the first 30 days

- You will......

I knew I had to pay attention, so I could figure out how I could avoid the cheat and stay out of trouble. If I looked arrogant or disinterested, I would get labeled as a snotty, spoiled know-it-all princess (which I was) before I even met the other inmates.

I was bouncing between realities. I just completely lost my freedom, no car, no apartment, no friends, no family, none of my favorite foods, no choice, no money, no drugs. I was about to cope with all this in front of total strangers in this program. And my body would soon ache, my nose would start running, and my eyes would start watering, my gut would start cramping, then my legs and my back would seize up.

I would curl up in a fetal position, sweating heroin from every pore, and throwing the covers. I would not even sleep for one minute. I would be fighting with people who would want me to bathe when the sensation of water on my skin would surely send me over the edge, maybe for good.

All those rules, I thought. *I should have told Judge Ritzi I would go to jail. I could be living with murders, rapists, and thieves here! Someone is about to strip me naked and look at me in ways that will shatter my modesty and pound on my shame. I will never stop using drugs forever, no matter how bad they brainwash me. How am I going to live through this?*

"Jackie! Are you with me here? Do you understand the rules?" Roseanne gave me a Resident Agreement to sign and then led me into a bathroom. I needed to be led. I was stunned and weak-kneed. I could feel myself giving up the fight. I was tired, it was time, and it was all just over.

Two women walked into the bathroom with supplies. They seemed like robots carrying out a duty they were trained to do while being as nice and empathic as they could pretend to be. They pulled a towel and someone else's clothes out of a paper bag. They told me to take off all my clothes and move under the shower, facing the curtain.

I complied. One woman with latex gloves conducted the body search while the other got the shower going. They looked in my mouth and under my tongue. They inspected behind my ears and ran their fingers through my hair. I was led into the shower and told to scrub from top to bottom and to wash my hair twice. I complied. It occurred to me that I did not even know the names of my robots, and that repulsed me.

I was led to a private office that was intentionally pleasant.

"Jesse, this is Jackie Mendelson. She just arrived and was sent by Judge Ritzi. She should be feeling pretty sick in about two hours," my escort left the room.

I was standing in front of the extraordinary Jesse W. Pratt, Founder and Executive Director of one of the toughest and most successful drug programs in the country. He was a black man with a shaved head and a bright dashiki tunic over knit slacks. He was wearing sandals and a huge diamond pinky ring. I figured he stood about 5' 9" and weighed close to 400 pounds. He had a Foo Man Chu mustache and clear manicured nails. He was oozing with charisma, and he leaned forward in his seat.

"Well, now, Miss Jackie. It looks like you lucked out by getting diversion to Tuum Est. You will get better if you stick to what we suggest you do and stick and stay even when it gets unbearable or tough. Everyone living here and working here has been where you are now, so they know you better than you know yourself. You will no longer be able to hide, and we will tell you about your sick ass when you slip into your dope fiend behavior. Your first job, after you kick that dope, is to start telling the truth!"

I stood there quietly. I had no idea what to say or what I was supposed to do next. Say thank you? Kiss his ring? Run out the door and keep running?

Jesse sensed my confusion, "Get your trifling ass out of here, and I will see you after you kick…if you make it that long. Good luck Mis Jackie."

Jesse W Pratt, Founder of Tuum Est

Diana escorted me down the stairs and into the main room of an old Craftsman Bungalow on a walkway on Vista Place in Venice. I was introduced to dozens of other people in various stages of recovery, all working and milling around like they knew what they were doing and what was expected of them. I figured that would be me someday if I stayed around.

A guy named Danny entered the program that day as well, so I had someone to bond with. He was already starting to kick, and his eyes were darting all around the room. I suspected that he had drugs hidden somewhere on the property, and he was trying to calculate how and when to retrieve them. I was right because Danny looked at me and mouthed the words, "I have smack in the bushes. Want some?" I nodded, yes.

When Danny's strength, a bodyguard of sorts, turned to talk to someone in the next room, he got up and walked out the front door while I watched through the picture window. He grabbed a small package out of the rosebushes and shoved it in his pants. He turned to see me watching him, looked around, shrugged his shoulders, and ran down the walkway, never to return.

I was numb, and I could feel the sick coming on.

My *strength,* Cindy, walked me through the food line to get dinner. It was ladies first in that program, and everyone was instructed to think of their brothers and sisters when they portioned out their meal on their plate. Wasting food was a sign of selfish behavior along with anything and everything else you do in that place. Everything gets confronted in Tuum Est.

After dinner, on nights when there are no groups, the residents pull back the tables in the living room and dance until bedtime. I danced until I was too sick to even move or stand. I wanted everyone to see how cool I was until I was totally the opposite. One of the guys signaled for Cindy to take me to the room where I would kick heroin for several days. It was time to get started.

There was a bed in the room and a chair for the women who would take shifts to monitor me throughout the process. Cindy was curled up asleep in the chair while I shook and poured out sweat in the bed. Every hour, a guy on the night shift would go into each room and count the occupants. *

Boutique Johnny slid in the door with a flashlight to count heads and to check on me to make sure I was safe. He leaned over my bed with a sly smile and whispered, "Are you okay, baby? Do you need anything? How about a nice back massage to work those cramps out?"

I focused on a large erection stretching out of Johnny's fly. My sarcasm always bloomed when I was dope sick, "No thanks, Johnny. I'm good... but thanks for making me feel so safe."

I rolled away, faced the wall, shook like a leaf, and quietly wept.

How could that be me? How did I get to this place? How in the hell was I going to get out of there? The faces of all my family passed right before my eyes. My grandmothers, was this my punishment for loving one grandmother and hating one grandmother? Was Nana right to be repulsed by me?

My parents, we were all so restless from moving around and adapting to change that we never really settled into safety enough to just be with each other. It made me so lonely. And Marilyn, my substance abuse must have been a colossal disappointment and energy drain for her, and in addition to all the obvious things that fueled the friction, I may have been a giant asshole a lot longer than I thought I was.

I prayed that night that God would see to it that Tuum Est is exactly what I need to stop the madness so that I can redeem myself and have a good life.

Epilogue

Entering a Residential Therapeutic Community on Venice Beach was an ending in one way while offering a new beginning in another. The days, weeks, and months after my admission to Tuum Est Inc. were the first steps in a brand new cycle of change in my life that lasted decades. The wild child and young hippie I was in this book was launched into another reality: this time, one of recovery. The loose Latin translation for Tuum Est is *"It's Up To You."* It was up to me to accept help... no one can do it for me.

Even the craziest episodes with family and friends or living in several hippie communes were no real preparation for the murders, scam artists and thieves I lived amongst in the drug program. I had to learn to stand my ground and hold a boundary while confronting an old, seasoned dope fiend that killed a guy in prison over cigarettes, and he didn't even smoke! I struggled to understand and achieve my own sobriety and learned to care about supporting those battling the same demons.

Recovery was more than scratching at my pain in front of total strangers. It was more than contemplating my navel to get to the revelation that not being breastfed was at the root of my addiction.

Recovery is complex, requires being vulnerable, being humble, opening up, being honestly sorry, baring my most vulnerable self, taking responsibility for my actions, and making amends when possible. It includes deep reflection, feeling my real feelings, and tolerating painful physical and emotional withdrawal. Doing jobs and tasks that seem senseless, nasty, and beneath me, such as cleaning toilets and scrubbing out dumpsters, because I was told it would change my life, is recovery.

Knowing the other people around me, actually caring about who they really are, how they feel, and what they need is recovery—understanding for the first time the reality of diversity, as taught from the mouths of men and women in ethnic groups other than my own. And, coexisting for one reason only, RECOVERY, shattered my dogma and created a space for real growth. Recovery is a way of life. But recovery isn't easy, and it isn't guaranteed, and it definitely isn't for the faint of heart (as you will soon see). One doesn't achieve "recovery" and simply move on with life. I had to learn all that. Stay tuned for the next installment. Natural Born Guilt: The Truth Will Set You Free.

NATURAL BORN GUILT

JACQUELINE MENDELSON